SOUTHERN ILLINOIS UNIVERSITY PRESS
Carbondale and Edwardsville

A PRAGMATIC THEORY OF RHETORIC

by WALTER H. BEALE

Copyright © 1987 by the Board of Trustees, Southern Illinois University
All rights reserved
Printed in the United States of America
Edited by William F. Cahill
Designed by Barbara Jahn King
Production supervised by Natalia Nadraga
90 89 88 87   4 3 2 1

Library of Congress Cataloging-in-Publication Data

Beale, Walter H.
  A pragmatic theory of rhetoric.

  Bibliography: p.
  Includes index.
  1. Rhetoric. 2. Discourse analysis. 3. Pragmatics.
I. Title.
P301.B37   1987   808'.00141   86-11807
ISBN 0-8093-1300-6

Permission to reprint the following is gratefully acknowledged: Ellen Good-
    man, "Participants Not Patients," from *Close to Home*. Copyright © 1979 by
    The Washington Post Company. Reprinted by permission of Simon &
    Schuster, Inc.
Mollie Panter-Downes, "Letter from London," *The New Yorker*, January 8,
    1981. Reprinted by permission; © 1981 Mollie Panter-Downes. Originally in
    The New Yorker.

*To Georgia, Buster, Carl, and Dorothy
with love and thanks*

A small circle is quite as infinite as a large circle; but though it is quite as infinite, it is not so large.

—G. K. Chesterton, *Orthodoxy*

CONTENTS

ACKNOWLEDGMENTS

Like most forms of scholarship, the theory of discourse is a lonely occupation that nevertheless creates communities of its own. One doesn't complete a task such as this without bending many ears, listening to many objections, and stealing many suggestions passed along in seminar or over coffee. I'm grateful first to fellow rhetoricians, especially to Wayne C. Anderson, Frank D'Angelo, and James Kinneavy for serious conversations, correspondence, and encouragement; and to my own students, for some lively engagements of the theory presented here.

The theory of discourse often sends one scurrying for help from friends in other disciplines. I appreciate both the creative listening and positive direction I got from Tony DeCasper and Sherrell Logan in psychology, Henry Levinson and Charles Orzech in religious studies, and most particularly Lawrence Shornack in sociology.

For readings of either the entire manuscript or parts of it, and for powerful suggestions, criticisms, and creative disagreements, I am also grateful to Frank D'Angelo, Mary Ellis Gibson, William Irmscher, Henry Levinson, and Beverly Wall.

For a semester's leave of absence an embarrassingly long time ago, and for a small grant to cover permissions, I am grateful to the University of North Carolina at Greensboro.

For everything, thanks also to Sarah Beale.

A PRAGMATIC THEORY
OF RHETORIC

INTRODUCTION: PRAGMATIC THEORY AND THE WRITTEN WORD

Is it either possible or useful to talk systematically about "kinds of discourse," as opposed to "processes of discourse"? Can anything beyond the sorts of rough-and-ready generic distinctions that one makes in ordinary parlance contribute substantially either to criticism or to general understanding? Should rhetorical theory attempt to deal with the motives and substance, as well as the forms and processes, of discourse? In this book I want to provide affirmative answers to these questions by suggesting a more coherent and provocative perspective on written discourse than is currently available, either from rhetoricians or communication theorists. My primary aim is to construct a theory of written rhetoric which will provide both a rationale and a foundation for the study of rhetorical literature, a field firmly established within the discipline of speech communication but much neglected by students of writing, literature, and the written word.

The method and scope of this book are informed by two perspectives that at least partially differentiate it from other books on rhetoric: The first lies in the concept of "pragmatic theory," by which I mean, first of all, a theory that is concerned primarily with *what human beings do with discourse*, rather than with the linguistic and cognitive conditions that underlie the doing. Such a theory will focus inevitably on *acts* of discourse—their kinds, functions, typical settings, and the strategies that are employed in their construction—instead of unconscious underlying processes. It is vitally concerned with "the composing process," insofar as that term encompasses the human motives and social conditions that bring discourse into being, as well as the processes by which acts of discourse are begun, shaped to fulfill certain goals, and concluded. However, a pragmatic theory will be concerned with these things as matters of conscious choice or typical action rather than as underlying mental disposition. It will make no claims about the nature of creativity or the dynamics of conceptualization. It is primarily concerned with the act of discourse as a human action, in its typicality and in its uniqueness.

1

These concerns are central to classical rhetorical theory and pedagogy, a tradition that now stands not so much in need of revival (as it did a quarter century ago) as of reassertion and revision, in the modern context and in the light of modern competition. This is a context in which language and discourse have become major, even dominant foci of every discipline, every field of inquiry that is in any way concerned with human action. In our own age dramatic theoretical and methodological advances, not merely in linguistics and communication studies but also in psychology, philosophy, and sociology, have made other kinds of discourse theory possible and desirable. These disciplines offer a wealth of insight about the nature and processes of human communication; they have underscored its essential orderliness; they point to solutions to some traditional rhetorical problems; and they pose new questions of their own. But these disciplines cannot replace the discipline of rhetoric, nor can the discipline of rhetoric afford to become too much like them in its methods, though it has much to gain from their insights. For these disciplines constitute, first and last, studies of human behavior; and rhetoric is, first and last, a study of human accomplishment.

Language itself may be, as some claim, the glory of humankind, the thing which most clearly sets humans apart from other species. It is certainly a wonderful thing. But it is not in any strict sense a human accomplishment. Acts of discourse—essays, poems, novels, memorandums—even dull ones, are human accomplishments. As "systems," they bear at times remarkable and fascinating structural likenesses to larger, encompassing systems of behavior or conceptualization. But they are nevertheless "made" things, the results of complex motives, responses to complex environments. And even though they may be unoriginal, they are not in any operational sense predictable. In this study I shall attempt to account for the nature and variety of such products in the realm of "rhetoric," at the same time exploring the vital relation they bear to other kinds of human discourse and to other kinds of human making.

The term "pragmatic" seems apt for a number of reasons: first, as a way of indicating the study of human performances in discourse, as opposed to discourse behavior in general; second, as the counterpart of what Frank D'Angelo has termed "conceptual theory," which undertakes something like an outline of "rhetorical competence" by relating patterns or modes of discourse to corresponding mental processes. The implicit analogy here to Noam Chomsky's celebrated notion of "linguistic competence" (as opposed to linguistic performance) is instructive, I think. Theories of "rhetorical competence" (conceptual theory) and "rhetorical performance" (pragmatic theory) should complement and illuminate one another, together providing a fuller comprehension of human discourse and a sounder basis for rhetorical criticism and pedagogy.

The principal reason, finally, for maintaining aggressively the posture of "pragmatic" theorist lies in the critical need to develop a system of explanations and characterizations that are at once rigorous and nonreductive. Discourse theory, criticism, and pedagogy have inherited a bewildering array of confusing and overlapping terminology, with inconsistent and contradictory descriptions of various entities, under such promiscuously used rubrics as "genre," "mode," "style," and haziest of all, "form." Clearly one of the first tasks of the theorist ought to be that of finding ways to organize, stabilize the meanings, and test the validity of such concepts. Such a project clearly suggests the need for "system" and "rigor"; a pragmatic theory will have no pretension to the connotation of "experimental science," however, for the price of certain types of rigor is far too high. In an essay which chronicles the failure of quantitative research methods to create a comprehensive science of communication in the twentieth century, Ernest Bormann has concluded: "As research accumulated, the analogy between Newtonian mechanics and behavioristic psychology proved more figurative than literal. The experimentalists in communication research stretched the analogy even more since they were, of necessity, interested in symbolic matters for which the behavior of subjects was often a poor index." Because it must deal with symbolic matters, rhetorical theory cannot be "a coherent, homogeneous body of principles," but rather must be a "collection of style-specific theoretical formulations to guide practice and criticism" (52). Such, in my view also, is the nature of a pragmatic theory, whose formulations, definitions, and guiding principles will not be so much predictive as relational and explanatory.

Bormann's requirement, in the passage cited above, that a rhetorical theory should be "style-specific" provides a rationale—above and beyond one's personal interest—for the second informing perspective of this book: its concern with the written word. Oral and written discourse have of course a common basis in the language of a community, and there are any number of instances where writing serves quite simply as a substitute for speech. But the view of writing solely as a graphic system for representing speech is limiting and distorting. Speech and writing are, or have become, separate media; they involve different sense perceptions, different modes of communicative interaction, and they have developed different formal characteristics. Also, even accounting for obvious elements of interplay and interdependence, they display differences of social function and cultural standing; they call into play different organizations of language, of thought, and perhaps even of consciousness itself.[1]

1. For provocative speculations on these issues, see Carothers, Jaynes, and Ong 1971.

Classical discourse theory and discourse education are concerned primarily with speechmaking, although ancient and Renaissance theorists and teachers were by no means oblivious to or uninterested in writing.[2] Several attempts were made to broaden the study in the eighteenth and nineteenth centuries; but whereas classical theorists looked upon purpose and social situation as major determinants of kinds of discourse (and consequently of form and style), moderns turned their gaze toward formal and psychological factors. From the standpoint of the teaching of writing, the most conspicuous modern fruit of this shift in perspective has been the composite rhetoric of "exposition, narration, description, and persuasion."[3] This rhetorical lore, while it has no doubt served as vehicle for a great deal of productive pedagogy, has never had much theoretical cogency and has fostered from the beginning a number of debilitating confusions among form, strategy, and purpose in discourse.[4] It has contributed virtually nothing to criticism, and it seems odd that teachers of literature should be primarily responsible for keeping alive for so long such a particularly arid tradition of critical concepts. That tradition's preoccupation with form and style has tended to divorce rhetorical pedagogy from its vital intellectual and cultural moorings, even among teachers who have no interest in such a separation.[5] Thus, in spite of the growing sophistication of formal and stylistic treatments of written discourse among students of literary art, we have yet to develop a fully adequate rhetoric of the written word, a rhetoric that comprehends and builds upon the major kinds and situations of writing as determinants of form and style, capable of casting critical and historical light upon the various orders of nonfiction prose that thrive in the contemporary world.

Two aspects of the written medium deserve special attention as we attempt to develop this rhetoric. The first is structural, and it involves the special dynamic of writer, subject, and audience that is occasioned by the absence of a definite situational context, by the removal of author from audience in space and time, and by the absence of literal voice— hence one's inability to call upon many of the communicative devices of spoken language. This medium places special, "unnatural" demands and limitations upon both readers and writers, calling into play certain artifices and conventions that have to be learned and practiced apart from the more regular processes of language learning in general; at the same time, this medium opens up new communicative possibilities, not merely quantitatively in the possibility of communication over great

2. See, for instance, Quintilian, X, iii–iv.
3. For surveys of the origins and currency of this set of distinctions, see D'Angelo 1976 and Connors.
4. Some of the deficiencies in this respect are noted by Kinneavy (28–29).
5. For an extended discussion of this point, see Young 1978.

expanses of space and time, but also qualitatively, in the special dynamic of author, subject, audience, and text.

At one level we can point to the distinct advantage of "not being there" on certain occasions, of avoiding certain interactions, of leaving certain elements of promise or threat in the range of implication; at another level, to the distinct advantage of "having it in writing," making the commitment publicly binding or the charge publicly sustainable; at another level, to the advantage of sustained and uninterrupted attention to subject matter, to one's ability to "go back over it," to produce and clarify complex hierarchies of analysis and classification; and at yet another level—perhaps the most fascinating—to the advantages of artifice and illusionism. Since the written discourse situation involves implicitly the imagining of a "real" discourse setting and the illusion of a spoken voice (Ong 1975), the medium implicitly encourages experimentation with different imagined voices, different imagined situational contexts, and different implied modes of interaction between author and reader. And thus a good part of the "communication" that takes place in writing resides in the calling to mind of established artifices and conventions, in the deliberate extension or violation of these conventions, and in the appropriation of familiar conventions or sets of conventions to novel or unexpected subject matters.

A second dimension of the written medium, closely entangled in the first, is social and cultural. From its earliest appearance in human societies writing has performed special functions—administrative, aesthetic, ritualistic—and enjoyed a special status in communication. In its functional dimension, as well as in the structural, it has developed historically in rich interaction with the spoken word and with speechmaking, and in both dimensions it has undergone important transformations—first in the manuscript civilization of the Middle Ages, and second in the present civilization that began with the European Renaissance, when the invention of moveable type enormously expanded the range and possibilities of written communication. We are now in the midst, some believe, of a third period of transformation, as the civilization of print merges into the civilization of electronic media (Ong 1971: 284–303).

This history holds some rich paradoxes. In one dimension it is a history of increasing specialization and differentiation. Structurally, it is possible to trace, as E. D. Hirsch has done, a progress from writing as a transcription of speech and quasi-speech events (even in local dialects) to writing as a standardized medium with its own special characteristics and conventions (1977: 51–72). Paradoxically, however, as writing moves more and more in the direction of a separate medium, its flirtations with the human voice become more intense, as do its capacities for being "conversational."

From the standpoint of cultural function, one detects similar sorts of divergences and convergences. On the one hand it is possible to envision, as Ong has done, the increasing specialization and differentiation of discourse functions as civilization progresses from preliterate, oral stages to the "relentless literacy" engendered by print technology and mass education. In the prose and poetry of primarily oral civilizations the ritualistic, political and instrumental, and aesthetic functions of language are more at ease together, and forms and genres of discourse are not sharply differentiated. The development of literacy, urban civilization, and the kinds of cultural specialization that follow from it urge also the specialization of kinds of discourse into different spheres of activity. And this leads eventually to an ever-increasing differentiation of writing and speechmaking. On the other hand, in a literate, technological society speechmaking itself is transformed and, in at least some of its manifestations, begins to perform some of the functions, adapting some of the formal characteristics, of the written word. The now-ubiquitous phenomenon of the speech delivered from a written text is the most conspicuous sign of such a development; the extreme of it (perhaps too extreme) is the scholarly "paper," delivered orally (with a handout) at the meetings of academic associations.

At the same time, it is worth speculating about the ways in which essay-writing and book-writing have recaptured some of the older styles and functions of speechmaking. Electronic technology, particularly television, has radically transformed the character of much public speechmaking, rendering egregiously old-fashioned what Weaver has called the "spaciousness" and what Ong (1971) has termed the "rhapsodic" design of older oratory; whereas writing, with its capacity for maintaining the illusion of nonelectronic discourse settings, and with its capacity for mimicking the spoken word, can often seem more like an oration than can an address delivered over television. Moreover, modernity has witnessed a vast proliferation of publications serving the literally thousands of religious organizations, special-interest groups, and civic organizations that now form the bases of cultural identity. Through these publications the written word often functions in ways analogous to older, communal and ritual forms of oral discourse.

All such speculation aside, however, there are some ineradicable discontinuities of medium that make the range of written discourse functions not only different in important respects from that of speechmaking but also more problematic to analyze. Speechmaking is a context and situation-oriented affair; its aims, genres, modes, and styles tend to cluster around occasions, forums, recurrent kinds of public situation and ritual. One's access to audiences is limited, it is relatively brief, and it is usually conditioned upon more or less definite expectations and conventions of a "live" audience. Aristotle's division of speeches into deliberative, forensic, and epideictic kinds is based principally upon this circumstance. These classes of speechmaking represent not merely different fields of subject matter and different specific discourse functions (exhort and dissuade, accuse and defend, praise and blame), but different settings and forums as well, with different structural constraints and different relationships of speaker and audience. The medium of writing, however, is not radically situation- or setting-oriented in the same way that speechmaking is, and this circumstance makes possible a much more fluid range of aims, modes, genres, and motives.[6] And thus the problems of classification are aggravated, as the possibilities of communication (as well as misunderstanding) are multiplied.

The situation is even further complicated by another set of modern circumstances—namely the relative cheapness of print technology, combined with literacy as a norm of culture, social conditions that make for increased leisure time, and work and travel schedules punctuated with hours of waiting and restless inactivity. These circumstances have created a vast public that is reading something almost constantly. Under such conditions the written word is not only an instrument of science, of information, of public debate or private reflection; it is also a commodity to be packaged and sold to mass markets. A good part of this modern commodity consists of contextless and trivial information merged into entertainment or diversion. A good deal of it is undoubtedly information we could do without, or perhaps even—as a celebrated critic of our civilization, Aleksandr Solzhenitsyn, has warned—information that we have a right not to be subjected to. It may well constitute both symptom and cause of "a culture overwhelmed by irrelevance, incoherence, and impotence" (Postman 76). Nevertheless, it is surely a distinct part of the reality which rhetorical theory must attempt to comprehend.

The fluid nature of the written medium, as well as the prodigious proliferation of writing in our civilization, places considerable strains on traditional discourse categories. And it is this fact, involving the great difficulty of dealing with writing at the levels of context, aim, and function, that has very likely determined the formal and stylistic drift of rhetorical scholarship and pedagogy centered on writing, as much as any preoccupation with form and style per se. Among literary scholars in particular, many of whom are also involved in the study and teaching of rhetoric, there is a general impatience with generic studies, born of the feeling that they are at best inconclusive and at worst damaging to the comprehension and appreciation of individual works. Such feelings are very often justified, particularly when critics and teachers attempt to

6. For further discussion, see chapter 5, pp. 107–9.

use classification as a substitute for understanding rather than as a critical tool of understanding. But these feelings are also often curiously coupled with uncritical assumptions about the nature of discourse, or uncritical acceptance of quasi-theoretical constructs that are at best inadequate and at worst illogical on the face of it.

My own view is that even though theories of discourse acts may "leak" even worse than grammars, some constructs are nevertheless clearly more adequate than others; the study *can* be conducted in a sensible and nonreductionist fashion, and it may have great intellectual and practical value. The human use of language is the center of the liberal arts, the starting point for our various understandings of reality, and the practical art on which the health of civilization depends. Because it affects the ways in which we view ourselves as individuals and as communities, and because it affects the way we teach the arts of language, we need the best rhetorical theory we can get.

OUTLINES OF A PRAGMATIC THEORY

The theory presented here is intended as a confirmation, refortification, and extension of the Aristotelian approach to discourse activity. That approach is fundamentally sound. It is comprehensive; it is nonreductionist; it concentrates upon the aims and substance as well as the forms and processes of discourse; and it is philosophical, energized by a principle that Plato established for all time: Questions of discourse, and especially of rhetoric, are inseparable from questions of truth and knowledge.

There can be no doubt, on the other hand, that there are both descriptive and theoretical weaknesses, even gaping holes, in classical theory. One part of this book's task is to shore up some of these weaknesses; another is to to extend that theory to the world of modern rhetorical writing. Some new categories are erected, some older ones discarded: To the traditional categories of *rhetorical, scientific,* and *poetic* discourse, I will add a fourth, the *instrumental.* Within the field of rhetoric itself I discard the category of forensic or judicial discourse, absorbing some of the rhetorical activity traditionally lodged there into a broadened notion of deliberation. I also attempt to redefine the traditionally troublesome category of *epideictic,* to extend the traditional category of *deliberation* into the world of writing, and to account for two additional categories of modern rhetorical writing—*informative* and *reflective/exploratory.*

These various adjustments are not isolated tinkerings, however, but integral parts of a broader, theoretical extension of Aristotle. They are grounded in a descriptive and philosophical framework whose full articulation was neither possible nor necessary in traditional theory.

The function of this framework is to show how the aims of discourse and the motives of rhetoric constitute a system, and how, since the aims of discourse constitute different methods of "arresting" experience in order to know it through language, this system relates to human constructions of reality in general.[7]

The relations and interpenetrations of "rhetoric" and "reality" have, of course, been concerns of rhetorical theory since Plato and Aristotle. However, while the goals of classical and modern rhetorical theory remain essentially the same, the modern theorist responds to descriptive and theoretical contexts that are in some respects quite different. The modern theorist faces not only a different set of phenomena, but different problems of conceptualization and method as well; dealing with these problems requires not merely different categories and different alignments of categories, but also more refined and more carefully articulated notions of "categories" themselves and of the relations among them.

Aristotle's theoretical accomplishment was to incorporate rhetoric into a "realist" or "formist" ontology established by Plato, at the same time rescuing both rhetorical and poetic discourse from the meanness and disorder that Plato had attributed to them. His moving target was rhetorical activity itself, which needed philosophical justification as an orderly construct and a respectable human art. The task of the modern theorist is rather different. The "defense of rhetoric" remains for us an important philosophical and ethical task, but in a theoretical context that is in some respects quite the reverse: The modern sciences and philosophies of language have established beyond question the fundamental orderliness of its processes, but they have at the same time uncovered language's own constructive role in those very notions of "being" and "reality" against which it has been traditionally defined and measured. Consequently, any notion of discourse "genre" or substance (as opposed to rhetorical process) must now run the risk of being dismissed as tautological or arbitrary.

As already noted, many students of rhetoric and literature do not consider the game worth the candle. And yet, as Kenneth Burke points out at some length in *A Grammar of Motives*, it is precisely the development of a "substantial" construct—an account of human motives and contexts—that is needed to comprehend without reductionism the complex unities of such purposeful and specifically human activities as rhetoric and literature. Moreover, what Kenneth Burke articulates so passionately about rhetoric and literature has become increasingly apparent in the understanding and teaching of literacy itself: The teach-

7. I borrow the metaphor of knowledge as an "arrest" of experience from Michael Oakeshott's *Experience and its Modes*, without any commitment to the philosophical idealism of his treatise.

ing of forms and processes is not enough (Hirsch 1980). Rhetorical theory, criticism, and pedagogy must rest ultimately upon an orderly
account of the motives and substance of discourse.

The theory attempted here is similar to what Burke envisioned in *A
Grammar of Motives*—a theory of rhetorical substance without ideological
or psychological commitments. Rather than attempting to resolve the
dilemmas of form and meaning along lines suggested by one or another
philosophical system or world hypothesis, I accept those dilemmas as a
given of the enterprise, and I develop frameworks of both a "formalistic" and a "semiotic" kind, along lines suggested by the analysis of language and discourse itself. The first of these frameworks I call the
"Discourse Hierarchy." It is constructed upon recognition of some
superordinate features of form that operate at every level of discourse
activity, and its purpose is to discover the status and stabilize the meanings of such concepts as *mode, strategy, genre,* and *aim* in discourse. This
framework is very useful in specifying "levels of form," and it provides
useful starting points for analyzing modes and strategies of discouse,
but higher levels of analysis require some account of kinds of meaning
and levels of meaning in discourse. This account is provided by a second and ultimately more important framework which I call the "Motivational Axes."

The "Motivational Axes" framework is constructed along lines suggested by two sources: the rhetorical and philosophical speculations of
Kenneth Burke, and contemporary speech-act theory as developed by
Austin and Searle. From Burke it derives the goal of relating patterns of
intention to a broader system that is neither a psychology or empirical
process-model on the one hand nor a fixed ontology on the other, but
rather a "grammar of motives." This broader system will not be a "philosopher's stone," that is, a particular theory of conceptualization or
world order, but "a system of placement"—in Burke's terms, a "philosopher's stone for the synopsis of writings that have sought the philosopher's stone" (56). Such a system is not in itself a construction of reality
but an objective model for talking about human constructions of reality.

Burke's version of this system was the "pentad." Perceiving that
the meanings of human discourse must be construed not merely as a
system of references but also as a system of symbolic actions, Burke
constructed a "dramatistic" model which urged the perception of discourse as a set of meaningful actions. My own "philosopher's stone of
philosopher's stones" is not a pentad—the *Action, Actor-Agent, Scene,
Means, Purpose* of Burke's *A Grammar of Motives*—but a quadrad, of
Action, Contemplation, Reference, and *Non-Reference.* This conceptual
framework, moreover, is not "dramatistic," as is Burke's, but semiotic,
and it draws upon what I believe to be a more precise and sophisticated
approach to the problem of language as symbolic action, namely that of

contemporary speech-act theory. It is represented in a pair of axes
extrapolated from the principal tensions inherent in the concept of
"meaning"—in any human attempt to arrest experience through language. Not surprisingly, these linguistic tensions relate to broader
dichotomies in the history of thought and culture: Action and Contemplation stand at the poles of a "constative-performative" axis (utterance
as *reflection-on-experience* vs. utterance as *participant-in-experience*);[8] while
Reference and Non-Reference stand at the poles of a "referential-tropo-
logical" axis (utterance as *designation-of-experience* vs. utterance as *sym-
bolization-of-experience*).

This particular "grammar of motives," like Burke's, construes discourse as a complex human activity, to be understood in terms not of
primary determinants but of *ratios*. These are indicated in figure 1. In
this figure the Contemplation-Reference ratio anticipates the "scientific" aim in discourse; Action-Reference anticipates the "instrumental"
aim; Contemplation-Non-Reference the "poetic" aim; and Action-Non-
Reference the "rhetorical" aim. My contention will be that this model

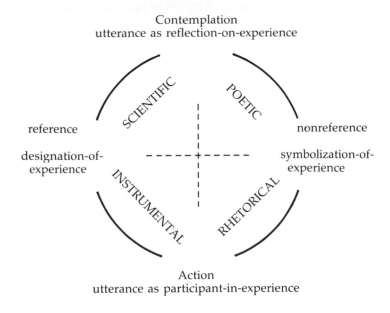

Figure 1. A semiotic grammar of motives

8. The notion of utterance as participant-in-experience, though not the precise terminology, is drawn directly from the speech-act theory of J. L. Austin and John Searle. There
are detailed engagements of this theory in chapters 1, 3, and 4.

constitutes a comprehensive and illuminating guide to the aims and substance of human discourse and to the "kinds of reality" that human beings discover in experience. I will also argue that rhetoric plays crucial educational, epistemological, and social roles in this scheme, and that rhetoric should therefore occupy a privileged place in discourse education.

All of this is by way of preview. It awaits a more patient and elaborate reconstruction, defense, and comparison with competing theories. It is not my purpose to announce an elegant formula and then, like Newton, to deduce all possible worlds from it. That would provide nothing for the theory and criticism of discourse but yet another dreary instance of the possibilities of conceptual reduction. Rhetorical theory and criticism must be responsive to the dappled, contradictory, paradoxical flux of rhetorical action, the achievements of creatures who are themselves contradictory, paradoxical, and—in Burke's ever-pregnant phrase—"rotten with perfection." If such terms describe both humanity and human discourse, they also describe the thicket of terminology that the one has developed to understand the other. It is a very deep jungle, in which one can get quickly lost without proper instruments. And so we must begin at the beginning, with some basic problems of terminology and conceptualization.

1. THE DISCOURSE HIERARCHY: A CATEGORIAL FRAMEWORK

I. CATEGORIAL AND SEMIOTIC FRAMEWORKS

The study of human beings using language is notoriously suspect because it must be conducted by human beings using language. The field of discourse is thus bedeviled by circularities and loopholes, the dangers of which can be avoided only by taking stock, from the outset, of guiding principles and theoretical foundations. It will not be enough to produce or stipulate a "workable" definition of rhetoric and then to proceed from there, thus using rhetoric to study rhetoric. Our first task is to discover and articulate larger frameworks which will provide bases for adequate definition.

At least two principles ought to guide any attempt to construct or organize a body of knowledge. The first is the principle of "appropriate measure," given timeless statement by Aristotle: "[I]t is the mark of an educated man to look for precision to each class of things just so far as the nature of the subject admits; it is equally foolish to accept probable reasoning from a mathematician and to demand from a rhetorician scientific proofs" (*Nic. Eth.* 1094^b). The second principle, really an extension of the first, may be designated the principle of "intrinsic nature." It dictates, quite simply, that a body of knowledge about any phenomenon or area of experience should be organized around a set of principles relating directly to that phenomenon and not some other related or encompassing area. This principle does not of course require that any particular source of insight be ignored or left unsearched, but merely that the starting points of a discipline should bear intrinsic relation to the object of study, employing a set of concepts that are directly relevant to the subject at every level of analysis. Basing one's inquiry on a set of extrapolations from a particular philosophical, psychological, or sociological approach to human interaction or intelligence would not only throw the study into immediate and unresolvable competition with other points of view, but—equally damaging—it would abstract the subject of discourse from its essential nature as a set of organizations of linguistic acts. These acts, and the principles inherent in their organization and meaning, must claim the first attention of a pragmatic theory; and they must, in fact, provide frameworks by which insights from various other disciplines can be effectively incorporated into the study of discourse.

An immediate burden of any set of framing concepts for the study of discourse is to provide criteria for, to validate, and to organize a set of classifications answering these questions: What are the basic materials and processes of discourse, and what are the basic entities and actions into which they are organized? And since in the case of discourse we are dealing with human products—deliberate organizations of language acts, as opposed to the organization of language itself—we will also inevitably be taking a stand on the status of various concepts as they relate to human purpose: What things constitute means as opposed to ends, lesser ends as opposed to higher ends, materials as opposed to strategies, forms as opposed to functions? We shall have to develop a "grammar of motives" that sheds light upon the motives of rhetoric, and at the same time a framework of categories for comprehending its genres, modes, and strategies. Providing the set of classifications called for is an enormously difficult task. It is not that there are so few points of entry but that there are so many, the principal cause of this being the condition already cited—the centrality of discourse to all human capability and all human action. Actually the range, diversity, richness, beauty, and complexity of discourse activity at any stage in civilization constitute an important signal. Little wonder that theorists and critics from the Greek rhetoricians onward have spawned such a bountiful confusion of classifications, grouped generally under such rubrics as "form," "mode," "genre," "tradition," all notably vague, overlapping, and reflecting different critical and cultural preoccupations. James Britton, the British theorist and educator, has remarked that "there is simply no fully satisfactory way to classify discourse" (1). But there are dozens of ways that are at least partially satisfactory, as the survey of classifications in James Kinneavy's *A Theory of Discourse* well illustrates (51–57).

Given this embarrassment of riches, one of the tasks of theory should be to test various ways of classification against the evidence of texts, perhaps arriving at some conclusions about their various degrees of validity and explanatory power. But it is obvious from the outset that many such classifications have a good deal of validity from one or another perspective. The first task of theory, it follows, is not merely to establish a new and more powerful partition of discourse (or to correct an old one) but to elucidate a framework able to test and accommodate various ranges of classification, organizing them so as to reveal their respective levels of application for a particular medium. Hence the usefulness, and the necessity, of a set of initial concepts that have immediate application to discourse (as opposed to some other field of inquiry), that are independent of any particular psychological or philosophical perspective, and that are powerful enough to comprehend the subject at all important levels of analysis.

Having accepted that these fundamental concepts should emerge from the study of linguistic acts, we must confront a dichotomy which permeates this study at every turn, the dichotomy of form and meaning. This dichotomy is inevitable because the linguistic act is an act of symbolism, with no essential or organic relationship between signifier and signified; and for this same reason the dichotomy is fundamentally unresolvable. Virtually every controversy in the language arts, whether of linguistic theory, of criticism, or of pedagogy, turns upon it in some way; and virtually every school or approach to language or discourse constructs a framework that attempts a resolution in one direction or another—either formalist or semantic, structural or cultural. For reasons that will become readily apparent in the pages that follow, "formalist" approaches to discourse generally break down more quickly, leak worse, and account for less that is interesting than "semantic" approaches. The theory of discourse presented in this book may be said to lean distinctly in the latter direction. Nevertheless, I do not wish to begin with a framework that resolves the form/meaning dichotomy in one direction or another, because the very unresolvability of the issue is too important a fact to ignore, and I wish to make the most of it. My procedure will be to erect successive conceptual frameworks, at key stages of the investigation, aiming at both sides of the dichotomy: a "categorial" framework and a "semiotic" framework. The crucial point of interchange between these frameworks, and the ultimate focus of this book, lies in the notion of "genre," a concept which in itself denotes a particular coalescence of characteristic meanings/purposes and characteristic forms/strategies in discourse. What is remarkable is that this process of coalescence appears in its most volatile and most freewheeling forms in rhetorical discourse, a fact of enormous significance for the theory of rhetoric and the relation of discourse to knowledge and culture.

II. THE DISCOURSE HIERARCHY

The hierarchy of discourse categories presented below constitutes the outlines of a pragmatic theory of written discourse. It is not a direct extrapolation from any operational model of discourse activity, nor is it an extrapolation from any "root" system of classifications derived from the structure, the psychology, the philosophy, or the sociology of language. It derives its justification, *although not the specific content of its vari-*

Aim	Strategy	Mode	Medium (Writing/Print)
Instrumental	Generic	Discursive	A. Format
Scientific	Material	Expressive	essay
Rhetorical	Dialectical	Objective	dialogue
Poetic	Formal	Affective	interview
	Stylistic		etc.
	Modal	Narrative	
		Expressive	B. The Paragraph
Rhetorical Genus		Objective	
Deliberative		Affective	C. The Sentence
Performative			
Reflective/Exploratory		Dramatic	
Informative		Expressive	
		Objective	
De Facto Genre		Affective	
(e.g., book review,			
obituary editorial,			
etc.)			

ous identifications, from a set of purely formal considerations, and that is why our attention for the present will be confined to its "categorial" elements—the hierarchy of concepts leading down (left to right) from "aim" to "medium."

The "formal considerations" that justify this framework derive from a set of answers to this question: Are there salient features or characteristics of discourse in every application of the term, from grammar and phonology to the study of texts in their cultural settings? I want to suggest that such features do exist; that their analysis can guide us in the attempt to discover and organize a system of discourse classifications; and that, while necessarily very broad in scope, they offer some particularly useful insights about the nature and the effects of the written medium.

It has become commonplace since the advent of generative-transformational linguistics to affirm that language is a "rule-governed" activity. And certainly the notion can be generalized to all levels of discourse. The production of a book review takes place under the guidance of certain "rules of the game" in a way that is analogous to the production of a word or a phrase or a sentence. It is obvious, however, that there is a difference, and the closest indication of this lies in the kinds of "mistakes" that are made in the process. At the levels of phonology and grammar, mistakes are the exception in ordinary discourse. When they occur they are usually quickly noted and compensated for. At the level of "speech acts," which Austin and Searle have shown to be governed by strict norms of context and usage, mistakes do rather frequently occur. We "apologize" or "offer condolences" in the wrong way or at the wrong moment; requests are "taken as" insults; mere "compliments" are interpreted as binding commitments of devotion. At the level of extended discourse, mistakes both of transmission and of interpretation are legion. In fact, the arts of rhetoric and hermeneutics have as their practical ends the construction of systematic procedures for conducting discourse successfully and avoiding these mistakes.

The higher the level of activity—the more closely it approaches the conscious shaping of discourse transactions in the performance of distinct social functions—the less constraining and more subject to extension and manipulation the "rules" become: they are now "norms," rules of the game, conventions to be followed, broken, or toyed with. In this discussion I will be primarily concerned with identifying such features as underlie, illustrate, and help to clarify this set of circumstances.

Asymmetry

The first feature is that of asymmetry, the pervasive condition that form is not intrinsically "locked into" meaning and can never in and of itself fully predict meaning. Discourse does, of course, involve at all levels the production and organization of certain "forms" in the communication of certain meanings; and hearers or readers do characteristically "understand" what a particular organization of forms has been designed to convey. They do not do so by virtue of any lockstep relation of form to meaning, however. Their understanding involves a complex interaction of factors, including the context of surrounding forms, the extralinguistic context or "field" in which the communication is embedded, and clarifying messages within the discourse itself, as well as intuitions about the *characteristic* range of form-meaning relations in the language and in the various modes and genres of communication at a given time (Halliday 1964: 87ff.).

As generative-transformational grammarians have eloquently demonstrated, these intuitions at the level of grammar and phonology are extraordinarily precise and systematic, and they are acquired by children in the regular processes of language learning; at other levels they are looser and more volatile, more responsive to the external historical forces that shape them. Such "higher" intuitions have to be cultivated, refined, and sometimes consciously adjusted. But even grammar and phonology are subject to change, albeit gradual and unconscious, and this is our surest sign that form and meaning at all levels are fundamentally asymmetrical.

In linguistic analysis all of this is commonplace. Individual sounds or phonemes have no intrinsic value, and the relationship between the form of a word and its meaning is usually arbitrary. At the level of syntax the phenomenon is even more striking: Different surface patterns will express the same functional or logical meanings, and conversely, a single pattern will yield a variety of such meanings. Imperative form, for instance, will express not only commands, but also warnings, instructions, well-wishes ("Break a leg!"), or even casual valedictions ("Have a nice day!"). Such dynamics as these underlie the determination of language philosophers that the basic unit of communication is not the sentence but the "speech act," a particular nexus of form, function, and context.

Naturally there are counter-tendencies, and they contribute to those "cultural" intuitions we develop about forms of communication at higher levels. Words, phrases, and habitual styles or methods of organization do acquire certain associations and connotations by virtue of provenance and repeated usage. It is possible to "sound like" a gangster or a sociologist. But while the processes of history may attach certain associations to certain forms, there is actually no necessary relations between them, and the associations themselves can be transcended, shucked off, or placed in dramatic opposition to other associations. The processes of linguistic and social change (as well as sheer human inventiveness) are usually victorious in this respect, and the feature of asymmetry, along with the possibility of infinite use it entails, remains intact.

Remarkably, the human impulse toward innovation and play is countered by an impulse toward stabilization and restriction—through education and regulation—of forms to specific contexts. The springs of such impulses run deep in human consciousness (deeper than can be comprehended in the reasonable demands of civil usage) and bespeak radical uncertainties about the possibilities of human knowledge and community. They are the source of Plato's musings about the relations of words to reality in the *Theaetetus*; and they are manifest in various forms of mysticism as well as some forms of scientism and aestheticism. Such impulses are all the more remarkable in face of the paradox that, if things were really any different, language would not exist as we know it; and not merely the possibilities of communciation but those of consciousness itself would be severely curtailed. A creature in command of a wholly symmetrical communication system would have to be either a creature of limitless possibilities, for whom the means of communication would be at one with the infinite range of experience itself, or a very limited creature indeed, using a finite range of signals to communicate an equally finite number of messages.

Human language uses a finite range of signals to discover an infinite range of meanings. This is made possible at one level through the recursive structures of grammar and phonology; but where lexical meanings come into play, the most conspicuous agency of infinite use is metaphor, the process whereby meanings associated with one form are transferred to another. Finally, at higher levels involving the organization of language into discourse modes and genres, something akin to the process of metaphoric transfer takes place in the various devices of masking and of stylisitc and generic appropriation. Here forms are used in novel ways, so that a "normal" range of meanings, values, or expectations conventionally associated with these forms can be transferred into new situations. These devices can make strange or difficult subjects easier to grasp, and they can create new ways of approaching and understanding experience. They can also fail, like bad metaphors. Jonathan Swift's condemnation of British practices and policies by means of a "modest proprosal" for slaughtering and eating Irish babies was an act of moral genius; the recent informative article on anatomy that begins, "I am Joe's gall bladder," is somewhat less captivating.

The generalized notion of metaphoric transfer, based on the principle of asymmetry, illustrates directly a central problem of discourse theory and pedagogy, namely their traditional inability to distinguish form from function, material from formal from final causes, and their inability to discover stable relationships among such terms as *genre, strategy,* and *mode.* The causes of the problem are not so much the dullness or recklessness of rhetoricians as the richness and trickiness of discourse itself: What is "act" in one instance may be "agency" or "vehicle" in another; and explicit formal clues are often entirely absent.

It is important not to overstate the case. The sort of generic appropriation and metaphoric transfer we are discussing here is not so much a rule as a possibility of discourse, one that is expanded greatly in the written medium. There are very significant stabilities in the form-function relationship among many poetic and rhetorical types and among virtually all scientific ones (in modern times at least). Specific "genres" of rhetoric are in fact mainly distinguishable by particular convergenes of function, form, and strategy. One may give ready assent both to Campbell and Jamieson's definition of genre as a "constellation of substantive, situational and stylistic elements" (18) and to Herbert W. Simons' insistence that rhetorical genre must be conceived as a "distinctive and recurring pattern of similarly constrained rhetorical practices" (42). However, the point that I wish to stress is that such stabilities as do exist inhere not so much in the nature of things as in cultural and literary convention. Even such generic concepts as "romance," "book review," or "obituary editorial," which carry fairly concrete expectations of purpose, strategy, and form, have a fundamental volatility about them. Not only do the characteristic motives and stylistic appointments of such entities change over time; they are subject to extension, transformation, or appropriation into alien territory in the hands of a single creative author. Furthermore, it is crucial to realize that, even as we attempt to discover rhetorical types on the basis of recurrent features of situation, form, and style, we are still dealing with a medium and a class of discourse wherein innovation in form is itself a pervasive strategy.

Naturally, not all things are possible. It is hardly conceivable that the American Declaration of Independence could have been cast in the form of a dialogue, let us say between Leo and Aquila. But a general condemnation of British policy might have taken such a form, perhaps with the eagle threatening to fly away, or worse. Conversely, the form and style of the Declaration itself might be appropriated to a satiric treatment of some modern constituency. To be sure, a heavy element of play enters into such transactions and gives them a turn toward poetic. But what an impoverishment of theory if we cannot comprehend such instances in a treatment of rhetoric.

The asymmetry principle is immediately relevant to questions of theory because it locates the ambiguity and volatility of categories such as "genre" and "mode" in the intrinsic capability of discourse at all levels for turning act into agency; and the recognition in itself points to ways in which stability might be imparted to these terms. At the outset a confusing or promiscuous application of a discourse concept can be immediately related to the fact that it is being used to indicate material and causal or purposive dimensions simultaneously—or that a term most commonly associated with one dimension is being extended into the other. The notion "exposition" in modern composition pedagogy is a conspicuous case in point. In some texts exposition is used as a purpose-oriented concept—albeit a defective one: the quasi-genre of "writing that explains." In such treatments, narration and description are comprehended as "methods" of exposition, alongside definition, classification, and the rest. In other treatments, exposition is more formally conceived, as a method of writing involving certain characteristics of form and coherence; in these partitions categories like description and narration are set off as separate, equivalent notions.

Recognizing the causes of these kinds of confusion prepares one to recognize that in asking such a question as "What are the modes of discourse?" we are asking an empirical question only in part. The question must really be framed in this way: Given a range of concepts that have some bearing upon the way or manner or proceeding in discourse, what different sorts of things do they refer to? And how do these different sorts of things relate to one another? The set of concepts and descriptions that we eventually call "modes" will take its definition partly from the *place assigned to it in a larger system of concepts*. The primary device for arranging these notions will be dictated by the asymmetry principle: While most discourse concepts are involved in potential ambiguities of form and function, some are less so than others. Some refer more clearly to "materials" that are unrelated to any specific purpose; others refer to "ends" subject to fulfillment by a variety of means; and others lie somewhere in the middle. We envision, then, a scale of concepts ranging from form to purpose, from material to final causes of discourse. The progression from Medium to Mode to Strategy to Aim reflects this organization.

The asymmetry principle is not the only informing factor in the designation and arrangement of these categories, however; the framework proposed here takes additional support and specificity from the examination of three other superordinate features of discourse: hierarchy, continuum, and context-sensitivity.

Hierarchy

Hierarchical arrangements are indispensable to any organization of diverse entities into purposeful action. Language is the primary human form of such a system, and so are the products of language—essays, poems, books. At every level of analysis we encounter the grouping of entities into categories and the arrangement of categories into higher categories; the production of speech acts and acts of discourse involves the subordination of certain features and designs to larger features and designs.

What is remarkable about these orderings is that they inhere in the inescapably linear, temporal flow of discourse, existing in a kind of structural tension with primary linearity. They constitute orderings, not physical features, of the primary signaling system. A sentence "conjoins" a subject to a predicate, but each of these units contains "head" elements to which various modifying and complementary structures are subordinated. The flow of meanings, likewise, displays this tension. For example, the sentence

> Jack has become a competent pianist simply by working hard at it; but he'll never be a true artist because he has no talent

has an essentially binary, forward-moving logical structure of the pattern "concession/assertion." But to each side of the conjunct are subordinated other conjuncts, first one of "effect/cause" (competent pianist/ work hard), and then one of "inference/premise."[1] And the entire structure would of course be subordinated to other structures in a particular text (perhaps a letter of recommendation).

As we look more broadly at discourse products in their cultural settings, we encounter the phenomenon of "wholes-within-wholes," wherein units of discourse that could conceivably have the status of sep-

1. This analysis owes a good deal to Pitkin, "X/Y: Some Basic Strategies of Discourse."

arate discourse acts (and perhaps at one time actually did have such status) are framed into larger units, subordinated to larger structures of
meaning. Pikes's example of the *sonnet* in a *sermon* in a *church service* is a
good one because it reminds us that in considering the external "framing
contexts" of discourse we are looking at phenomena that are fundamentally continuous with the process of discourse itself (79). This is, in fact,
the point at which the study of discourse merges with the study of social
and cultural behavior and history. The student of discourse, who is interested in the sermon as act of rhetoric, will need to draw upon this larger
study because the nature of church services in general (as well as of the
particular service) will be a factor in determining what kind of rhetoric is
involved. And the student of history or social behavior will need to draw
upon the study of discourse, because the church service itself may be an
act of what Kenneth Burke has called "administrative rhetoric," framed
by some larger program of action (1950: 158–66).

Although hierarchies are largely intuited rather than "seen," they
can be signaled in various ways: by suprasegmental patterns of pitch,
stress, and transition; by function words that signal embeddings and
logical subordinations; and even by explicit verbal directions which
speakers will, from time to time, inject into a conversation or a speech.
To all of these devices writing adds a spatial, visual element, which cuts
even more radically across the temporal flow of discourse, intensifying
the urge toward hierarchical order, and in fact rendering this order
more efficient, through various devices of punctuation, numbering (I.1,
2, 3, . . . II. 1, 2, 3), spacing, headlining, and even in some cases the
arrangement of print on a page.[2]

Hierarchy is itself a variable concept that has varying ramifications
for the theory of discourse. Of particular relevance, first of all, is the
distinction between the hierarchy of forms and categories that constitute the system of communication itself, and the functional hierarchies
that human beings incorporate into acts of discourse.[3] In the one case
we are talking about a static construct—a progressively inclusive series
of discourse categories; in the other a dynamic process, wherein writers
and speakers subordinate certain speech-acts to others, certain forms to
larger formal matrices, and certain functions and effects to more encom-

2. Ong (*Rhetoric, Romance, and Technology* 37) has taken note of the "loosely strung-out,
episodic style" of earlier narrative, as opposed to the more intricately woven plots that are
made possible when composition is in writing and designed for print. It is paradoxical
that only very late in the history of narrative fiction, after the possibilities of the print
medium had been exploited to a very high degree, did authors hit upon the possibility of
representing the rhapsodic "stream of consciousness." It is as if such representations
could succeed only against the backdrop of highly developed expectations of more hierarchical sorts of order.
3. This distinction corresponds to the distinction between paradigmatic and syntagmatic
order in structural linguistics. See also Willis Pitkin, "Hierarchies and the Discourse
Hierarchy."

passing elements of purpose. The intricate relations between these two kinds of hierarchy are of the utmost importance to theory, for it is by observing the dynamic process that we can test the accuracy and consistency of the static construct. The Discourse Hierarchy represents a series of categories ranging from material to final cause, and the resulting arrangement constitutes a hierarchy of discourse forms, strategies, and functions that can be tested against the kinds of dynamic hierarchies exhibited by texts. Thus of a particular discourse notion (such as "mode") we can ask not only the hypothetical question: Does it refer (or shall we stipulate that it refers) more closely to material, means, or ends of discourse? We also ask the related empirical question: To what extent is it subject to appropriation and transformation—that is, to being subordinated to larger ends in a particular act of discourse?

This procedure can have an immediate clarifying effect. A persistent error of the prevailing textbook tradition in written composition has been the identification of such items as *comparison, description, definition* (actually the classical topoi) as forms or modes of discourse, coupled with the explanation that such forms are usually "combined" or "mixed" in actual discourse products. In the case of the items named, what we are dealing with are *strategies*—a middle level of concept—that can be employed in a variety of *modes*—a lower level of concept—and which fit into more or less elaborate discourse hierarchies toward the fulfillment of certain *aims*—a higher level of concept, referring more closely to the final causes of discourse as they relate to different sorts of cultural circumstance. Within the aims, it is worth noting in advance of extended treatment, the category of "de facto genre" (book review, obituary editorial, travelogue)[4] is assigned the lowest position. The rationale of such positioning is that "de facto genre" represents a category wherein certain typical functions are associated fairly consistently with certain conventions of form and strategy; and, as we have already noted in the discussion of asymmetry, anything *perceived* as a conventional form is subject to metaphoric transfer—to subordination to other ends. This happens, for instance, when what *appears* to be a book review turns out to be an extended presentation of a counterthesis or an extended promotion of the ideas contained in the book. A "form" associated with the function of evaluation has been appropriated to the ends of a different order of deliberation.[5]

4. The term "de facto genre" is borrowed from Harrell and Linkugel.
5. The opposite of this procedure occurs when a subordinate unit such as might have existed as part of a larger whole is extracted from that larger context and presented as a discourse act in some other context. Polonius' rather stuffy advice to Laertes in *Hamlet* has often been extracted from its aesthetic context and presented to modern young men as a serious piece of epideictic rhetoric, for example.

An additional relevant distinction among kinds of hierarchy in discourse is that between *categorial* and *generic* hierarchies. A categorial hierarchy involves successive orders of concepts, each more inclusive and "higher" in the sense of involving complex forms of organization that include lower categories as units or items. Generic hierarchies, on the other hand, involve successive layers of abstraction. Here the "higher" categories "contain" lower ones only in the sense of being more general orderings of types. They are not qualitatively different forms in themselves. ("Epideictic rhetoric" is a higher, more inclusive concept than "obituary editorial," for instance, but they are not different things.)

The arrangement of concepts from Medium to Mode to Strategy to Aim—obviously constitutes a categorial hierarchy. The Aims of discourse designate certain general types which "use" or organize certain Strategies; these in turn involve various organizations and manipulations of discourse Modes; and the Modes in turn involve characteristic organizations of the forms and conventions of the written medium. Particular instances of written discourse will involve the organization of all of these elements into functional hierarchies, which are sometimes highly conventional and sometimes highly novel.[6]

The arrangement of concepts under the heading of Aims in the list above (p. 16) is primarily a *generic* hierarchy. "De facto genre" names a more particular type of writing than "genus" which names a more particular grouping than does the general heading of "rhetorical discourse." These types are "included within" each other. At the same time, however—owing to those peculiar features already discussed under the heading of "asymmetry"—this group exhibits something in the nature of a categorial hierarchy as well. The Aims involve primarily a series of motivational and functional concepts; but because particular genres and groups of genres come to be perceived as conventional forms, they become items to be used and organized into larger discourse hierarchies, in ways not dissimilar from that associated with units from lower stages of the categorial hierarchy. Hence there is a special sense in which these concepts could be arranged in a scheme such as represented by figure 2.

This arrangement, or rather the insight about the structure of discourse categories that it represents, has a direct bearing upon the phenomenon of "overlap," which Pike in particular has identified as a

6. The kind of categorial arrangement presented here makes sense not only from the standpoint of one's observation of superordinate features of discourse; it also stands in accord with the logical requirements of categorial frameworks in general. Philosopher Stephen Körner notes that the highest categories in such frameworks must be "logically ultimate"—"possessors of characteristics but not characteristics themselves"; and "ontologically fundamental"—"objects which exist apart from and independently of other objects" (2).

AIM	Rhetorical Genus	De Facto Genre
Instrumental	Deliberative	(book review,
Scientific	Informative	obituary,
Poetic	Performative	editorial, etc.)
Rhetorical	Reflective/Exploratory	

Figure 2. The aims as categorial hierarchy

regular feature of discourse hierarchies (409). In figure 2 the series of items identified as "strategies" are "laid flat" to indicate this phenomenon: When particular discourse modes are used in highly conscious and uncharacteristic ways toward certain rhetorical ends, they become strategic devices, as do particular genres when they are appropriated in the ways that we have already identified. By accounting for these areas of overlap, incidentally, we provide further confirmation of the placement of the category of Strategy midway in the categorial hierarchy between Mode and Aim.

Continuum

A third superordinate feature of immediate relevance to discourse theory is that of continuum. Of the two types of linguistic continuum identified by Pike, the "stream of continuous speech" and the "continuum of physical characteristics of members of a class of units" (94), the latter bears most directly upon the problem of organizing discourse categories. In discourse, as in most human behavior, categories tend to "run together," particularly categories of roughly equivalent status. At every level of analysis, from phonological types to genres of discourse in their cultural settings, we encounter continuous phenomena: categories of form and function which extend into one another by gradual stages, and in which the value or consistency of a particular form is approached by the value or consistency of neighboring forms. The fact that categories do "run together" in this way does not imply that the study of rhetorical types is futile, any more than it implies that the study of language itself is futile. It does predict that some of the most interesting examples of discourse are going to reside at the frontiers and hinterlands, where both the risks and rewards of communication are sometimes greater; but even such examples are best accounted for in terms of their departure from (or alteration of) certain norms and their approximation of other norms.

As with the features of asymmetry and hierarchy, relationships of continuum reveal at the level of linguistic system highly systematic properties and configurations, which are mirrored at higher levels but greatly complicated by conscious human manipulation. With regard to greatly complicated by conscious human manipulation. With regard to the sound system, it has become a linguistic commonplace that individual phonemes are perceptual classes which exist in continuum with other classes, and whose individual members often approach the physical status of other classes without losing their fundamental identity. Two sounds resembling /t/ might actually belong to two different categories (the medial consonants of "butter" and "rudder," for instance); conversely, two sounds that have distinct physical differences might belong to the same category (Cockney pronunciations of the medial consonants of "butter" and "bottle," for instance).

The principle of continuum thus underscores even more pointedly than the asymmetry principle the futility of understanding discourse notions in terms of unitary formal or functional criteria. It is important in every case to comprehend a larger configuration of relationships and to know what things *mean in context*. Moreover, like hierarchy, the principle of continuum becomes an important tool for defining and organizing concepts, particularly concepts of equal status in the categorial hierarchy. Important discourse notions do have some empirical basis, of course, and important features should be described in detail; but the ultimate definitions and understandings of these concepts will be relational. At every level we will look for formal and functional continuums within categories, as a way of bringing fuller definition to individual concepts, and as a way of creating a fuller understanding of the dynamics of discourse activity. In chapters 3 and 4 it will emerge that the category of rhetoric is uniquely open-ended, forming lines of continuum with each of the other aims of discourse—instrumental, scientific, and poetic. And this will be an important defining feature of rhetoric itself.

Relationships of continuum are especially important in what they reveal about discourse categories as "clusters" of features. Categories of equivalent status do not simply "slide into" one another in some vague and mysterious way; rather, they approximate certain features of neighboring categories, while retaining distinctive features of their own. Each unit of discourse is properly defined as a cluster of such features, and individual instances will begin to approximate other norms in certain features only. One salient feature of English consonantal sounds, for instance, is that of "voicing," and it is in terms of this feature that the sound of /t/ in words like "butter" and "writer" begins to approximate the sound of the neighboring phoneme /d/, while retaining perceptually the status of /t/.

At the level of grammar there are analogous situations. One feature of transitive verbs, for instance, is their ability to accept complements or objects; another distinguishing feature is their ability to undergo certain transformations like the passive. But there is a middle category of verbs, between transitive and intransitive, which can take objects but which cannot be transformed into the passive: We say, "Little Simon resembed Big Simon," but not, "Big Simon was resembled by Little Simon." Moreover, as John Robert Ross has demonstrated, even such discrete-seeming categories as noun and verb come together in terms of certain transformational features along a grammatical continuum. Some nouns are "verby" and some verbs are "nouny."

If such relationships inhere at the level of grammar, how much more likely are they to inhere at higher levels, which are much more responsive to the pressures of history and human invention? It is clear that they do. But a further point stands in need of emphasis here: Definition and classification by clusters or matrices of features are even more a necessity at the levels of Aim, Genus, and Genre, if one is to gain any precise understanding of how the various kinds of discourse converge upon one another in actual instances and of how they change over time. The aims and genres of discourse are typical or "normal" interpenetrations of features: of immediate purpose or act (illocution); of the demands of situations; of typical kinds of subject matter; of author-audience relationships; of success and spoiling conditions; and of special conventions and traditions of strategy and mode. The extension or alteration of one or more of these features (some of which may be more crucial than others for a given type) in a particular instance may give the discourse a turn toward a neighboring category, and it may bring new forms of historical or social participation into play, altering for better or for worse the conventional dynamic of author, subject, and audience. Defining discourse categories in terms of clusters of features, then, is fully in accord with what is known about the nature of linguistic categories in general, and it leads to precise discriminations, rather than impressionistic reflections, about the relationships among different categories.

Context-Sensitivity

Each of the principles examined so far has pointed at every turn to the need to look at features in context, and thus a good deal of what might be said under the heading of context-sensitivity has already been accounted for. It is obvious that, in a system in which meanings are not absolutely predictable on the basis of form, one must (and characteristically does) look to the contexts in which those forms are embedded. The statement, "Abraham Lincoln is a Republican," might be an answer to a question of fact, a warning, a rebuttal, a moral judgment, an insult, or even a promise, depending upon that pattern of hierarchies and surrounding circumstances that we call its "context." The same is true also with higher units of form and function: Expressive, referential, affective, or playful (aesthetic) uses of language cannot in

themselves predict or determine kinds of discourse; rather, they constitute varieties of language use (or at best lower categories of intention)
embedded in larger contexts which do a great deal to determine their
ultimate status.

These notions are fairly commonplace. What is worth emphasizing
here is that discourse operations at every level are dominated by "con-
text-sensitive" rules (Chomsky 112), and that discourse categories at
every level are definable not merely on the basis of form but also on the
basis of the contexts in which they characteristically or potentially operate. Moreover, a form that is generally aligned with a particular category may be given new status by a change of context. A conspicuous
lower-level example is the lexico-grammatical phenomenon of "functional shift," wherein verbs like "shave," "smoke," and "rage" are
transformed to nominals by being placed in grammatical contexts (slots)
that yield "a shave," "a smoke," "a rage." Something analogous to
functional shift takes place when an essentially static and classificatory
system such as the "Seven Liberal Arts" is presented in the allegorical
narrative form of Martianus Capella's *The Marriage of Mercury and Philology*. One of the things to be gained from such a presentation is that the
dynamic and experiential elements of a system are highlighted by a
mode whose ordinary alignments are with changes in time rather than
with conceptual hierarchies.

A higher-level example of this kind of functional shift would be the
piece of discourse that "looks like" or "reads like" the sort of personal
testimonial that one would normally associate with ceremonial or
epideictic rhetoric, but whose fundamentally deliberative status is
revealed primarily by its contexts—those which it establishes by internal reference and those which are implied by the circumstances of
publication.

If discourse categories at every level are defined at least partially by
typical or potential contexts,[7] and if these units are arranged in a categorial hierarchy wherein higher units are to some degree "contexts"
for lower ones, then it stands to reason that the range of categories will
involve progressively broader and more encompassing notions of context. It follows that in the "clustering" of features whereby each category is defined, those features which refer to contextual dimensions
will take on increasing importance as one ascends the hierarchy. The
category of "mode" will involve clusters of primarily formal features
and conventions, with some contextual ties which, although clearly
identifiable, are not constraining. The category of "de facto genre"
names a specific type of discourse employed in a specific cultural func-

7. For a provocative attempt to devise a taxonomy of writing based solely upon the criterion of context, see Mathes.

tion, in fairly predictable circumstances, and usually operating under certain formal constraints. The higher category of "genus" involves discourses participating in specific classes of discourse acts or functions, embedded in broader types of context, with fewer formal constraints. The "aims," finally, involve even broader purposes and contexts.

In concluding this section on the Discourse Hierarchy, it would be remiss to avoid noticing under the heading of "context-sensitivity" the fact that most writing is removed from literal "contexts of situation"—a circumstance several of whose implications have already been noted. This fact does not of course mean that writing lacks *context*, but merely that one of its special burdens is to simulate forms of *contact*. It does mean, nevertheless, that specific occasions and forums of discourse will not predict as much about writing as about speech-making: Lacking the direct defining constraint of context-of-situation, genres of writing tend to be much more various and continuous than those of speechmaking. But the possibilities of contextual influence are actually broadened, not lessened thereby, and this circumstance will prompt, in Chapter 3, the search for a framework that goes considerably beyond the hierarchy of forms and focuses primarily upon meaning.

2. MODES AND STRATEGIES OF DISCOURSE

Modes of Discourse	Strategies of Discourse
Discursive	Generic Strategies
Expressive	Material Strategies
Objective	Dialectical Strategies
Affective	Dispositional Strategies
	Stylistic Strategies
Narrative	Modal Strategies
Expressive	
Objective	
Affective	
Dramatic	
Expressive	
Objective	
Affective	

An extended discussion of modes and strategies comes logically at this point, because these are form-oriented categories whose definition is directly related to the formalistic framework discovered in chapter 1. However, readers who wish to pursue directly the larger theoretical argument of this book may wish to skip this discussion for now and go directly to chapter 3.

Before launching into separate discussions of the modes and strategies of written discourse, it will be useful to lay out some provisional definitions of terms, anchoring them in the Discourse Hierarchy. Within that framework, both modes and strategies are situated lower than the level of "de facto genre," a category naming quite specific convergences of subject, purpose, and method in discourse. A distinct implication of such placement is that the modes and strategies are not *types* of discourse but *operations* of discourse: They do not stand alone but exist within functional hierarchies of individual works of discourse, fulfilling the particular purposes and expectations of those works. They are *ways* of conducting discourse rather than *reasons for* conducting discourse.

As ways of conducting discourse the modes and strategies can be distinguished from one another by their separate placements in the Categorial Hierarchy. The strategies have a more direct application to, and look upward to, the functions of discourse; the modes have a more direct application to, and look downward to, the forms of discourse. Strategies represent operations that are directly functional in the fulfillment of generic expectations and goals. For instance, the strategies of description, enumeration, definition, climactic arrangement, and others may be used to fulfill an informative motive; the same strategies could be used to fulfill a deliberative motive.

The situation is complicated somewhat, though not in any debilitating way, by the fact that common usage confers multiple status upon single terms. Thus "narration" names a "material strategy" when an author fulfills a deliberative or informative purpose by inserting a story into either an argument or a discursive presentation of information; it names a "formal strategy" when it applies to one of the divisions of classical arrangement; finally, as a discernible pattern of coherence based upon items in temporal sequence, narration is not a strategy at all but rather a mode.

The modes of discourse, occupying a lower status in the Discourse Hierarchy than either de facto genres or strategies, represent operations that are less directly functional than formal. They constitute methods of proceeding coherently in discourse, and at the same time, methods of simulating contact between author and reader, given certain exigencies of subject matter. In this final qualification—exigencies of subject matter—lie enormous complexities, however, as will become apparent in the discussion that follows.

I. MODES OF WRITTEN DISCOURSE

Considering the multiplicity and diversity of usage in literary and rhetorical theory, criticism, and pedagogy, it is no understatement to say that there is no designation more riddled with confusion and paradox than that of discourse "modes." Frank D'Angelo's bibliographical survey of various descriptions and partitions gives an admirably clear picture of the variety of thought on the subject, but it hardly begins to explain the widespread variety and confusion itself (D'Angelo 1976). The asymmetry principle, which encourages novel appropriations of both modes and genres as strategic devices, will explain a great deal, and a careful delimitation of usage to a certain set of boundaries within the Discourse Hierarchy will do much to lend stability to the term. Consider, for instance, the following groups of concepts, used fairly commonly by rhetoricians and literary critics:

narrative mode	autobiographical mode
discursive mode	epic mode
dramatic mode	prophetic mode
ironic mode	epic mode
allegorical mode	mimetic mode
naturalistic mode	romantic mode
symbolic mode	ironic mode
descriptive mode	

Differences of status among these four groups of concepts can be fairly easily dealt with by observing the different aspects or operations of discourse that they attempt to realize. Among the four groups, only the first—narrative, discursive, dramatic—could be said to represent modes in the strict sense of *formal methods of proceeding coherently in written monologue*. The second group—autobiographical, epic, prophetic—links the notion of mode with matters of genre, or of techniques and voices characteristic of certain genres—not with formal concerns alone but with peculiar convergences of form and purpose. The third group—ironic, allegorical, naturalistic, symbolic, descriptive—links the notion of mode with matters of material and stylistic strategy—operations that fulfill particular purposes within individual works of discourse. The fourth group, categories advanced by Northrop Frye in *Anatomy of Criticism* (33–35), uses the notion to name traditions of literary representation and consciousness—characteristic existential stances of presentation, reflecting different cosmic views of humanity.

These distinctions are useful ones, and if applied rigorously they would clear up a good deal of the confusion that now exists in rhetorical criticism and pedagogy. However, it will be impossible to stabilize the notion of "mode" as a formal method of proceeding coherently in discourse—and thus to avoid confusion with functional and generic properties—unless we take into account an additional, deeper source of volatility: namely the paradoxical truth that different modes, even as formal operations, are vitally connected to different dimensions of reality and consciousness.

The distinction between narrative and discursive[1] modes may serve as an illustrative example, since it is recognized in virtually all of the

---

1. I have chosen the term "discursive" over the more familiar term "expository" for three reasons: First, it is broader, encompassing a good deal of what is commonly called "descriptive" as well as what is usually termed "expository"; second, it matches the terminology of Suzanne Langer, whose work I call upon for theoretical support; and third, because the term "expository" has been subjected to such varied and promiscuous usage

various attempts to discriminate modes of discourse. On the one hand, it is crucial to recognize—as many composition textbooks do not—that to "tell a story" or alternately to conduct an exposition of a subject do not constitute reasons for conducting discourse but rather *methods of conducting discourse.* In many situations authors may choose one or the other: Faced, for example, with the task of defending a point of view, an author might choose to present that point of view as directly as possible, offering a series of "good reasons" for its validity; or the author might elect to "tell a story" that illustrates in a vivid and highly affecting way the validity of the position; the author might even elect to tell the story of how he or she arrived at this point of view, how experience gradually forced and sustained a recognition of its powerful truth.

But the matter does not end there. Up to this point we are dealing with modes as matters of rhetorical choice. However, there is no way of avoiding the circumstance that, having made a particular choice, one's motives undergo some channeling, involving those particular extensions, restrictions, clarifications, or indeed new insights into the subject that a particular mode may encourage. An almost universally testified experience of authors is the experience of discovery *in the process* of composition. Authors always "get into" things they had not anticipated, discover things they didn't think they knew before. This element of discovery is both activated and limited by the author's mode of discourse.[2]

We now approach the paradox of form and discovery. The asymmetry principal, so useful up to this point, runs up against its contrary: Form and meaning are arbitrarily connected in one sense, intimately related in another. How then are we to understand and describe discourse modes? If we proceed from the assumption of an organic unity between operations of language and varieties of meaning and consciousness, the analysis may run aground in circularities. We become the prisoners of intuition and preconception, and we overlook the essential arbitrariness, freedom, and playfulness of language. On the other hand, if we proceed in strictly formalistic way, from the assumption of the arbitrariness of language and discourse operations vis-à-vis varieties of meaning and consciousness, the analysis may run aground in particulars.

---

in composition pedagogy, it is better to avoid it whenever possible in any kind of rigorous discussion.

2. This remarkable circumstance, extensively explored and pondered over in modern literary criticism, is mirrored in the historical development from oral to literate civilization and the consequent development from narrative and drama to logical discursiveness as principal shapers of consciousness (Ong 1971: 1–22). The romantic critical notion that literature exists to restore earlier or more primitive states of consciousness, though a dangerous one and subject to various kinds of abuse, nevertheless rests upon profound intuitions about the nature and history of discourse modes.

We shall never come to grips with this dilemma of description unless we confront thoughtfully the fact that we are dealing with a paradoxical truth. It was Samuel Butler who reflected that "an essential contradiction in terms meets us at the end of every inquiry," and it should come as no surprise that theoretical constructs about language and discourse, phenomena so closely linked to essential humanity and the conditions of knowing, should be similarly beset. The very unresolvability of these problems, however, points to a way out of the methodological dilemma, for in the end we must choose a course that recognizes both sides of the truth and still allows for some precision of definition and classification.

The essential contradiction in terms does, after all, meet us *at the end* of every inquiry, not necessarily at the beginning or the middle. The paradox of discourse modes is visible at the extremities of perception. This lowest rank of classifications in the Discourse Hierarchy "looks back" and entangles itself in the highest rank of categories by entangling itself in the realm of motivation and discovery. And yet it is not in the nature of such entanglements to be precise, to allow for analytical discriminations, or to be usefully descriptive of particular works of discourse except as matters of rhetorical choice. Profound intuitions about the entanglement of the modes in states of reality or consciousness will not lead successfully to precise discriminations about the actual conduct of discourse, any more than the knowledge that all scientific activity involves metaphor will say anything useful about the day-to-day conduct of science, or than the insight that poetry is a form of knowledge will provide useful instruments for practical criticism. In fact, coming as they do from the extremities rather than the center of perceptions about discourse, they are likely to generate a good deal of confusion if one attempts to forge them into practical instruments of criticism.

I am stressing this point because I believe that it uncovers a confusing factor in both scholarly and pedagogical treatments of the "modes" of written discourse: namely, the tendency to start from assumptions about the entanglement of modes of discourse and modes of thought, rather than what I believe to be a sounder approach to form in written discourse. That approach is to start from observations about the actual conventions that come into play as solutions to the problem of addressing an extended monologue to an audience removed in space and time from the situation of actual delivery. If the pattern of forms that emerges from such an investigation *then* suggests an approach to modes of perception or consciousness, then the pattern will be confirmed in both a descriptive and a theoretical sense.

The nineteenth-century founders of the pervasive "modes of discourse" tradition, to the extent that they attempted to bring theoretical cogency to their formulations, looked primarily to the psychologistic theories of Campbell and Whately, which were themselves mechanistic in orientation and sought correlations of discourse activity with the "laws" of thought and association. However, in the pedagogical treatments of Bain, Genung, Cairns, and the hosts of imitators that followed them, there is a conspicuous absence of rigor, both in the correlation of modes and psychological categories and in the descriptions of the modes themselves. As a result, these treatments immediately involve themselves in two sets of confusions which inhabit the whole tradition: grossly overlapping rhetorics of "description" and "exposition," and the introduction of "persuasion" into the picture, thus confusing modes with motivations or genres.

Alexander Bain, more rigorously than either Genung or Cairns, defines mode as a specific correlation of purpose, subject, and method—actually a formulation that comes closer to defining the notion of "genre"; the concept would have some cogency, nevertheless, were it not for some damaging circularities and equivocations in the basic terms of the definition itself. Thus according to Bain the *purpose* of description is "to describe," the *subject* is "an object," and the method is "the art of description" (153). And considering that characteristic "objects" of description include feelings and intellectual processes as well as physical things, one is not surprised when Bain capitulates and announces: "Description is involved in all the other kinds of composition"; and "Exposition, or Science, is frequently made up in a great measure of description" (163). Actually, recognition that "description" occurs in various other kinds and permutations of writing is evidence in itself that description is not a *mode* of discourse at all. It is a material strategy of discourse that is realized in all the modes—in discursive writing, narrative writing, and dramatic writing. Bain's thoroughgoing identification of exposition with science, signaled in the quotation above, makes his treatment of exposition more principled than later ones, as a comprehensive method of scientific discourse, as opposed to a series of devices for ordering the pseudo-discourse of composition classrooms; nevertheless, there remains a debilitating confusion of aims, modes, and strategies in the overall construct.[3]

3. James Kinneavy's reorganization of the modes of discourse (35–37; also Kinneavy, Cope, and Campbell) makes an admirable attempt to clear up some of the blatant confusions in the tradition of Bain, Genung, and Cairns; but it does not significantly improve upon them, and it does in fact continue the practice of founding the modes not on any firm descriptive basis but upon reputed correlations of discourse operations and states of reality. Eschewing the psychologism of Bain and Genung, Kinneavy bases his partition of modes on a scheme of propositional status analogous to the Aristotelian predicables (*Topica* I. iv. 4–12), in which each category represents a different approach to experience and makes a different subject of experience. The four modes of description, narration, classification, and evaluation are concerned with particles, change, logical conceptualization, and normative perspectives, and they align ultimately with four major dimensions of systematic inquiry.

Avoiding these circularities and confusions will not require a rigid or thoroughgoing structuralism. What is required, though, is an approach that looks first to observable structural regularites in identifying and defining the modes, and then explores theoretical alignments of the modes with patterns of motivation or consciousness, as a relational and confirmatory device, not as a discovery procedure.[4]

The starting points for a structural examination of written discourse modes are to be found in three sets of artificialities that inhere necessarily in any attempt to communicate by means of extended monologue. To these I have applied the terms *stance, direction,* and *contact.* Stance involves a continuum of feigned situational focusings, imagined to be either coincident with or disjoined from the setting in which reader and script converge; *direction* involves patterns of directional and coherence devices, occupying a continuum from author-orientation to subject-orientation to audience-orientation; and *contact* involves a number of imagined interactional circumstances either coincident with or different from the actual fact of a single person's encounter with the text.

Stance: Discursive, Narrative, and Dramatic Modes

Any monologue, lacking as it does the opportunity for direct interchange between speaker and hearer, engages the problems of achieving coherence and sustaining interest. In genuinely oral monologue, without scripts, these problems are complicated by the additional problem of fluency—keeping the discourse flowing without lapses into stammering and silence. Traditional solutions to these problems include the cultivation of elaborate systems of mnemonics, as well as the memorization of verbal formulas for negotiating different subjects and situations. In written monologue the problem of fluency vanishes, but the problem of coherence is complicated in other ways— by the physical and temporal separation of author and audience, by the absence of a literal forum or situational context, and by the consequent loss of even the meager opportunities for interaction (eye contact, applause, laughter) afforded by oral monologue.

Extended monologue, either oral or written, can achieve coherence in one of three ways: through the logical connection of ideas and con-

---

For all its remarkable orderliness, this scheme does not, however, clarify a great deal about the operations of discourse, and like earlier schemes it introduces confusions between form and function. What are we to say about evaluative narration (or evaluative description or evaluative classification for that matter), except that the modes are always intermingled in actual discourse? The fact is that Kinneavy's "modes" are actually functional/strategic designations which, because they are presumed to exist in lock step with formal operations, suffer from the imprecision and confusion that is bound to follow upon any such presumption about discourse.

4. Two other theorists who use a similar approach, with results different from mine, are Hernadi, esp. 153ff; and Longacre, esp. 197ff.

cepts; through temporal connection of actions and developments; or through the meaningful interplay of motives and actions in a dramatic situation. Naturally it would be fatuous to think of exposition, story, and drama solely as solutions to the problems of coherence; but the written medium, where problems of coherence are intensified and complicated, will tend to intensify and regularize these three methods, as devices for holding and organizing the attentions of an audience along the linear path of discourse.

These methods constitute ways of focusing audience-attention in time and space, and they differ from each other not merely in terms of separate linking devices but also in the special way in which they treat the moment of contact between reader and text. The *discursive* mode focuses attention upon a present time and place *coincident with the convergence of reader and text*. The persistent illusion involved in this mode is that of being spoken to directly in a present situation. Even if the subject matter involves happenings in the past or speculations about the future, these are now matters of present concern. The formal orientation to the present is reinforced in the reader's consciousness by a battery of logical connectives, of evaluative and generalizing terms, and by verbal indications of authorial presence. These elements are italicized in the following discursive passage:

> *A dozen years ago,* when William Shockley first began talking about improving the stock of the human race, nobody knew that he was going to try to do it all by himself. *Back then, you may recall,* the man who won a Nobel prize for making transistors started talking about making babies. He believed that the world would be better off with *more smart people than dumb people*—and that intelligence was inherited.
>
> *Therefore,* he suggested that the best way to improve the world was to set up sperm banks for very smart men and impregnate very smart women. *As an amateur geneticist,* he sounded like an expert in making transistors.
>
> *Well, now it turns out* that a 74-year-old California businessman, Robert K. Graham, has *actually* founded an exclusive sperm bank. *In what sounds like a Woody Allen script,* he solicits donations from Nobel Prize scientists only. . . . (Goodman 1980)

The sample passage contains a number of logical connectives, but it is also rich in other sorts of coherence devices. I chose it deliberately for this reason, hoping to emphasize that while logical coherence is an outstanding feature of the discursive mode, it is not the defining feature. What most closely defines discursiveness is the sense of present time and place that logical coherence helps to create, often coupled with the illusion of authorial presence. So pervasive is this fiction in most discursive prose that we seldom take note of it, except in those rare instances in which an author shatters the illusion by making reference to the circumstances of composition. Such a reference always calls attention to the necessary disparity between time-and-place of production and time-and-place of reception, as happens in the following passage:

> Changes of idiom between generations are a normal part of social history. Previously, however, such changes and the verbal provocations of young against old have been variants on an evolutionary continuum. What is occuring now is new: it is an attempt at a total break. . . . There is a terrible, literal image in "stone-deafness," in the opaque babble or speechlessness of the "stoned.". . .
>
> But are there no other literacies conceivable, 'literacies' not of the letter?
>
> I am writing in a study in a college of one of the great American universities. The walls are throbbing gently to the beat of music coming from one near and several more distant amplifiers. The walls quiver to the ear or to the touch roughly 18 hours a day, sometimes 24. The beat is literally unending. It matters little whether it is that of pop, folk, or rock. What counts is the all-pervasive pulsation morning to night and into night, made indiscriminate by the cool burn of electronic timbre. A large segment of mankind, between the ages of thirteen and, say twenty-five, now lives immersed in this constant throb. (Steiner 41)

The effectiveness of the "modal strategy" in this case depends upon the excitement accompanying the shattering of discursive presentness, the sudden shift to a new, dramatic presentness, and the skill with which the author then modulates back into discursive presentation.

The modal stances occupy a continuum from the illusion of direct or indirect authorial presence in time and place coincident with the convergence of reader and text (*discursive*) to the illusion of a fictional present—often containing no "author" at all in the conventional sense—in a time and place completely removed from the convergence of reader and text (*dramatic*). In the middle of this continuum stands *narrative*, the most versatile of the modal stances insofar as the possibilities of illusionism are concerned. The most conspicuous feature of narrative is, of course, temporal coherence; but the distinguishing feature of narrative stance is the focusing of time and place *away from* the time and place either of oral delivery or of the convergence of reader and text. The experience of "losing oneself" in a story involves a conventional forgetting, in varying degrees, of present time and situation—absorption into a fictional past. In oral narrative this is accomplished in spite of the literal presence of a narrator, who may have a reputation as a spellbinder. In written narrative the problem is in one sense compounded, since a characteristic method of entry involves the narrator in feigning at first a discursive or dramatic presence and then "modulating" into narrative; on the other hand, the written medium's absence of literal contact makes the literal author easier to forget, and it invites a host of illusion-fostering devices—masks, personae, narrative perspectives (points of view), as well as the appropriation of generic forms (letters, for instance) which are only clumsily available to the oral narrator.

The third modal stance is *dramatic,* and its distinguishing character-istic is the illusion of a present time and place *not coincident with the literal present in which reader confronts text.* This modal stance involves the greatest degree of illusionism among the modes, presenting a speaker talking to someone else, a speaker talking to himself (thinking out loud), or a group of speakers talking to one another, as in a dialogue. In any of these cases the reader is normally placed in the position not of literal addressee but of a fictive on-looker or eavesdropper. This is the case in much lyric poetry, for which dramatic can be considered a nor-mal stance:

> Whose woods these are I think I know.
> His house is in the village though;

In this example, as in most dramatic prose also, the situation unfolds gradually as the discourse progresses. The fictive speaker may be con-strued as the poet, as a character created by the poet, or as the poet's caricature of himself; but there can be no doubt about the role of the reader as eavesdropper. The fictive audience is the speaker himself, and in this case the literal audience does not enter into the dramatic situa-tion. However, there is a kind of dramatic stance which does engage the literal audience directly, and it occurs most frequently in personal letters:

> Dear _____,
> I've been reading papers all morning and have just now moved the whole operation over to the Gardens (lapboard, sunglasses, bandanna); it's getting close to lunchtime (where is my watch?) and people are beginning to stroll around as usual. There's old Smiley, punctual as ever. . . .

There is nothing particularly unusual or outstanding about such writing as this; what is worth noting is the integration of the reader as the actual addressee, and the simultaneous inclusion of the reader in the time-space reference of the writer. Paradoxically perhaps, this extension of dramatic mode carries it full circle, tapping on the back door of dis-cursiveness, with its illusion of authorial presence in a time and place coincident with the convergence of reader and text. But of course it is not the same: Here the reader is brought directly into the situational reference of the writer, whereas discursive writing puts forward a kind of present tense neutral ground or no-man's-land of contact.

The existence of a modal continuum from discursive to dramatic, with various points of transition and overlap, is fairly well indicated in the fascinating range of possibilities offered in the middle territory of narrative. A crucial observation point lies in the area of narrative beginnings and the kinds of "modulations" that occur there. Narrative shares with discursive the feature of direct address to a literal audience (which most dramatic lacks), and it shares with dramatic mode the feature of removal-in-place (which discursive lacks). A crucial feature that narrative lacks, and which dramatic and discursive share, is the consistent illusion of present time; consequently, there is a special sense in which a narrative must be "gotten into" or "focused into" past time, away from the present. Of course, many written narratives will open directly, with no more in the way of a focusing device than "once upon a time" or "On the 15th of January, 1945 . . ."[5] Nevertheless, traditional literary narrative reveals a good deal of skittishness about brazen leaps into narrative mode, and both traditional and contemporary narration, literary and non-literary, often choose to modulate into the narrative past either from a discursive or a dramatic present. Chaucer's "reverdie" opening to the *Canterbury Tales*, whose main clause announces in present tense, "Thanne longen folk to goon on pilgrimages," is discursive, as is Virgil's "Arma virumque cano." Milton's invocation to *Paradise Lost*, with the main clause "Sing, heavenly muse," is dramatic.

Another indication of the continuum from discursive to dramatic lies in the texture of narrative itself. Historical writing, of necessity focused on the past but engaged fundamentally in interpretation and causal explanation, often hovers between the two modes, often modulating back and forth. But even a good deal of distinctly narrative writing has a discernible discursive element, evoked by verbal reminders of authorial presence, by judgmental and interpretive characterizations, by the logical coherence clues characteristic of discursive mode, and by the framing of narrative passages with topic sentences. Some of these devices are italicized in the following sample:

> At 11:20 the caravan of klansmen drove *without warning* down Everitt Street toward the *100 or so still-unassembled* marchers. The two groups began yelling obscenities at each other. Some of the marchers laughed and began to pound the klansmen's cars with fists and sticks. The klansmen stopped and got out of their cars. Someone *(no one is now sure whether it was a Worker*

---

5. To a certain extent the problem is automatically solved for the author who "tells his own story" or imposes a first-person narrator, because the interference of a mediating "author" in the present is dissipated thereby. This may partly account for the popularity of the device in late medieval narratives—*Roman de la Rose, Piers Plowman, Commedia,* and most of Chaucer's works—which effected a transition in writing from the status of performance manuscripts to the status of "books" to be read by individuals or by small groups of individuals taking turns.

or a Klansman) began firing shots into the air. Suddenly *it was all a whirling chaos* of fists, sticks, and shouts. Klansmen, *with calm precision,* removed weapons from car trunks and began shooting. . . . The survivors instantly began shouting Communist slogans and "Where were the pigs?," ignoring the fact that they had asked the police to stay away. (Watson, "Mediamartyrdom," 96)

In this kind of "discursive" narrative, interpretive and framing elements are externalized in the consciousness of the narrator, of whose presence we are periodically reminded. As narrative modulates further away from discursiveness, however, these elements tend to be internalized into the consciousness of the subjects of narration, diminishing further the signs of authorial presence, as in the following passage:

Onto the list of women with whom he planned to have this relationship went Barbara Coles. There was no hurry. Next week, next month, next year, they would meet at a party. The world of well-known people in London is a small one. Big and little fishes, they drift around, nose each other, flirt their fins, wiggle off again. When he bumped into Barbara Coles, it would be time to decide whether or not to sleep with her. (Lessing 12–13)

There is even more here in the way of commentary and generalization than in the previous passage; but the crucial difference is that the commentary is not authorial but representational. It belongs not to the narrator but to the subject (he), and it comes to us not as an explanation but rather as a portrayal of his attitudes.

Deeper into the continuum, bringing the submergence of both exterior and interior consciousness, narrative begins to modulate toward dramatic, where situations and relationships must unfold before an onlooker or eavesdropper. A preponderance of dialogue, sparsely cued, adds to this effect. The following narrative passage exemplifies this movement:

At the lake shore there was another rowboat drawn up. The two Indians stood waiting.

Nick and his father got in the stern of the boat and the Indians shoved it off and one of them got in to row. Uncle George sat in the stern of the camp rowboat. The young Indian shoved the camp boat off and got in to row Uncle George.

The two boats started off in the dark. Nick heard the oarlocks of the other boat quite a way ahead of them in the mist. The Indians rowed with quick choppy strokes. Nick lay back with his father's arm around him. It was cold on the water. The Indian who was rowing them was working very hard, but the other boat moved further ahead in the mist all the time.

"Where are we going, Dad?" Nick asked.

"Over to the Indian camp. There is an Indian lady very sick."
"Oh," said Nick.
Across the bay they found the other boat beached.
Uncle George was smoking a cigar in the dark. The young Indian
pulled the boat way up on the beach.
Uncle George gave both the Indians cigars. (Hemingway 91)

In order to grasp the full impact of this passage it is necessary to
keep in mind that it actually begins, not continues, a story. It does not
merely describe a scene, introduce characters, and reveal their circumstances; it makes the reader an intimate spectator from the beginning,
with linguistic presuppositions of dramatic presence: "*the* lake shore"
(not *a* lake shore, or the shore of Lake Huron); "*another* rowboat," (forcing the reader onto the lake, and forcing the presupposition of other
rowboats); "the two Indians" (not "two Indians").[6] As the story progresses it modulates back toward some interior commentary in the consciousness of the character Nick; even this is muted, however, and the
extension of narrative toward dramatic is apparent throughout. It is
precisely this extension, in fact, which accounts for the peculiar mood
and tone of the story.

Theoretical Alignments of the Modes of Discourse

It is important to recognize the modes, and the possibilities of
experimentation and modulation within a work of discourse, as dimensions of rhetorical choice—as methods of conducting discourse that are
not locked into different purposes or different subject matters. Various
cases of experimentation with narrative and dramatic modes by practitioners of "new journalism" are only the most conspicuous and flam-
boyant examples of a phenomenon that has been present in written
discourse at least since the advent of print technology. Having made
this recognition, however, and having explored the empirical and formal bases of the respective modal stances, it next becomes important to
recognize also the fundamental alignments of the modes with different
ways of approaching reality. Choices among the modes would not be
significant if not for their impact upon consciousness. A journalist
assigned to produce a background "story" based on travels and inter-
views with a particular political figure might produce either a richly
detailed discursive piece, arriving at a set of generalizations about the
character and style of the person; a narrative of the travels and inter-
views, with intermingled coloring and commentary; or a dramatic rendering of the same events (perhaps appropriating the form of the
personal journal). But the choice of modes would in itself be partially

6. This analysis owes a great deal to Ong 1975.

conditioned upon intuitions about which aspects of the reality examined were most outstanding, or which avenues of exploration seemed most productive of insight: the static, logical, classificatory, analytical dimension (*discursive*); the dynamic dimension of process and change over time (*narrative*); or the dynamic interactions of character, feeling, and events within a delimited temporal context (*dramatic*).

Surface intuitions provide an initial point of observation. Most readers, for instance, even without the framing cues of titles and names of authors, would immediately recognize the passage quoted from Hemingway above as literary. From the outset one is aware of language in a condition of play, of an experiment in representation associated with literary art. Ordinary intuition extends so far, as a matter of fact, as to recognize discursive as the normative mode of scientific and instrumental discourse, with narrative and dramatic as normative for poetic. Insofar as it reflects its historical lineage from speech-making, rhetorical discourse retains discursive also as a normative mode; but in its broader development in the written medium, rhetoric makes use of narrative and dramatic modes as well.

Beyond these common sense intuitions about the character of modes lies the critical speculation that certain fields of reality may be available only (or at least *especially*) to certain modal stances. Outstanding in such speculation is the utility of narrative and dramatic modes in discovering and conveying realities that are experiential and not fully available to or discernible within the analytical and classificatory potentialities of the discursive mode. (Nietzsche, in *The Birth of Tragedy*, pitted the dramatic religious consciousness of the tragic poets against the discursive philosophical consciousness of Socrates and Plato.) Students of religion have long been fascinated by the profound connections between religious experience and *story* as a mode of discourse; and also by the inevitable tensions that arise with the development of theology, and the rational discursive exposition of religious principles. One contemporary religious thinker describes the problem in this way:

> When Paul Tillich was transplanted from Germany to the United States, the tenor of his thinking changed profoundly. When Reinhold Niebuhr moved from Yale to become a pastor in Detroit, and again after he had visited Germany and seen the rise of Hitler, the content of many of his concepts shifted. Basic experiences often alter one's cognitive life. It does not follow that one's ordinary cognitive methods suffice to give a full account of these experiences.
>
> One of the functions of 'story' in philosophy is to meet this gap in our cognitive methods. 'Story' articulates a change in experience. It is a particularly apt method for expressing the sort of experience that alters one's fundamental 'standpoint' or horizon. (Novak 175)

As a matter of theoretical alignment, though not always of practical application, the dramatic, narrative, and discursive modes correspond to the comprehensive cognitive viewpoints of particle, wave, and field identified by tagmemic theorists (Young/Becker/Pike). Dramatic presentation has an affinity for the specific event in the single moment, with little *explicit* rendering of past developments or conceptual understandings; narrative has an affinity for the item-in-flux, in a process of change, in the context of broader developments; discursive, finally, has an affinity for logical analysis, definition, and classification. These affinities may be characterized alternately as ways of approaching experience or as separate dimensions of any experience or attempt to understand experience. They also constitute *ways of experiencing* or *ways of symbolizing experience*, suggesting a somewhat broader set of theoretical alignments than expressed by the framework of particle, wave, and field.

One of the profoundest and most systematic philosophical explorations of the relationships between symbolic forms and modes of consciousness is that of Suzanne K. Langer, whose typology of symbolisms in *Philosophy in a New Key* suggests a more provocative set of theoretical alignments for the modal stances. Langer begins with the insight that discursiveness—the property of verbal symbolism that "requires us to string out our ideas even though their objects rest one within the other" (118)—is a defining characteristic of linguistic symbolism, but that there exist, nevertheless, "matters which require to be conceived through some symbolistic scheme other than discursive language" (120). This leads to a broad distinction between "discursive" and "presentational" modes—one which makes an exact parallel to the distinctions already set forth here, between discursive as a modal stance that maintains a focus on a time-and-place coincident with the convergence of reader and text, and narrative and dramatic as "presentational" stances that maintain a focus away from that convergence.

Langer identifies three modes of presentational, as opposed to discursive, symbolism. Furthest removed from the discursive forms of language is the mode of *music*, "a kind of symbolism peculiarly adapted to the explication of 'unspeakable things'" (121). Between the extremes of discursive and music lie two additional modes: *ritual*, which *in extremis* involves the dramatic interactions of visceral symbols and archetypes; and *myth*, which begins in fantasy and evolves into higher and more philosophical types of narrative such as epic.

These modes of symbolism form an exact theoretical compass for the modes of written monologue. The discursive mode inclines to Langer's designation of "language"; narrative mode finds its ultimate bearings in "myth"; and dramatic mode relates in an ultimate way to Langer's category of "ritual." Music, as the one form of symbolism completely discontinuous with language, has no direct modal stance in literary monologue, but both of the presentational literary modes (narrative and dramatic) contribute forms that incline in this direction: the ballad as a characteristically narrative form, and the lyric as a characteristically dramatic form, have their roots in musical presentation. An outline of all these relations is presented in figure 3.

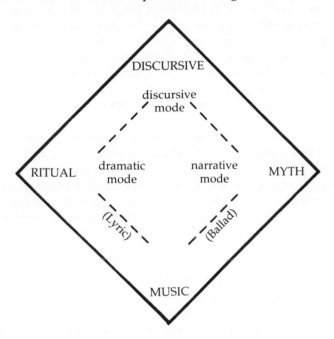

Figure 3. Theoretical alignments of the modes of discourse

Other Determinants of Mode: Direction and Contact

While the modal stances are the primary determinants of mode in written monologue, two other sets of formal criteria, related similarly to illusionary projections of speakers and audiences, help to clarify these divisions and at the same time to account for some other variations in ways of conducting discourse. The first of these is what I have termed "direction," a concept that refers to a monologue's relative degree of alignment with or direction toward the three other operational components of a communication situation—author, subject, and audience. Accordingly, the three modal "directions" are *expressive, objective,* and *affective.* These constitute variations that can occur within either discursive, narrative, or dramatic modal stances.

Expressive direction is characterized by the sense or illusion of personal involvement on the part of the writer; by language heavily laden with subjective, evaluative terminology; by such overt markers as *I*, *I feel*, *I believe*; and by an overall pattern of coherence that relates more closely to private associations of the author than to independently discernible features of subject or method. These expressive features are characteristic of personal journals, letters, and testimonials of various sorts.

Objective direction constitutes what most readers consider the normal form of scientific and instrumental discourse. It is distinguished by a relative paucity of self-referring expressions; by referential vocabulary; by a persona who, if he or she intrudes into the discourse at all, does so in a way that is largely incidental to the subject or argument of the discourse; and by an overall pattern of coherence that relates to the logical, temporal, or spatial dimensions of the subject more than to the author's reactions to it.

Affective monologue is aimed at the audience in an immediate way. It has a tendency toward the manipulative and incitive, and it coincides with a good deal of what is normally thought of as hortatory, emotionally charged, or imagistic language. It may be characterized by evaluative and incitive terminology; by a high frequency of imperative forms; by affective imagery; by the frequent use of the second person pronoun; or by series of short, clipped locutions—either sentences, fragments, or sentence modifiers—designed to emphasize feeling or imagery over logical and syntactic connection, and attempting to engender what Burke has termed "formal appeal" (1950: 65). *Affective* is the dominant "direction" of consumer advertising.

A final determinant of mode is the one that I have termed "contact," a concept designed to account for the condition of writing as a "secondary" form of communication that often simulates primary forms. It does so by using verbal clues to maintain illusions of direct contact between author and addressee. While written discourse is inherently isolative—usually only one person can read a text comfortably at a time—it will sometimes mimic the "aggregative" nature of oral monologue, feigning an audience of readers being addressed all at once. Alternately, it will sometimes capitalize upon the intrinsically isolative nature of writing, focusing on the individual reader, even while hoping that there will be thousands of such individuals.

Because the various illusions of contact involve different permutations of feigned "presence," they form variants primarily of the discursive mode. Since the notion of contact necessarily implies two variables, addresser and addressee, we can delineate the varieties of contact with reference to the different ways in which these two may be constructed or assumed by the discourse. On the side of addresser, there are basically three forms of simulated contact: *personal*, where there is something like the presence of a single speaker, conducting a lecture or one-sided conversation; *collective*, where the illusion is of a group of speakers conducting a monologue in unison; and *impersonal*, where the pretense of a speaker communicating with an addressee is dropped altogether and is replaced by the pretense of a *book* communicating with the addressee. This last form is made possible by the notion of the book as a repository of information, as a "container in which 'things' are neatly ordered rather than as a voice which speaks to the reader" (Ong 1977: 88).

A good deal of contemporary discursive prose is indeterminate with respect to contact, whereas in the discursive prose of oral and manuscript cultures the boundaries are usually clearcut. There is no mistaking the *personal* character of Ecclesiastes, for example, or the *impersonal* character of Proverbs. The variations do persist in modern writing, however, as the examples that follow illustrate:

Personal Contact

> Bravery is a complicated thing to describe. You can't say it's three feet long and two feet wide and that it weighs four hundred pounds. . . . It's a quality, not a thing. Lots of men have tried to describe what it is, and most of them have done pretty well, though the definitions vary a bit.
>
> One of the most widely quoted definitions of courage is the famous one of Ernest Hemingway's. I bet I've seen it quoted fifty different times, though at first I didn't know it was Hemingway who made it up. . . . Hemingway used that short common word that my father used—guts. He said, 'Guts is grace under pressure.' (Mantle 11)

Collective Contact

> We affirm the students' right to their own patterns and varieties of language—the dialects of their nurture or whatever dialects in which they find their own identify and style. Language scholars long ago denied that the myth of a Standard American dialect has any validity. The claim that any one dialect is unacceptable amounts to an attempt of one social group to exert its dominion over another. . . . We affirm strongly that teachers must have the experience and training that will enable them to respect diversity and uphold the right of students to their own language. ("Secretary's Report No. 65")

Impersonal Contact

> The observed adrenal hyperplasia in the tumor-bearing rats may have been produced by the high prolactin secretion, but it did not contribute to inhibition of LH release. . . . It is not known whether the enlarged adrenals of the tumor-bearing rats secreted increased amounts of steroids.

The present study is believed to further clarify the mechanism by which a PRL secretary pituitary tumor reduces gonadotropin release and results in a decreased gonadal function in the rat /2/ and perhaps also in man /1/. (Hodson et al. 10)

On the side of addressee there are just two variations of contact, as already indicated: the isolative and aggregative. Although a good deal of contemporary discursive writing is also indeterminate in this respect, the differences are clearly exemplified in the passages that follow:

Isolative Contact
In hundreds of ways you may have been not a growing developing, choice-making individual, but a shadow of somebody else. Even your name implies it—Mrs. Edward Smith, your name completely dissolved into someone else's. Now the situation has changed, and it is time to rediscover who you are. Essentially it means doing what feels right to you—that is, making the right choices—and that means re-examining old habits, old patterns, old influences. (Singleton 62–63)

Aggregative Contact
Looking back now, we can see that it was almost inevitable that by the seventies, those of us in English departments would eventually be made to feel particularly responsible for doing something about social ills. When Kennedy turned university faculties into a farm system for the Federal League, and when the population bulged onto the campuses a few years later, the sheer numbers of young people made them—and many of us—feel we had a special mission. The embarrassing truth was, though, that it was the social scientists who got The Call and not English teachers. (Williams 8)

II. STRATEGIES OF WRITTEN DISCOURSE

The strategies occupy a place in the Discourse Hierarchy between modes of disourse and de facto genres of discourse. Like the modes, they are discourse operations rather than purposes; but unlike the modes, which are in a primary sense "formal," the strategies are in a primary sense "functional." Because the notion *strategy* is inherently less problematic than aim, mode, or genre, and because the strategies have received extensive treatments in both classical and contemporary rhetoric, their discussion here will be somewhat briefer than that of the other categories. I will be concerned primarily with identifying a continuum of strategies and relating this continuum to the larger framework of the Discourse Hierarchy.

The pivotal position of the strategies, between the purpose-oriented categories of *aim, genus,* and de facto genre on the one hand, and the form-oriented category of mode on the other, determines the character of the continuum of strategies themselves. At one end of the continuum, directly linked to the category of de facto genre, lie the "generic" strategies, conscious appropriations of generic forms and conventions in unexpected settings; at the other end, directly linked to the modes, lie the modal strategies, conscious appropriations of modal stances and directions, as well as strategic modulations from one stance or direction to another. Between these outposts lie more familiar groups of strategies, which form the traditional arts of invention, disposition, and style. These are the material, logical, dispositional, and stylistic strategies.

It is obvious that these elements are often bound up in one another and exist in varying degrees of interdependence in actual instances of discourse. The choice or appropriation of a certain genre, for instance, necessarily commits one to certain material, logical, dispositional, stylistic, and modal choices as well. However, we must once again insist that these things do not exist in absolute lockstep with one another, that they can be isolated from one another, and that there exists a good deal of variation in actual practice. The outline that follows will serve to indicate something of the range of possibility.

Generic Strategies

Every individual discourse performance, even though it may achieve a certain uniqueness, may be said to participate or reside in a certain genre, involving distinctive and characteristic purposes, strategies, forms, and constraints. Some genres are more determinate than others in one or more of these areas. The rhetorical-informative genre of the journalistic "portrait" is less determinate, for instance, than the genre of the "obituary tribute"; and both of these are less determinate than the instrumental genres of "last will and testament" and "recipe." *Generic strategy* involves appropriating the strategies and formal operations familiar to one set of purposes and circumstances for use with another set of purposes and circumstances. This strategy involves a kind of metaphoric transfer, the appropriated genre acting as "vehicle" for the communication of uncharacteristic or unexpected fields of meaning. Usually the vehicle in such operations is fairly determinate and recognizable in form, while the tenor is less determinate. This would be the case if an author chose to do a rhetorical portrait and assessment of a living political figure by writing a feigned "obituary tribute," projected twenty years into the future. Like verbal metaphors, generic appropriations can be delightful and fascinating or they can be tasteless and gratuitous. Also like metaphors, they can be hackneyed—witness the bounty of "recipes" for good marriages, happy homes, and the like in popular inspirational writing.

Generic appropriation is a stock device of traditional and modern lyric poetry, with individual poems taking on the forms of love letters, last wills and testaments, charters, epitaphs, invitations to dinner, and a host of other things. Owing to the possibilities of dramatic modal stance, vehicles can include not only written genres but oral ones as well: speeches, debates, religious confessions, television commercials, telephone conversations, welcoming speeches. To a somewhat lesser degree than in lyric poetry, generic appropriation is a device of modern prose fiction as well. Phillip Roth's *Portnoy's Complaint*, for instance, is cast as a series of psychiatric conferences, with the narrator presumably lying on the couch and confessing all. (There are of course more familiar and time-honored conventions: The use of epistolary forms is virtually as old as the novel itself.)

Generic appropriation is also a possible strategy of modern rhetorical literature. For the present, a single deliberative example will suffice: In January 1980, the Superintendent of Public Schools in a southeastern city ordered removed from all school libraries a novel thought by some parents to be obscene. There followed, predictably, a controversy which raised issues of censorship as well as of the novel's merits and appropriateness for young readers. One of the most striking of the pieces that appeared in the local press was a "review" of the book, written in the manner and format of a typical book review, even though the novel in question was eight years old and, in fact, out of print at the time. Quoted below are the opening and closing sections of the "review."

THE CAR THIEF. By Theodore Weesner. Random House. 1972. 370 pages. Also available in paperback for $1.50.

The Car Thief is one of the best novels published in the last decade. Theodore Weesner in his story of the 16-year-old Alex Housman is both relentless in his moral vision and compassionate for the boy's intense suffering. The setting is Flint, Michigan, a factory town, and the year is 1960. . . .

I highly recommend this book to parents, high school and junior high school students. Selections from it were printed both in *The New Yorker* and *The Atlantic Monthly*. It contains some gutter language but only where appropriate, mostly spoken by the juveniles in the children's prison. These are words that every child over eight—unless he is kept locked in a closet—has heard again and again but probably has the sense not to use at the family dinner table. The book contains no explicit sex scenes. No drugs either: It took place before drugs became widespread in our culture.

After a reading of this book, everyone young or old will know what it is like to be in Alex's shoes. The young will never want to make the wrong choices Alex did in stealing; the old will feel lucky that they never gave in to his temptations. (Watson "The Car Thief")

One of the most interesting advantages of generic appropriation is that in almost every case the appropriated genre specifies a form of modal stance and contact, thus solving what may be a problem for the writer who finds himself in a situation of rhetorical indeterminacy. Walter J. Ong has commented upon the tendency of writers in manuscript cultures to cast what we would call treatises and essays in the forms of letters and speeches, partly as ways of fixing a modal stance (1975: 71). By contrast, a literate culture in which reading is a commonplace activity is much more comfortable with the prospect of a voice speaking out of a book, and even of the book itself as an impersonal repository of information. Nevertheless, the problem is to some degree a permanent one. Authors speak routinely of the struggle to find an appropriate "voice."

Material Strategies
Dialectical Strategies

Aristotle's *Rhetoric* contains lists and descriptions of at least two basic kinds of argumentative device. One type, more readily classified and codified, consists of the logical and quasi-logical strategems of dialectic: the familiar "places" of classification, division, definition, cause, *a fortiori*, comparison, and so on. These places apply to all kinds of subject matter and operate in all types of rhetoric. They are here designated as "dialectical strategies." The other type consists of strategies that attach to the subjects and purposes of specific kinds of rhetoric, and these are here designated "material strategies." Aristotle's list of twenty-eight *topoi* actually contains both kinds of strategies. Some of them are clearly drawn from dialectic, but others, such as the device of turning an opponent's utterance against him (*Rhetoric*, 1398[a]), or the treatment of a conceivable motive as an actual motive (*Rhetoric* 1399[b]), are not dialectical topics at all but rather manipulations of typical deliberative or forensic matters and situations. In succeeding ages the Latin rhetorics of speechmaking developed a rich tradtion of material strategies that came to be known as "commonplaces"—set arguments or expostulations on various subjects and for different occasions.

The study of material strategies has a great deal of relevance to studies of rhetorical genre, since these strategies do relate more closely to the separate purposes, subjects, and situations of individual genres than do the dialectical topics. One recent study, for instance, identifies the strategy of "enactment," in which the "speaker incarnates the argument" and is "the proof of what is said," as a dominant strategy of the "keynote address" genre (Campbell and Jamieson 9–10). Another study identifies the material strategy of "synthesis"—whereby controversies about one's character or action are "subsumed into a higher frame," demonstrataing the authenticity of one's conduct or views on life—as a defining strategy of the rhetorical genre of "apologia" (Black 156–58).

The distinction between dialectical and material strategies forms an exact parallel to Max Black's distinction between formal and material fallacies (1952: 232–39). The former are violations of logical principle, while the latter represent objections from some moral or philosophical standpoint to certain manipulations of subject, situation, or audience. Circularity, the undistributed middle term, and affirming the consequent are formal or dialectical fallacies; *ad hominem, ad ignorantiam,* and *ad misericordiam* are material strategies. The idea of "intentional fallacy" in literary criticism amounts to a philosophical objection to the use of a particular material strategy in critical argument.

Dispositional Strategies

Dispositional strategies encompass the whole field of rhetorical arrangement, especially in cases where either the overall design of a work or special internal orderings are matters of rhetorical choice rather than of generic or situational constraint. Classical formulas for deliberation, Whately's distinction between deductive and investigative order (142ff.), and various studies of the ordering of arguments are all concerned with strategies of disposition.

Stylistic Strategies

Stylistic strategies encompass a wide range of verbal and syntactic devices, which exist in close interdependence with the other groups of strategies, and which in particular combinations or states of interdependence are often singled out as definitive of the overall character of a work. Examinations of and prescriptions about stylistic strategies have been a preoccupation of rhetorical pedagogy and criticism, especially in the modern period.

In general, stylistic strategies can be comprehended under five headings: (1) *register,* which identifies levels of diction, idiom, and syntax from highly casual to highly formal; (2) *provenance,* which identifies particular collocations of diction, idiom, and syntax as characteristic of particular sociological, geographical, professional, or ideological groupings, e.g. "frontier," "academic," "posh," "black," "female"; (3) *schemes* and (4) *tropes,* which encompass patterns of language and reference traditionally grouped under these headings; and (5) *tone,* which identifies various projections of attitude toward subject, audience, or both. These various projections are identified by such terms as "sarcasm," "belligerence," "geniality," and so on. ("Irony" is either a trope or a tonal projection, depending upon circumstances.) To the extent that tonal projections involve implicit characterizations of author and audience and of the relation between the two, stylistic strategies merge into consideration of mode.

Modal Strategies

Just as the generic strategies form a continuum with a higher categorial grouping (that of de facto genre), so do modal strategies form a continuum with the lower one. Modes are very often, of course, determined by the choice of genre or subject. To the extent that modes are adapted for specific purposes above and beyond such considerations, or to the extent that "modulations" within a single work acquire significance for what is being communicated or the power of what is being communicated, they become matters of strategy. The generic and modal strategies, even as they occupy opposite ends of a strategic continuum, are in this respect often bound up in one another, illustrating once again the Möbius-like tendency of items at the ends of continuums to loop back upon one another.

CONCLUSION: MODES, STRATEGIES, AND THE CONTEXTS OF DISCOURSE

Both the modes and strategies always occur in broader generic and situational contexts, and they take on different, sometimes unique colorations and variations in different contexts. As a pedagogical activity, it is a mistake for rhetoricians to attempt to construct extensive drill or practice in modes and strategies without tying them into distinct contexts and purposes and situations of discourse. As a descriptive and analytical activity, however, it is possible for rhetoricians partially to "segment" them out of these contexts, precisely because they do not march in lockstep with contexts. They remain "ways of conducting discourse," not "reasons for conducting discourse." They can be accounted for fairly accurately and readily through empirical description and through identification of the hierarchical placements, lines of continuum, and regularities of context discoverable within the framework of the Discourse Hierarchy.

With the modes and strategies, however, we have reached the limits of such a procedure, even though all of these things—empirical description, hierarchical placements, lines of continuum, regularities of context—will remain important in the identification and characterization of aims of discourse. The farther one travels up the hierarchy of categories, the broader and more influential relationships of context become. It is now widely recognized that cultural features impinge upon forms and operations of discourse at all levels. However, as we pass over the line from "ways of conducting discourse" to "reasons for conducting discourse," these features become definitive: We have passed over from the description of categories of form, which have different uses and permutations in a variety of contexts, to the description of categories of purpose and context, which absorb and channel a variety of forms. In this altered situation we require a broader framework of motivations than can be provided by the Discourse Hierarchy alone.

3. MOTIVATIONAL AXES: A SEMIOTIC FRAMEWORK

The Discourse Hierarchy is a powerful instrument for identifying and stabilizing such intrinsically murky concepts as aim, genus, strategy, and mode. Because it is a formalistic construct, however, it can provide very little help in "filling in the blanks," that is, in specifying the content of these categories, particularly at higher levels. For this task we need a systematic way of talking about the "motives" and "intentions" of discourse—about the kinds of meaning that discourse is called upon to express, as well as the kinds of cultural role that it is called upon to perform.

One convenient way of approaching this task would be to look for a theory of discourse aims in one or another general theory of human culture. (See the survey in Kinneavy, 51–57.) But such an approach has obvious shortcomings. Aside from being entirely deductive and reductive, it would be entirely "committed" to a particular view of human nature and society, thus in immediate and unresolvable competition with other views. In fact, it would not be (strictly speaking) a theory of discourse at all, but rather an application to discourse of some other kind of theory.

In addition to whatever losses to criticism would result from deriving a theory of discourse from a theory of human culture, we would also lose the opportunity to see what light the theory of discourse can throw upon culture itself, as well as upon theories about it. Such an opportunity seems within reach when we reflect upon the constitutive (as opposed to the expressive or communicative) function of discourse in human culture and human knowledge. All human making, all human systems, all human institutions involve convergences, which we are hard pressed to understand, of mind and matter, intelligence and action, knowing and doing—*understandings of reality* and *participations in reality*. Without this mixing, intelligence on the one hand and action on the other are lifeless and meaningless.

The primary form of this mixing is of course language. The word itself is an organization of matter (physiological manipulations, acoustic phenomena) in the framework of a conceptual system (underlying phonological and morphological rules). It is in the word, moreover, that thing and idea come together; so that human utterance, itself a synthesis of the material and conceptual, repeats the function of synthesizing at ever higher levels of application. The human utterance is ideational—a signification of the "world" other than itself—and at the same time pragmatic—an action within that world.

If language, then, is a primary form of the mixing which underlies all human making, the products of language—works of discourse—are of primary importance to the human sciences. For these products, the instruments by which the human sciences are constructed and communicated, are themselves forms of human making in the primary medium, themselves forms of human culture. Hence the need for a broader, ideologically "uncommitted" framework for understanding the ways in which discourse and works of discourse "mean" and construct understandings of the world.

The critic-philosopher who has written most profoundly and provocatively on this matter is Kenneth Burke. In *A Grammar of Motives* Burke proposed a "dramatistic method" for revealing the constitutive role of discourse in human culture and knowledge. Burke hoped to gain an Archimedean point for critiquing a welter of seemingly irreconcilable twentieth-century ideologies, and he also hoped to construct a literary humanism free of both theology and ideology. The key to that humanism is the Pentad, a dialectical rather than a philosophical construct, a "system of placement" rather than a system of specific ideas, based upon the analysis of discourse as both "action" and "substance": "One might hypothetically grant," Burke states, "that the treatment of motives in terms of 'action' and 'substance' is wholly fallacious, yet defend it as central to the placement of statements about motives. Relinquishing all claims for it as a 'philosopher's stone,' we might then make claims for it secondarily, as a 'philosopher's stone' for the synopsis of writings that have sought the philosopher's stone" (56).

Burke's pentadic framework of concepts—Act, Scene, Agent, Agency, Purpose—is based upon the insight that discourse "means" not merely by referring (as positivists would have it) but also by participating in human action. The pentad is a powerful device for discovering motives within the symbolic actions that constitute human discourse. It lacks, nevertheless, a linguistic base. The pentad remains a self-consciously "dramatistic" and not fully a semiotic framework, at least in the sense of identifying a "pattern of or play of forces which we can detect inside language" (Eagleton 188). Its starting point is not a perspective on the "symbolic act" as a key to motives; it is a perspective on "action" itself, into which symbolic acts are assimilated. As a result, Burke produces brilliant accounts of the involvements of discourse in culture and in human knowing, but he does not develop a theory of discourse itself.

In *A Grammar of Motives* Burke makes a movement toward developing such a theory, with a set of speculations about the "master tropes" of metonymy, metaphor, synechdoche, and irony (503–17); the discussion is fragmentary, however, and laced with considerations not strictly focused on understandings of the aims of discourse. A clearer and more rigorous linguistic basis for the construction of a semiotic framework, I believe, lies in the speech-act theory of Austin and Searle, which has made possible a rapprochement of linguistics and the philosophy of language that would not have seemed possible when *A Grammar of Motives* appeared. In the pages that follow, I will articulate a semiotic framework suggested primarily by this development. First, however, it will be useful to take note of the fact that different sorts of semiotic frameworks are possible, and to examine another particular semiotic framework that has gained widespread attention, particularly among students of writing.

THE COMMUNICATION TRIANGLE

In recent theorizing about discourse, the most useful and powerful sets of organizing concepts have been provided by application of the now-familiar "communication triangle," a model of linguistic behavior adapted from modern communication theorists but actually implicit in traditional theories of rhetoric. In its simplest and most commonsense application the communication triangle can serve as a heuristic device, isolating the various components of the communication situation for any given text or segment of a text. (It is readily apparent that any text will exhibit and depend upon the features of encoder, decoder, signal, and reality; and that for a given text one or more of these features may be more conspicuous or more fruitfully analyzed than others.) In another application the communcation triangle may serve as a kind of theoretical compass, pointing to the various orientations any particular discussion or theory of discourse may exhibit. (Thus there may be expressive, affective, mimetic, or formal theories of discourse or of a particular branch of discourse.[1]) In its most elaborate application, in Kinneavy's *A Theory of Discourse*, the communication triangle serves as a semiotic model for organizing the entire field of language and discourse (figure 4); but Kinneavy's most productive and provocative use of the communication triangle is as a device for discovering and predicting the "aims" or basic kinds of discourse at the highest level of classification. This application evokes the principle that "the language process seems to be capable of focusing attention on one of its own components as primary in a given situation, with the result that the other components function in a subordinate role" (59). Accordingly, if attention is focused

1. For a successful application to literary theory, see Abrams, *The Mirror and the Lamp*.

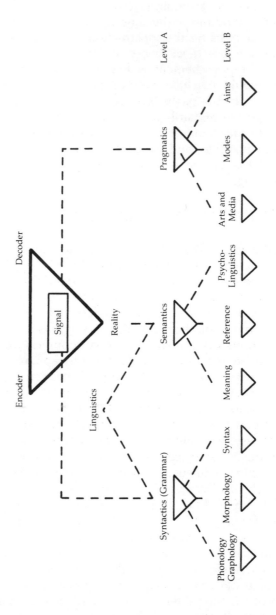

Figure 4. The study of language (after James Kinneavy, *A Theory of Discourse*, 25)

primarily on the encoder, the discourse is Expressive; if on reality, the discourse is Referential; if on the decoder, Persuasive; and if on the discourse itself, Literary (figure 5). The basic theoretical claim is that these points of focus correlate with final causes of discourse, and that these in turn predict certain logical, formal, and stylistic modalities.

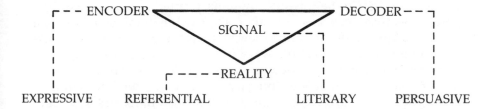

Figure 5. The aims of discourse (after James L. Kinneavy, *A Theory of Discourse*, 61)

In spite of the obvious success of some of these applications, I have rejected the communication triangle, particularly in the last-named application, in favor of what I believe to be a more powerful semiotic framework that I term the "Motivational Axes" of discourse. In doing so I do not reject the communications triangle as a model of linguistic behavior but rather as an overarching framework relating linguistic behavior to the world of action and motivation.

It must be acknowledged at the outset that Kinneavy's theory has brought a great deal of needed clarity to the study of discourse classifications. His model is based on intrinsic observation, it is free of psychologism and ideology, and it is highly elegant. Nevertheless, as some literature in the field suggests, the classifications of aims themselves are not entirely successful (Fulkerson), and the entire system suffers from at least two notable deficiencies. The first, already noted in a preliminary way, is that the communication triangle simply does not provide sufficiently rich or powerful criteria for classifying written discourse products. The principal reason for this defect is that it is insufficiently able to account for the qualitative differences that arise between "speech acts" and "discourse acts"—that is to say, between any particular instance of linguistic behavior, on the one hand, and "made things" of language on the other: deliberate, extended, complete, and unified productions of discourse.

This distinction between "speech acts" and "discourse acts"[2] demands that we view the discourse act as a composite unity of speech acts, brought into being by a complex set of interactions among author, subject, and audience in a special or typical situation. The totality, moreover, may be at least partially predicated upon or transacted in the awareness of similar events that have been produced in the past, under similar circumstances; it also suggests that distinctions among the basic kinds of discourse should reflect different orderings of these complex relations. If this line of reasoning is correct, the "ultimate aims" of discourse ought not to be classified by unitary criteria (as Kinneavy proposes), because they are not, after all, fixed natural or conceptual categories but complex historical developments; they need to be understood in terms that reflect the ways in which clusters of motives and traits come together in a discourse situation. Even if we can identify traits or principles that are "primary" and which tend to subsume others, the names that are extrapolated from such traits and applied to whole categories of discourse will not denote any special feature but a special way in which various features tend to be clustered.

A second defect of the communications triangle is its relative weakness as the "system of placement" that we hope to find in a semiotic model—that is, as a device for understanding the ways in which discourse interpenetrates and "understands" experience. The source of this defect is the same as that of the first: namely, the behavorial or operational posture of the entire model. Such a posture allows the discovery of statements focused on "reality," as opposed to "audience" or "self," but not of the ways in which various focusings constitute or lead to different constructions of reality. Not the least casualty of this defect is our ability to penetrate and understand either the social or intellectual functions of rhetorical discourse. By atomistically separating rhetoric from reference, Kinneavy's application of the communication triangle forfeits any hold on this crucial area of understanding. These considerations and others have led me to seek an alternate framework for discussing the ultimate aims of discourse, one that is less mechanical and reductive, more unified, and better equipped to explore the interpenetrations of discourse and culture.

MOTIVATIONAL AXES OF DISCOURSE

One of the virtues of the communication triangle is that it avoids the quagmire of epistemological and psychological speculation that often accompanies the search for comprehensive theories of "mean-

2. This distinction is based upon the work of Karl Wallace, *Understanding Discourse,* and is treated at length in the next chapter.

ing." Is it possible to construct a more powerful "system of placement" for the relations of discourse and "reality," "action," and "motivation," while still avoiding this quagmire? It is indeed possible, I believe, if we attend not to definitive answers but to persistent questions. What we seek is not a complete and unified adjudication of all the problems of semantic theory, involving necessarily a position on broader philosophical questions, but an analysis of these problems that relates them directly to the conundrums of both discourse and "reality."

Taking this analytical view, one finds the relations of utterance to "meaning" or "motivation" problematic in two persistent and recurrent ways. In any discussion of language and discourse, in fact, two sets of paradoxes emerge; both are involved in the problem of language *description* as well as of meaning, and more importantly, both relate to traditional axes of rational thought and speculation.

Referentiality and Non-referentiality

The first paradox is the paradox of *referentiality* and *non-referentiality*. All meaningful discourse is necessarily referential in some way, even where the referential motive is marginal. It is simply unavoidable. The most inchoate expressive utterance points to a condition separate from the utterance itself, and the most convoluted "metalinguistic" utterance must assume an entity, "language," that is conceptually different from the "language" that is the utterance itself. It is doubtful that language even more blatantly nonsensical than Lewis Carroll's "Jabberwocky" could be said to be entirely without reference. The restrictional features that attach willy-nilly to verbal forms and structures, and the temporal/ spatial presuppositions of grammar (now, then/here, there) always assure a certain degree of referentiality.

At the same time, even though all "common sense" notions of meaning speak in terms of reference, such notions are undermined by the circumstance, more apparent to moderns than to ancients, that discourse is irretrievably cut off from the experience it names or directs. The forms of language, arbitrary significations at the outset, are finite, and metaphor supplies the principal mediation to the infinity of experience. "Experience" itself is in a sense unreachable, can never be known directly. Its infinity can only be "reduced," "arrested" by structures that are finite and other.

The antinomies of reference and nonreference pervade discussions of language and its relation to experience. In philosophy and intellectual life they anticipate the dichotomy between objectivity and subjectivity—or, in antinomies articulated by Ernst Cassirer, between the "object pole" and the "ego pole" (1961: 93). They reflect dual urges and capacities of human language and human intellect: Dialectically, they

reflect the function of analysis, partition, and the delineation of differences, as opposed to the function of synthesis, drawing connections,
discovering points of identification. Epistemologically, they reflect the
orientation toward "outer reality," comprehending an experience *as it
really is*, as opposed to "inner reality," comprehending it "as perceived," or in terms of some other experience. In the broadest sense,
they point to separate loci or realms of reality: the realm of the phenomenal and the realm of the phenomenological.

In the history of ideas, these antinomies are expressed repeatedly:
in Platonic agonizings over the relations of words to things; in positivist
attempts to rid language·of extra-referential contaminations; in humanist defenses of poetic and rhetorical language; in philosophical recognitions of the metaphorical bases of all science; in aesthetic claims that
poetry "reflects" reality; and in counterclaims that poetry creates its
own reality. The paradox is as unresolvable at the level of linguistic
analysis as it is philosophically and culturally, except in a practical way:
Some speech is more referential than other speech, in certain contexts.

Participation and Non-participation

The second paradox is the paradox of *participation* and *non-participation*, or in broader terms *action and contemplation*. Though philosophically just as pervasive as the paradox of reference and nonreference,
this paradox has come under active scrutiny *as a linguistic matter* only in
the present half-century, with the advent of speech-act theory, pio-
neered by Austin and Searle. The paradox is this: All saying is doing,
and no saying is doing. There is a sense in which all language and all
discourse activity is radically divorced from action and experience. In
this sense, verbalizing is inherently disjunctive, reductive, postponing,
and abstracting from participation, as an instrument of intellection and
speculation. (Even the command "Off with her head!" does not participate directly in the off-taking, which in rare instances may be happily
circumvented.) But in another, diametrically opposed sense, all speech
is inherently participatory, performing actions of one sort or another,
bound up in the temporal and material existence it seeks to understand.
Not merely those directly "performative" utterances such as "Off with
her head!" "I dub thee knight!" and so on, but even abstract philosophical formulations constitute doings of a sort within a particular communal framework. Contemplation itself is a form of human action.

Like those of the reference/nonreference dichotomy, the antinomies
of participation and non-participation pervade discussions of language
and its relation to reality. They are expressed in philosophical and linguistic debate over the "constative" and "performative" dimensions of
speech acts; in mystical attempts to bypass or transcend language alto-

gether, in the attainment of pure, "passive" comprehension of reality; and most pervasively, in popular sayings about the disparity between words and deeds, rhetoric and results, lip-service and real service: "Actions speak louder than words," goes the saying. "It's what you do, not what you say / that's going to count on judgment day." This popular wisdom is undercut by what every statesman knows intuitively: that eloquent and forceful articulation of a communal value is an important form of political action in itself. However, as with the paradox of reference and nonreference, there is no final resolution of the problem. We can only say, in a pragmatic formulation, that some speech is more "performative" than other speech, in certain contexts.

In intellectual life, the paradox of participation/non-participation anticipates the paradox of action and contemplation, along with a host of dichotomies related, once again, to fundamentally different orientations toward experience: On the one side we encounter the orientation toward the realm of the concrete, the particular, the natural, and the practical; on the other, we have the orientation toward the realm of the abstract, the general, the intellectual, and the theoretical. Dialectically, there is the predilection for description of individual entities, as opposed to the classification of these entities into a system. In the language of traditional philosophy and metaphysics, these dichotomies are reflected in such distinctions as "the one and the many," "mind-body," the realm of intellection vs. the realm of appearances, the province of pure forms vs. the province of coming-to-be-and-passing-away.

Historically, different philosophical schools locate "reality" in different places, setting forth different adjudications of the epistemological and ontological issues implicit in these dichotomies. These issues persist, moreover, in the humanities and the human sciences, where they are revealed in orientations toward substance as opposed to process, toward the formal and static as opposed to the processive and dynamic. In theoretical dispute, they tend to be expressed in such terms as positivism vs. formalism, mechanism vs. mentalism.

THE AIMS OF DISCOURSE

These discussions of the Motivational Axes have been necessarily far-ranging. If we may now return to the original, semantic distinctions, but keeping in mind some of their broader philosophical implications, we may obtain a broad theoretical preview of the aims of discourse. Taken together, these paradoxes—of *reference and nonreference* and *participation and non-participation*—constitute a map to the entire range of linguistic and intellectual activity. Although they may not anticipate absolutely everything of any interest to students of meaning, they certainly encompass enough to constitute the essential components of a "system of placement" for dealing with the problems of motivation in discourse. The two paradoxes suggest two axes or lines of continuum for the placement of speech acts: The first I call the "literal-tropological" axis, indicating the broad continuum between referentiality and non-referentiality; the second is the "constative-performative" axis (borrowing terms from J. L. Austin), indicating the broad continuum between participation and non-participation.

On reflection it is apparent that no utterance, especially no extended utterance, can call into play one of these axes without simultaneously invoking the other. No utterance can be "placed" simply as "literal" or "tropological"; it must be "literal/performative," or "literal/constative," and so on. Consequently, without any distortion we may graph one of the axes against the other, producing a conceptual map of four motivational dimensions of discourse activity: a referential/non-participatory dimension, a referential/participatory dimension, a non-referential/non-participatory dimension, and a non-referential/participatory dimension. As figure 6 indicates, these dimensions both anticipate and confirm theoretically the four "aims of discourse" to be discovered and described in chapter 4: Scientific, Instrumental, Poetic, and Rhetorical. Scientific discourse, we may say, rests theoretically in an objective/contemplative

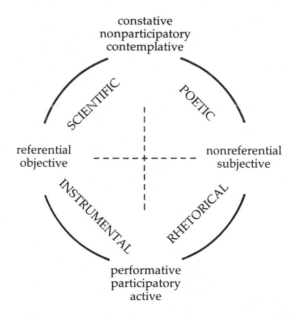

Figure 6. The aims of discourse

dimension; Instrumental discourse, in an objective/active dimension; Poetic discourse, in a subjective/contemplative dimension; and Rhetorical discourse in a subjective/active dimension. For important reasons also discussed in chapter 4, the dimensions located by these ratios also antici-pate the major subclasses of rhetorical discourse itself. Rhetoric, I hope to show, is the most "comprehensive" branch of human discourse, with the most responsibilities to the fullness of experience and knowledge; and one of the cultural and intellectual functions of rhetoric lies in the per-spective it provides on overspecialized and truncated constructions of reality. However, we must pull back from these as-yet incomplete identi-fications for the moment, both to anticipate some problems and to com-prehend some broader dimensions of the Motivational Axes.

It cannot be too strongly stressed that the model presented here is a "motivational" and not a "formalistic" construct. It is a map of the motives and not necessarily the forms of discourse. In fact, the principle of asymmetry that governs the form/meaning relation in speech acts argues against attempting to map both of these dimensions at a single stroke. Meanings are always determined in context. As an example, consider the following three statements, each fundamentally alike in outward form:

1) A sentence must be given an identical subject and object before the reflexive transformation is indicated.
2) The cooling system must be thoroughly drained and flushed before a new type of antifreeze is added.
3) The city of Carthage must be completely destroyed before it once again rises against us.

On reflection it should be clear that in spite of their formal sameness, these statements not only mean different things but have fundamen-tally different sorts of motivations, *when considered in the contexts where one normally encounters them.* The first statement normally appears in a descriptive grammar and is "scientific" in aim. The second normally appears in an "operations manual" and is "instrumental" in aim. The third normally appears in a political speech and is "rhetorical" in aim.

It is better, however, to speak of *aims* in connection with unified, extended discourse rather than with individual statements, and in such a connection the form of utterances, while not irrelevant in cer-tain circumstances, is even less a factor in the total picture. It is cru-cial to avoid misunderstanding at this point, even at the expense of redundancy: There is no claim being made here that "rhetorical" dis-course consists primarily or even substantially in either "performa-tive" or "tropological" utterance per se. The claim will be that rhetoric is "performative" in a teleological rather than a formal sense:

it aims at participation in the actions of a community. It would also be a grave mistake and a reduction to regard non-referentiality as a practical condition of rhetoric. Once again, rhetoric is "nonreferential" only in a teleological sense: It does not aim, finally, to create a fit or exact correspondence between language and reality. In practical terms, all the quadrants of the Motivational Axes constitute complementary dimensions, potentially, of any particular work. The great danger of reductionism in formulations of this sort is the primary reason that I will insist, in chapters 4 and 5, on more empirical identifications and descriptions of the aims of discourse.

CONSTRUCTIONS OF REALITY

The Motivational Axes would not constitute such a powerful system of placement for the aims of discourse if they did not simultaneously anticipate some pervasive philosophical and dialectical antinomies involved in human understandings of reality. As we have already seen, several pairs of concepts provide the primary terms of these dichotomies, but the particular terms that provide the conceptual map to aims of discourse are literal—tropological and constative—performative. Graphed against one another, these axes generate ratios of concepts that anticipate four broad categories of discourse, corresponding to broad categories of intellectual and cultural motivation.

We need at this point to fix upon an appropriate set of primary terms that will generate a map of constructions of reality. For just as every coherent utterance must call into play both sets of dichotomies simultaneously, so every coherent view of reality must do the same. The construction of reality involves two major axes, two sets of decisions that have to be made—either consciously, as a matter of principle, or unconsciously, as a matter of assumption. These derive from two sets of possibilites about the locus and nature of reality, independently of any actual observation of it:

1. We may think of reality as either exterior (strict objectivism, realism) or interior (strict relativism, subjectivism) or somewhere in between. Reality is perceived as "out there," existing independently of consciousness, or "in here," as something that includes one's consciousness or in fact is primarily a matter of consciousness.

2. We may think of reality as either abstract (strict formalism) or concrete (strict empiricism) or somewhere in between. In traditional terms, reality is perceived as "up there," in the realm of abstract essences, or "down here" in the realm of concrete realities. In more contemporary terms we may say that our knowledge is of the *gestalt* or formal pattern of things—observable regularities of form within experience—or of the diverse experiences themselves.

These constructs may be mapped as in figure 7, ready to be placed congruently on the maps already constructed. Keep in mind that such terms as "formalism" and "empiricism" are not meant to name specific philosophies but specific philosophic approaches or "corroborative structures" (Pepper 329).

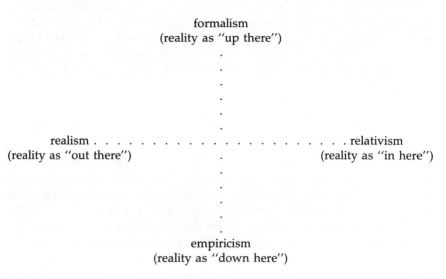

Figure 7. Constructions of reality

The primary axes specify and delimit different ways of knowing, different cognitive approaches to experience. Looking along the constative/performative (formalism/empiricism) axis from bottom to top, we see that we can approach experience either as becoming (action, process, series of actions, series of processes); or as being (substance, part of a larger substance, system). Looking along the referential/tropological (realism/relativism) axis from left to right, we can insist upon approaching experience *in itself*, in contrast or comparison to other experiences; or *as interpreted*, either in terms of or by analogy with other experiences. In sum, along one axis we "arrest" experience either as static (product, system, or substance) or as dynamic (process or action); along the other, we arrest experience either as a thing-in-itself, different from other things and isolated from the observer, or as a thing-as-experienced, in interaction with the observer, and absorbed into other experience.

Traditional philosophy, metaphysics, and theology in the West are preoccupied with pairs of concepts along the vertical axis: mind and matter, contemplation and action, being and becoming, the one and the many, transcendence and immanence. Modern thinkers, by contrast, tend to focus speculation and debate along the horizontal axis, dealing with such antitheses as object and subject, outer and inner, phenomena and perception, fact and value. In the history of ideas we see at particular times and within particular communities certain resolutions or states of balance achieved. But we also see these resolutions come unstuck, either through the pressure of new perceptions and discoveries or through the logical extension of a particular resolution to the point that inner contradictions become apparent. It is commonplace that old disputes surface with new combatants, especially on the battlefields of philosophy and psychology, and especially where questions of language are involved.

Dialectical Relations

It is natural that such basic antinomies as we have been discussing should express themselves in fundamental dialectical relations (ways of thinking, ways of representing thought). Dialectical relations we may define as instruments of understanding that relate one thing to another as subject and predicate. Not all subject-predicate relations are "dialectical" in this sense. For instance, "The dog is in the corner" contains not a dialectical but a simple or categorical relation: item/location. "The dog is a mammal," however, does represent a dialectical relation—the predicate is a term that understands the dog, by placing it in a class. Thus defined, all dialectical relations congregate into two basic types which correspond to the linguistic continuums of the motivational axes: difference/sameness and parts/wholes. Shifting to more familiar terminology, we can express these correspondences in the following way: Along the referential/tropological axis there is a movement from *analysis* to *synthesis*—from discovering differences and dividing things into parts to discovering likenesses and experiencing things as wholes. (Extrapolating from this fundamental contrast, Pascal distinguished between the "geometric spirit" and the "acute or subtle spirit," viewing the latter only as adequate for comprehending the quality of human life.) Along the constative/performative axis, on the other hand, there is a movement from *description* to *classification*—from identifying discrete identities to grouping those entities into categories and subcategories.[3]

It is important to keep in mind that this very way of talking about dialectical relations is itself an "analytic" construct, and obviously it would be foolish to forget that the "experience" of thinking is a whole

3. I believe that the Viconian/Burkean "master tropes" of metonymy, metaphor, synecdoche, and irony actually constitute dialectical relations along the Motivational Axes: irony and synechdoche along the constative/performative axis, and metonymy and metaphor along the referential/tropological axis. Burke's analysis generates enormous complexities (along with its penetrating insights), however, by obliterating the possibility of "degrees of referentiality."

thing, involving all these processes. Nevertheless, common sense indicates that there are characteristic habits of thought, ways of approach, even personality types involved in and related to these contrasts. Corresponding to analysis and synthesis, we find the objective as opposed to the evaluative account; the detached as opposed to the "engaged" viewpoint; the analytic as opposed to the holistic approach. Corresponding to description and classification, by contrast, we find the specific as opposed to the general focus; the concrete as opposed to the abstract account; the empirical or nominalist as opposed to the formalist approach; the "close-up" as opposed to the overview, the temperamentally particularist thinker as opposed to the temperamentally theoretical thinker. All of these considerations are important for understanding constructions of reality, because all systems of thought make use of dialectical relations and particular concentrations of dialectical relations, at the same time reflecting certain dialectical predispositions of their authors. The various distinctions represented here obviously do not circumscribe all thinking or communication of thought, for there are infinite subtleties and permutations of process. The convergence, nevertheless, of so many fundamental relations along the motivational axes does give one confidence that the construct is capable of casting considerable light on the *results* of thought—on human discourse and its ways of comprehending experience.

WORLD HYPOTHESES

Up to this point we have been dealing with "primary" concepts—with the separate poles of the motivational axes and the continuums between them. But acts of discourse are "secondary" phenomena: As indicated earlier, no act of discourse can bring one continuum into play without simultaneously activating the other, because the paradoxes of participation and non-participation, reference and nonreference inhabit every utterance. A "performative" statement can still be either "referential" or "tropological." A science that locates reality "out there" (realism) can in addition be either formalist or empiricist in orientation. For the placement of specific kinds of human discourse and specific ways of constructing reality, we must develop, therefore, a system of secondary concepts generated by ratios of primary concepts. Using the "naive" primary concepts developed earlier, we derive four secondary pairs to fill in the quadrants of our diagram:

out there/up there—realist and formalist in orientation
out there/down here—realist and empiricist in orientation
in here/up there—relativist and formalist in orientation
in here/down here—relativist and empiricist in orientation

It is difficult to find uncommitted terminology for these secondary dimensions, and the following labels must be offered with the caveat that they are not meant in this case to designate actual philosophies or world views: The *formalistic* dimension (out there/up there) is concerned with the general pattern or underlying logic of experience; the *operational* dimension (out there/down here) is concerned with actual events and with the general pattern insofar as it leads to prediction and control of these events; the *imaginative* dimension (up there/in here) is concerned with an inner, intuited order or design of experience; and the *ethical/pragmatic* dimension (down here/in here) is concerned with that sphere of actual events controlled or mediated by human choice. It is important to keep in mind that these terms designate not different experiences but different dimensions of experience—different potentialities for "arresting" experience into knowledge. The remaining question, of course, is whether these ratios bear any correspondence to actual philosophical systems.

Philosophers and historians of philosophy are not by any means completely agreed on the question of "fundamental types" of philosophical system, and many in fact are content to bypass the question, treating different philosophical systems serially, in order of their chronological development. Among those who approach the question analytically, however, there are some interesting confirmations of our semiotic model. The most cogent and influential of these is Stephen Pepper's *World Hypotheses*, which posits four basic theoretical approaches to reality: Formism, Mechanism, Contextualism, and Organicism. While admitting that there are historically more than four sorts of world hypothesis and that there are many combinations and permutations, Pepper insists that among fully developed and "relatively adequate" systems, there are only four types, based upon four different "root metaphors" and four different sets of epistemological assumptions (141).

(1) Formism, also known as "realism" or "Platonic idealism," is best represented by the philosophies of Plato, Aristotle, scholastics, and neoscholastics. (Plato and Aristotle represent transcendent versus immanent versions of this world hypothesis.) Its "root metaphor" is that of *similarity*: Because various particulars have identical qualities, reality may be organized into classes (151). Formism's basic epistemological view or corroborative principle is the "correspondence theory" of reality. ". . . [S]tatements of empirical uniformities are only half-truths. Full truths are descriptions which accurately correspond with facts that have occurred or with laws that necessarily hold (183)."

(2) Mechanism, also known as naturalism or materialism, is represented by the philosophies of Lucretius, Hobbes, and Locke. Its root metaphor is the machine, and while older versions are attached to the

correspondence theory of truth, modern mechanism is associated with the "causal theory of truth" or the "causal adjustment theory." The truth of a hypothesis is corroborated by a "system of connections which holds between an environmental stimulus and the response of the organism" (228).

(3) Organicism, also known as absolute idealism, is represented by the philosophies of Schelling, Hegel, and Royce, and its root metaphor is that of the organism, a unity above and beyond individual constituents. Its epistemology is the "coherence theory," or the "positive organic relatedness of material facts." Features of the organic whole are inclusiveness, determinateness, and organicity. The ideal of truth is "the absolute" (280).

(4) Contextualism, also known as pragmatism, is represented by the philosophies of Peirce, James, and Dewey. Its root metaphor is the "act in context," the "total given event," the "rich concrete thing, in which features interpenetrate" (233). Alone among the world hypotheses, contextualism is a philosophy in which *change* is categorical. Order may be defined in any of a variety of ways, "so long as it does not deny the possibility of disorder or another order in nature also" (234).

This implicit pluralism of outlook is combined with a qualified relativism. The corroborative principle connected with contextualism is a combination of "successful working" and the "verified hypothesis," in which successful working is only the "final factor in the constitution of truth" (270–72). This implies a process in which certain types of truth are "made," not merely discovered, and it leaves the door open to situations in which "reality" is at least in part a function of what James termed "the will to believe." It is not a full-blown subjectivism, however, or an idealism of the type that sees all constructions of reality as "airy fabrics of the mind, which express not the nature of things, but the nature of mind" (Cassirer 1953: 7). Such cases are limited to certain spheres of operation, particularly those involving human action and belief. Moreover, as Pepper notes, contextualism "is only a special truth theory," and it does not deny that other types of truth exist (268).

Pepper's four world hypotheses find congenial resting places as secondary concepts in our semiotic framework: Formism in the "formalistic" (constative/referential) dimension; Mechanism in the "operational" (performative/referential) dimension; Organicism in the "imaginative" (constative/tropological) dimension; and Contextualism in the "ethical/pragmatic" (performative/tropological) dimension. Even more promising than this convergence, moreover, is the fact that Pepper's system is based upon a theory of "root metaphors," which is like a semiotic framework in that it locates the ultimate placement of constructions of reality in the potentialities of language. Pepper's articulation of the theory of "root metaphors," however, is less than completely satisfying, even as the overall analysis remains brilliant and provocative. He often seems uncomfortable in locating the particular metaphor for a particular hypothesis; and such notions as "the total given event," while wonderfully suggestive, do not immediately strike one as metaphors. Pepper is somewhat at a loss, moreover, with the question of why there should be four (and only four) metaphors productive of world hypotheses, and he suggests only that there might be others which have not been developed (340). The Motivational Axes may provide a fortification for Pepper's system, by providing a closer specification of the relation between ways of seeing the world and ways of using language. They also provide an answer to the question, Why four? The semiotic model may be said (with qualifications to be broached in the next chapter) to circumscribe the possibilities of meaning in language. This "reconstruction" of Pepper's system is represented in figure 8.

Figure 8. A reconstruction of Pepper's world hypotheses

Among attempts to delineate philosophical systems, Pepper's is the most convincing and useful because it is the most analytical and systematic. There are others, however, which confirm the general set of relations posited in the diagram above. William Pepperell Montague, in

The Ways of Knowing, identifies in the history of philosophy "four methods of interpreting the meaning of truth or knowledge," based upon four distinct answers to a primary epistemological question which experience and observation alone cannot answer: "whether or not the object . . . apprehended can retain its existence and character apart from its relation to the apprehending subject" (237). The positions he identifies—Objectivism (or realism), Dualism ("the copy theory of knowledge"), Subjectivism (idealism), and Relativism (pragmatism)— correspond directly to Pepper's categories of Mechanism, Formism, Organicism, and Contextualism, respectively. Moreover, these categories fit very well as secondary terms within the Motivational Axes, as can be gathered from Montague's characterizations of them: Objectivism is the belief that "all the objects which are experienced exist objectively and are independent of mind" (292); Dualism is the belief that not the immediate objects of sense but rather the "conceptual objects which are inferred as the true causes of expression exist independently of the self and are never identical with the objects of consciousness" (306); Idealism is the belief "that objects . . . cannot exist independently of a consciousness of them, and that therefore all reality consists exclusively of conscious being and its states" (265); finally Relativism is the belief that "all truth depends upon or is in part created by individuals. It is, therefore inseparable from them and relative to them; and as such, it changes as they change" (165).

DISCOURSE AND THE HUMAN SCIENCES

A construct as powerful and inclusive as the one we are dealing with carries implications not merely for philosophy and discourse but also for such areas as politics, religion, education, or any of the "human sciences," where behavior, motivation, and understandings of behavior all come into play at once.[4] It would be well off the track to enter into discussions of these implications at this stage, but we can indicate something of their tenor and usefulness. Sometimes the theoretical compass provided by the Motivational Axes can spot either gaps or redundancies in existing explanations. In a discussion of religion, for instance, the philosopher William Ernst Hocking identifies three areas of root motivation: the speculative, the ethical, and the emotional (17). Depending upon the ways in which they were elaborated, these terms

4. *Metahistory*, Hayden White's fascinating study of "the historical imagination in nineteenth-century Europe," draws upon Burke, Pepper, Frye, Mannheim, and other works in criticism and the sociology of knowledge to construct an anatomy of historical writing and historical consciousness that strikes some parallels to the anatomy of discourse I am proposing in this study. White's ecclecticism and "Burkean" mode of presentation introduce complexities that would completely derail the present line of investigation, however.

would fit either as primary or as secondary concepts within the Motivational Axes. As primary terms, they correspond to the constative, performative, and tropological poles; as secondary terms to the formalistic, ethical, and imaginative dimensions. It is apparent that this explanation omits the "referential" pole and the "operational" dimension from view, and on reflection it is equally apparent that the operational motive—the comprehension and control of natural events—is a conspicuous feature of religious systems. Though associated primarily perhaps with primitive religions, the operational motive retains a strong foothold in modern religious concerns (and claims) about psychological and even physical health.

The overall picture that emerges, with this dimension added, is confirmed by the anthropological view of Anthony F. C. Wallace, who outlines five basic goals of religious ritual: technology (control of nature), therapy and anti-therapy (control of human health), ideology (social control), salvation (identification with supreme being), and revitalization (discovery of "new ways" through inspiration and memory of past inspiration) [106–215]. Allowing for a slight schematic redundancy, we can say that this more comprehensive view is anticipated by the Motivational Axes: "technology" and "therapy" come together in the operational dimension; and ideology, salvation, and revitalization fall in the ethical/pragmatic, formalistic, and imaginative dimensions respectively. Such examples as this both confirm and enrich one's sense of the categories provided by the Motivational Axes. Wallace's notion of "revitalization," for instance, provides a very powerful and suggestive set of adumbrations on the "imaginative" dimension—its reliance not only upon individual intuitions but also upon traditions of past intuitions; its connections with the prophetic character and prophetic vision; its affinities for metaphors of wholeness; its tendency to hold communities and nations accountable to absolute values. The example also reveals something of the framework's usefulness, not merely as a system of placement but also as a check against various sorts of blindsidedness in the human sciences. Some of the milder forms of blindsidedness, such as historical and cultural myopia, are eminently correctable; the more virulent forms are those of theoretical and ideological reductionism, and our framework is sensitive to their tendency to reduce one dimension of experience to the terms of the other, or to ignore whole dimensions altogether.

The natural condition of the humanities in the modern world, Walter J. Ong has said, is a state of crisis. If this is so, it is so because the humanities are always properly in a state of self-definition, partly in response to the tug of changing historical circumstances, and partly in the effort to hold in balance different dimensions of human consciousness amid the din of conflicting world views. They face challenges from and are themselves affected by radical formalisms and mechanisms on the one side, and radical subjectivisms on the other. Natural battlegrounds in this perpetual state of crisis are language and the language arts, for language is the paradigmatic human subject. It should come as no surprise, then, that the search for an adequate framework for a theory of rhetoric has led us into such wide-ranging considerations. We are reminded that the subject of rhetoric itself, since the time of Plato and Aristotle, has gained urgency out of the battle against narrow conceptions of the art and against narrow conceptions of human nature.

RHETORIC, CONTEXTUALISM, AND THE AIMS OF DISCOURSE

Another philosophical confirmation of the Motivational Axes, and one that sheds additional light upon the connection between constructions of reality and aims of discourse, comes from Irvin Edman's *Four Ways of Philosophy*. Edman's four categories of philosophical motivation, which he believes to be "not only chronologically but psychologically typical" (19), are "logical faith," "mystical insight" "nature understood," and "social criticism." Within the Motivational Axes, these correspond to the formalistic, imaginative, mechanical, and ethical/pragmatic dimensions, respectively.

Edman's model is instructive because, while less rigorously worked out than Pepper's, it is broader and more inclusive. Whereas Pepper deals only with fully articulated, "reasonably adequate" world hypotheses, Edman is less concerned with specific philosophical systems than with "ways of approaching reality." These may be expressed as the controlling outlooks of particular world views, as the methodological preoccupations of different thinkers, or as the different dimensions of experience for which any coherent philosophy bears implications. Into this broad context Edman is able to bring a number of approaches to experience that Pepper systematically excludes. The inclusion of mystical insight, as a prime example, casts further light upon the "imaginative" quadrant of the Motivational Axes, and it also reveals how different levels of inclusiveness can shift the relationships between different points of view. Whereas in Pepper's system the idealisms of Hegel and Royce are separated from the Formism of Plato, all of these formal idealisms come together in Edman's system under the heading of "logical faith," as distinct from more mystical and subjective approaches to reality. There is nothing surprising or contradictory in such shifts. In looking at literature, for instance, we might make a distinction between the personal lyric, which we would place in the "imaginative" dimension, and the public, celebratory epistle, which we would place in the "ethical/pragmatic" dimension. In in a broader context, however, both of these forms we would count as poetic, in the imaginative dimension, in contrast to such distinctively rhetorical products as *The Federalist Papers*, which themselves contain an imaginative dimension that might, in some context, distinguish them from other examples or traditions of rhetoric.

The "contextual" principle that emerges out of these reflections is a matter of signal importance, because it helps to clarify the proper relations between the different aims of discourse and the "outlooks" or "corroborative principles" with which they are aligned in the Motivational Axes. The placement of scientific discourse within the "formalistic" dimension obviously should not indicate a theoretical or ideological connection between science and Formism, for it is a presupposition of discussion that differences of alignment among constructions of reality do in fact exist both among and within the various sciences. Such a connection would indeed be "out of context." What the placement does capture at this level is that, whatever the theoretical or epistemological framework, and even where the work is primarily descriptive, the *end* of scientific discourse is with the elucidation of general principles and laws, and never solely with individual operations.

Rhetorical discourse is a parallel case. The practice of rhetoric obviously involves no ideological commitment to contextualism as a world hypothesis; however, there are certain contextual principles that emerge as methodological imperatives of the study of rhetoric. Some of these are carryovers from the study of discourse in general, and they turn up in recognition of the impossibility of purely formalistic accounts of language. (The asymmetry principle, which comprehends the finitude of forms, their detachment from the infinity of meanings, and the possibilities of irony and metaphor, dictates a contextual approach not merely to meaning but to the analysis of forms themselves.) There are other connections, however, between rhetorical discourse and contextualism; and these are worth dwelling upon, because they provide insights not only about how the study should be conducted but also about the significance of the study itself.

Among the various features of contextualism as outlined by Stephen Pepper, there are four which bear a more than casual connection with traditions of rhetoric and rhetorical scholarship. The first is the contextualist's special attention to the elements of change and novelty in experience. Rhetoric is an art enveloped in change: It operates in the world of change, and its purpose is change—change of hearts, of minds, of the world itself. (The purpose of both poetry and prophecy, by contrast, is not change but transformation.)

A second suggestive feature of contextualism is its "special" epistemology, which insists upon certain areas of experience where consciousness and will play a role in the constitution of truth. It was in battle against the radical extension of philosophical relativism by teachers of rhetoric in the ancient world that Plato gave birth to rhetoric as a subject of formal inquiry. Aristotle, certainly no epistemological relativist, nevertheless articulated something like a contextual principle by insisting that rhetoric can be properly conceived as an art (as opposed to a set of gimmicks) parallel to the art of dialectic: The basis of such a claim is that there are levels of certitude and exactitude relevant to different spheres of operation; and that rhetoric, like dialectic, operates in a world of probabilities and probablistic premises, as opposed to a world of absolutes. It is partly this contextualist understanding, which rests as a presupposition of rhetorical art, that has led twentieth-century theorists such as Chaim Perelman—seeking a basis for ethical and juridical philosophy between the extremes of positivism and radical subjectivism—to the study of Aristotelian rhetoric and to the notion of "rhetoric as epistemic." Questions of how far one should go in this philosophical direction—to what extent the rhetorical process "constructs" (as opposed to "discovers") moral and social knowledge—are matters of continuing debate[5]; but in either case, a healthy society has a great stake in preserving the integrity of a process which deals with those sorts of questions that, as William James puts it, "immediately present themselves as questions whose solution cannot wait for sensible proof. A moral question is a question not of what sensibly exists, but of what is good, or would be good if it did exist" (*Will to Believe* 22).

A third contextualist feature relevant to rhetoric is the implicit pluralism of its outlook. The criterion of "successful working" or "truth in terms of action," notes Pepper, is not a comprehensive epistemology but "only a special truth theory," which does not deny that other types of truth exist (268). The contextualist holds that order may be defined in any of a variety of ways, *"so long as it does not deny the possibility of disorder or another order in nature also"* (234). In a modern contextualist like William James, there is even a celebration of the possibility of "many interpenetrating spheres of reality," tinged with the recognition that no single view can capture everything:

> The obvious outcome of our total experience is that the world can be handled according to many systems of ideas, and is so handled by different men, and will each time give some characteristic kind of profit, for which he cares, to the handler, while at the same time some other kind of profit has to be omitted or postponed. (*Varieties* 120)

---

5. In addition to Perelman, see Cushman and Tompkins, Brinton, Croasman and Cherwitz, and Grassi.

Now this type of ideological pluralism is obviously not a feature of traditional rhetorical theory (although there are shades of it in sophistic relativism); and in fact modern critics of classical rhetoric often list as one of its deficiencies the fact that it was constructed on the foundation of a realist epistemology and devised for service in the homogeneous value-world of the Greek city-state (Halloran, Berlin, Young/Becker/ Pike). These very criticisms testify to a perceived *need* to tie the art of rhetoric to a pluralistic outlook. Actually, though, modern critics some- times overlook a number of pluralistic features and presuppositions of traditional rhetoric. The idea that cogent arguments can be built on either side of many cases is an obvious case in point. More important, however, is the topical system for finding arguments, which in itself involves one in the presupposition that there are multiple sources of value (or at least of allegiance). A party who cannot be brought around one way may be brought around another way ("If I cannot appeal to you as a Christian, I appeal to you as a man!"); and different parties may be brought around to a single position from different "places" of persuasion.[6]

Finally, the most significant connection between rhetoric and con- textualist pluralism lies in the unspecialized and pluralistic character of rhetorical activity itself, in comparison with the other aims of discourse. This connection may be best approached in a roundabout way, through an analysis of prominent social and organizational character types. Searching the Motivational Axes for a broad classification of such types, we discover the scheme set forth in figure 9. Here we are able to locate (outside the undifferentiated middle, containing the mass of human beings) the *technician* in the "operational" dimension; the *theorist* in the "formalistic" dimension; the *poet* or *prophet* in the "imaginative" dimen- sion; and the *statesman* in the "ethical/pragmatic" dimension.

These character types form secondary concepts corresponding to the instrumental, scientific, poetic, and rhetorical aims of discourse. What is remarkable about them is that the first three tend to be highly specialized and solitary geniuses, with an impulse to generate "worlds of their own," to see reality from a single point of view—in special cases even to the point of monomania. Politically, these types reveal a ten- dency toward absolutism—toward utilitarian technocracy, philosopher- kingship, and theocracy, respectively. The statesman, by contrast with the other three, is a generalist, a "normal" personality, gregarious, and

6. This very point is emphasized by the modern Aristotelian critic, Richard McKeon: "Antagonistic formulations of purpose and methods, based on basic differences in philos- ophies and beliefs sometimes entail different and contradictory courses of action, yet they are often found to be compatible in practice or even identical in their broad lines of ulti- mate objectives. A common course of action may be undertaken and justified for different reasons based on different basic principles" (1951: 135).

Figure 9. Prominent social and organizational character types

accustomed to hearing and negotiating a variety of points of view. Recognizing the social and intellectual value of a variety of specializations, as well as their separate tendencies toward absolutism, the statesman may be motivated simultaneously to create protective structures for the other three types and to place limits on their claims. His or her watchword is balance, often to the consternation of "deeper," more solitary, more committed thinkers. Historically, it is this type that reveals the greatest affinity for mixed, at least partially consensual forms of government and for pluralism in the social sphere. We see something of this contrast between between the pluralistic and the absolutist cast of mind in Aristotle's famous criticism of Plato's *Republic*:

> The error of Socrates must be attributed to the false notion of unity from which he starts. Unity there should be, both of family and state, but in some respects only. For there is a point at which a state may attain such a degree of unity as to be no longer a state, or at which, without actually ceasing to exist, it will become an inferior state, like harmony passing into unison, or rhythm which has been reduced to a single foot. (*Politics* II. 5. 13–15)

Aristotle's critique of philosopher-kingship is conceptually parallel to his defense of rhetoric against the Socratean attacks in the *Gorgias*; for it is a defense of different ways of knowing, appropriate to different spheres of human concern. It is no coincidence that rhetorical education is traditionally oriented toward the cultural ideal of the statesman or "gentleman" (Weaver 1948: 53–62); for rhetoric as a branch of discourse forms an exact parallel to the statesman as a social character type. Not only is it the least specialized and differentiated of the aims of discourse in terms of its characteristic themes, forms, and conventions; as will be demonstrated in the following chapter, it is also the most assimilative, appropriating themes, forms, and conventions from the other aims of discourse. Moreover, as I also hope to demonstrate in the chapters to follow, the *genuses* or subdivisions of rhetorical discourse form a mirror of the entire system of discourse aims, making rhetoric both a comprehensive language art and a despecializing force in human culture.

These considerations indicate something of what I believe to be rhetoric's importance to modern education and intellectual life, but they also carry the argument well ahead of itself. Perhaps the most important "contextualist" principle that emerges out of these reflections is the desirability of viewing such a subject as human discourse in its concreteness and in the fullness of its contexts. Under the pressure of this principle, one's attention shifts to the "total given event," to the "rich, concrete thing, in which features interpenetrate."

4. RHETORIC AND THE
AIMS OF DISCOURSE

The aim of this chapter is to build from the ground up what the previous chapter has anticipated from the top down. The Motivational Axes provide conceptual anticipations and philosophical placements of the four aims of discourse: Scientific, Instrumental, Poetic, and Rhetorical. We now turn to empirical justifications and descriptions of these same categories, with particular emphasis on written rhetoric.

I. DISCOURSE PERFORMANCES

Traditional rhetorical theory does not sharply distinguish between rhetoric as *art or faculty* and rhetoric as *type of action* or *sphere of activity*. When Aristotle defines rhetoric as the "art or faculty of discovering the means of persuasion" and as the *antistrophe* or counterpart of dialectic, he clearly indicates an emphasis—in fact a shift of emphasis, given the traditions of his day—toward rhetoric as an art, one that can be founded, as Plato had envisioned in the *Phaedrus*, on principles of mind. At the same time it is clear in Aristotle, and even clearer in Cicero and Quintilian, that rhetoric is a *kind* of discourse, a particular sphere of discourse activity, defined not so much by the mental capabilities employed or addressed as by its status as a type of speaking developed to persuade popular audiences, on topics that are generally subject to diversities of opinion, and on occasions such as those provided by legislative assemblies, law courts, and public ceremonies.

This dual usage of the concept "rhetoric" is preserved in Aristotle's treatment of the *topoi*, or places of argument: Some of the topoi have a common application, representing fundamental operations of the mind, while others apply only to specific situations. Thus while Aristotle's *Rhetoric* gives rhetoric-as-faculty a philosophical or theoretical foundation, there is no corresponding effort to employ theoretical measures in defining and partitioning rhetoric-as-act. Aristotle did not construct a treatise on the aims of discourse. Had he done so, he would probably have employed a procedure similar to the one he uses in elaborating the partition of rhetoric, identifying a bundle or matrix of features covering the most important aspects of any discourse situation: function, author-audience relationship, field of subject matter, and typical strategies of reasoning and presentation (1358^b-1359^a). Richard McKeon's masterly attempt to reconstruct and synthesize Aristotle's theory of discourse employs just such a procedure, with its implicit concentration on "acts of discourse," rather than discourse (or the processes of discourse) in general.

One of the ablest modern formulations of this distinction—or rather the basic principles embodied in it—is found in Karl R. Wallace's *Understanding Discourse*. Focusing primarily on the rhetoric of speechmaking, Wallace distinguishes between the "speech act"—any meaningful utterance—and "rhetorical action"—a "rhetor's response to a rhetorical context." Rhetorical acts differ from speech acts in four ways: (1) they are "more complex and sustained"; (2) they are "more deliberate than are ordinary acts of speech"; (3) "more artistry is revealed . . . than in ordinary conversation"; and (4) "public speakers and their listeners are usually more or less aware of the factors that control a public speech. They are mindful of ends, means, methods, and principles" (71–72). In composite, these criteria suggest that in dealing with the rhetorical act—or more broadly with the "discourse performance"—we are dealing not merely with an act of speech or writing, or even a succession of such acts—but with a *unity* forged out of speech acts, dominated by and participant in a full complement of causes:

> First, the action is dominated by something analogous to the "final" cause. There is a situation whose immediate and remote facets constitute the full context of the reason for which a speech comes into being. Second, the materials of the action are constituted by the rhetor's experience . . . prior to his utterance and by the information he derives from the setting of his utterance. Third, there is a formal cause, revealed substantially as meaningful behavior and constructed in a temporal frame from a beginning to a conclusion. Fourth, there is obviously an efficient cause. . . . There is, finally, the speech—the product that is created by the interplay of the four causes. (72–73)

Proto-Discourse and Proto-Genres

One area that Wallace does not explore is the inevitable no-man's land between "speech act" and "rhetorical act," or—to revert to the broader terminology necessary for this discussion—between the utterance and the discourse-performance. However, by at least recognizing this middle terrain, especially in the world of written discourse, we can reduce a good deal of the agony and confusion that can accompany attempts at classifying discourse. There are a number of characteristic instances of writing—involving such proto-genres as shopping lists, bookkeeping entries, diary and journal entries, most personal letters, inter-office memoranda, and the like—which, by virtue of either the simplicity or indeterminacy of their motives and designs, as well as the restrictedness of their situations, do not fully constitute discourse performances.

Such instances are by no means primitive or uninteresting. Some of them are properly the subject matters of individual arts (as in the art of letter-writing); and most are, in fact, discourse performances *in potentia*, capable of elaboration and extension to formal or public contexts. But when not recognized at the outset as "proto-genres" or "proto-discourse," they can present unnecessary difficulties. First, they can make discourse classifications seem to leak more badly than they actually do, when in fact a theory of rhetorical writing should not be obliged to account for every instance of writing which may display rhetorical motives in some way. Second, they can either inspire or prop up categories that have only a dubious validity or stability. The notion of "expressive discourse" (Kinneavy 393–447), which has gained some currency in composition pedagogy, is one such category.

Recapitulating Wallace's criteria, with some refocusing and extension to the world of written discourse, we can identify the basic qualifying features of the "discourse performance" as the following: Extension, Unity, Design, Completedness, and Publicity.

1. EXTENSION

Although probably the weakest of the five, extension or extendedness is nevertheless an important criterion. Successful discourse performances can be surprisingly short, whereas a classroom roster filling ten pages would still be nothing more than a list of names and numbers. However, under most circumstances a certain degree of elaboration is a necessary condition under which other features—unity, design, completedness, and publicity—are brought into being. (In the case of haiku or very short lyric poems, which might otherwise be analyzed as single speech-acts, we are dealing with discourse performances for which the absence of extension is an integral feature of design and unity.)

2. UNITY

Unity is that constancy of purpose which, in extended monologue, generally results in the discernible subordination of certain speech acts or groups of speech acts to others. A complementary result is the discernible connection of successive units, so that the discourse is perceived as a single thing, as opposed to a mere collection of things. This *descriptive* criterion of unity, which qualifies any discourse performance, should not be confused with the more normative criterion of unity as a feature of *successful* performance. A discourse performance might well exhibit the former, while failing to achieve the latter.

3. DESIGN

Closely related to and overlapping with the feature of unity is that of design, involving the arrangement or coordination of parts in accommodation of subject or audience, or with implicit manipulation of audience response. Design should not be confused with "planning," which may not always have been present. In such a case, we are dealing with an arrangement of discourse that has been *validated* in an author's or editor's judgment, after-the-fact. Such validation actually consists in the judgment that the discourse has unity and that it fulfills some normal function of discourse. And whether correct or incorrect, this validation constitutes design. The great majority of diaries, journals, and personal letters do not exhibit this feature, although many are potential discourse performances. In some notable instances, such as the *Diary of Anne Frank*, validation is a process completely separate from that of composition, usually accompanied by some creative editing.

4. PUBLICITY

In Basil Bernstein's formulation, the shift away from a private or intimate context to a public, formal one activates a shift away from "restricted" and toward "elaborated" speech codes. Similarly in written discourse, the shift away from private or highly restricted purposes, subjects, and contexts activates the impulse toward the features of extendedness, unity, and design. Actual publication is not, of course, an essential feature of "publicity," although discourse performances are normally composed in anticipation (or hope) that what is written will be circulated in some way. What is salient is the accommodation that is made, under these circumstances, to the communicative needs of an audience that does not have access to one's private stock of signals and memories, and which does not have access to the complete range of assumption, implication, and values that are often shared by a few intimates.[1] Various forms of ellipsis and the use of private allusions and

1. The expectation of publication has immediate and inevitable effects on private writing. Consider the following testimony by Reinhold Niebuhr, in the preface to a volume of selections from his diary, *Leaves from the Notebook of a Tamed Cynic*: "It must be confessed in all candor that some of the notes, particularly the later ones, were written after it seemed certain that they would reach the eye of the public in some form or other. It was therefore psychologically difficult to maintain the type of honesty which characterizes the self-revelations of a private diary. The reader must consequently be warned ... to discount the unconscious insincerities which no amount of self-discipline can eliminate from words which are meant for the public" (v–vi).

mnemonics are stock features of proto-discourse. These constitute a sort of "restricted code" for communicating with oneself or with a strictly private audience. It is true that analogous forms of "shorthand" come into play in longer discourse performances, as they develop conventions of internal reference. The crucial difference, of course, lies in the exposition and elaboration of these elements *within the discourse itself*.

5. COMPLETEDNESS

Completedness is the counterpart of unity. Just as a discourse performance is normally perceived as *one thing* rather than several, it is also normally perceived as a *complete thing* rather than a piece of a thing. Like the other criteria of discourse performances, the notion of completedness is subject to questions of degree that can be adjudicated only by common sense. As a matter of theoretical principle, however, there should be no difficulty in recognizing the possibility of a discourse performance being simultaneously a whole thing and part of some larger thing. The principle of hierarchy allows not only for parts-within-wholes but "wholes-within-wholes" as well (Pike 79), although a particular work may acquire a different status and a different contour of meanings as it is placed into or extracted from larger contexts. The salient element is the sense of beginning and distinct closure that obtains in the discourse performance and gives it a certain degree of independence.

Unfortunately, rhetorical theory has developed no stable term for this minimum, unified, free-standing unit of written monologue—something equivalent to the notion of "a speech." Common usage does grope for such a term, further validating the notion to some extent. The term "essay" has lost a good deal of its historical connection with informal reflection and has come to be used, paired with such descriptors as "formal," "familiar," and "scholarly," to name a number of different kinds of writing. Similarly, in the world of journalism the term "story" has lost any absolute connection with narration, while a "piece" often refers to a production of considerable length and seriousness. Perhaps the most neutral term, most freely accepting of generic descriptors, is the term "article," although its ordinary usage tends to be restricted to performances actually published in conjunction with other "pieces."

More important, in any case, than one's choice of terminology is the definition of scope achieved by designation of something like "article" as the basic unit of study. We will be dealing with proto-discourse only to the extent that it sometimes constitutes the "stuff" of discourse performances, either by virtue of the appropriation of proto-genres or by their extension and elaboration into discourse performances. At the other end of the continuum, the making of rhetorical books, so prominent a form of discourse in contemporary culture, presents fascinating avenues of investigation that will be touched upon but not fully explored here. In some cases rhetorical books amount to extensions and elaborations of article-length performances; in others, they are simply collections of performances united in varying degrees by subject matter and by the general outlook of the author; in some interesting cases, they constitute composites of aim and genre—unities perhaps of a sort that cannot be achieved except in extended forms.

The Status of Generic Classifications

It is clear that the informal judgments that people make regarding the kinds of discourse they are experiencing—that is, the expectations and constraints that are felt to be normal in a given situation—are at least partly intuitive and conditioned upon various relations of form and function in the system of communication itself. Most of us have fairly stable intuitions (although we do make mistakes and we can be deceived) about whether the discourse we are experiencing is emotive, objective, or directive; referential or nonreferential; earnest or game, and so on. It is equally clear, however, that the informal judgments we make about kinds of discourse are historical and cultural, conditioned upon certain values, certain social arrangements and traditions, and certain developments over time. We have heard or read "things like this" before, and the meanings that they convey are partly contingent upon this fact.

Again, it is clear that the root functions of discourse are finite and that these functions are discernible in large measure according to the way in which they focus, respectively, upon individual components of the discourse situation. (Emotive discourse focuses on the addresser, directive on the addressee, and so on.) It is a crucial point, however, that *not all of these functions will extenuate into aims of discourse performances*. The reason is that the processes of monographic extension, design, and publicity that lead to discourse performances almost inevitably involve the subordination of certain functions to others into complex hierarchical arrangements, and they almost inevitably involve the channeling of discourse into culturally and historically recognizable forms, functions, and situations.

Because it is the most comprehensive and the most independent of psychological interpretation, the most useful outline of discourse functions is the one developed by the linguist Roman Jakobson and elaborated somewhat by the anthropologist Dell Hymes. The seven factors inherent in any utterance are, after Dell Hymes, the following:

1. Expressive (emotive)
2. Directive (conative, pragmatic, rhetorical persuasive)
3. Poetic
4. Contact (including not only such direct contact-establishing locutions as "Can you hear me?" but also the kind of everyday chit-chat sometimes called "phatic")
5. Metalinguistic (language about language)
6. Referential
7. Contextual (language used to clarify or stabilize the message). Examples: "as mentioned above"; "You can't talk like that here!" (117)

This outline provides an excellent heuristic for identifying the functions of various locutions in any setting; also for identifying the multiplicity of overt and covert motives that may inhere in any stretch of extended discourse. The latter can be quite important in literary and rhetorical analysis. For instance, it has been argued with some cogency that a motive of the disturbing 1978 Harvard commencement address by Aleksandr Solzhenitsyn was in the area that Hymes would call "contactual." According to this analysis the speech, which was highly critical of Western institutions, was for Solzhenitsyn a means of keeping open a line of communication with fellow Russians of like mind, assuring them of his continuing allegiances to a common cause (Carlisle).

Certainly it was no ordinary commencement address. However, the example serves to illustrate the principle of "channeling" already mentioned. The contactual motive of the speech (assuming that the analysis is correct) has been channeled into a type of rhetorical address traditionally known as epideictic, and into a specific tradition perhaps best identified as "prophecy." The contactual motive is in fact a traditional element of epideictic rhetoric, although it is normal for this element to involve the primary rather than a secondary audience.

Other discourse functions as well are commonly "channeled" into a finite group of aims, considered as cultural and historical norms: "Contextual" motives are commonly channeled into instrumental discourse (example: *Robert's Rules of Order*); metalinguistic motives are channeled into scientific discourse; directive motives into either instrumental discourse (The U.S. Constitution) or rhetorical discourse (advisory deliberation); and expressive motives into either poetic or rhetorical discourse. Interestingly, Hymes himself calls into question the idea that even primary discourse functions can be identified adequately with reference to individual features of the discourse-event, proposing instead that more attention be given to *relations* among factors and also to cultural norms (121). Such a backtracking constitutes an implicit recognition of the phenomenon of channeling, and it should place serious doubts upon any attempt to construct a theory of discourse on the analysis of speech acts or speech functions alone.

In the final analysis it would be better to recognize that "discourse function" (which relates primarily to speech acts) and "discourse aim" (which relates primarily to discourse performances) are concepts of radically different status. Whereas discourse functions are unidimensional, discourse aims are multidimensional, involving a full set of causes and *relations among* author, audience, form, and message, as well as considerations of historical and cultural context. Whereas discourse functions constitute identifiable forms and activities, the aims constitute identifiable *norms* of activity, inevitably involving not merely psychological and linguistic norms but also the values of communities. Finally, whereas functions of discourse can be determined without extensive reference to time and place, the aims are very much historical products, developing and changing in time. The range, the methods, the expectations and constraints of scientific, rhetorical, poetic, and instrumental discourse respond to the history of a civilization, and they help to shape that history.

In sum, the aims of discourse, even more than other discourse categories, have a composite nature: They are convergences of features, historical products, directions of specialization, and norms of discourse activity.

II. VIRTUES, SHORTCOMINGS, AND OMISSIONS OF ARISTOTELIAN THEORY

In his survey of approaches to the aims of discourse, James Kinneavy sees no radical difference of method or orientation between Aristotelian discourse theory and the modern theories that are placed beside it. In his view the Aristotelian categories of discourse are, like some modern ones, based on a single theoretical measure, in this case the "scale of probability." Kinneavy's characterization of the theory runs as follows: "Discourse which refers to certainties is *scientific*; discourse used in the pursuit of exploring the probable is *dialectical*; discourse aimed at persuading others to accept the seemingly probable is *rhetorical*; discourse aimed at pleasing through internal and fictional probabilities is *poetic*" (56).

While this view is in the main correct, there are some important deficiencies of focus and detail, which do not so much distort the Aristotelian view as they make it too easy to dismiss. It should be mentioned, in the first place, that the "scale of probability" does not just identify a set of basic discourse functions and then extrapolate from these primary units to the aims of discourse. Rather it identifies *fields* of discourse, which project readily into typical circumstances under which extended and elaborated discourse occurs. This latter procedure indicates an orientation radically different from the former because it places immediate emphasis upon *norms* of activity rather than the activities themselves. Because it deals with probabilities of action and understanding, rhetoric is a kind of discourse that operates under certain typicalities of form, strategy, and language; because it deals with probabilities that are established internally, poetic operates under different norms. In other words, the distinction between "speech act" and "discourse performance" is implicit in Aristotelian theory.

Second, even though the "scale of probability" is prominent in Aristotle, it is not rigorously schematized in its application, as is the case in medieval scholastic treatments,[2] and there is no attempt to erect a corresponding division of mental faculties to go with the arts of discourse. Although some types of language may be more appropriate to one sort of discourse than to another, the crucial factor in any given case is not the character of language but the purpose, or final cause, of the discourse. The "contextualist" or "pragmatic" character of these divisions has not been more effectively expressed than in the analysis of Richard McKeon: "In the philosophy of Aristotle, sciences and arts are differentiated by their subject matters and purposes, and the several uses of language lead to the differentiation of logic, rhetoric, and poetic as the proper arts of language" (1946: 193). Again:

> Aristotle's examination of the scientific basis of language seems both to prevent philosophical or semantic reductions of language to things, thoughts, or operations and also to discriminate among the arts those in which language is an instrument of knowledge and control relative to natural processes and things, those in which it is a medium of communication and understanding relative to men, and those in which it is a form of edification and pleasure relative to human products. (1946: 200)

The failure to recognize these distinguishing features of Aristotelian rhetoric leads, finally, to a slight confusion between what are implicitly in Aristotle aims of discourse and what are implicitly methods of reasoning; hence (in Kinneavy) the identification of "dialectic" as an aim separate from science. It is true that Aristotle distinguishes sharply between theoretical and practical sciences, but the question of whether two branches of science occasion two related aims of discourse or two subcategories of a single aim is not crucial, except as a matter of implication; and the implication that separate branches of reasoning determine absolute correspondences of discourse aim is faulty. "Sophistic" is also

2. For a summary of scholastic categories see Ong, "The Province of Rhetoric and Poetic."

characterized by Aristotle as a branch of reasoning and is the subject of a separate treatise; but it would not be seriously proposed that sophistic constitutes thereby a separate aim of discourse. It is fairly clear that Aristotle envisioned not four but three aims: Scientific, Rhetorical, and Poetic.

Method, then, is not a problem: Because of its comprehensive and nonreductive character, and because of its acknowledgment of the priority of purpose and range as factors in the channeling of discourse activity, the Aristotelian approach to discourse is fundamentally sound. Nevertheless, there are at least two important areas in which Aristotelian theory stands in need of extension and refortification, particularly with a view toward contemporary written discourse.

The first is, of course, the area of writing itself. No one in the ancient world could have foreseen the changes in society, in communication, and in consciousness that have accompanied the development of a technological civilization in which writing and print have played so crucial a role. The aims of discourse are at least partially historical developments, and rhetorical theory must keep abreast of their histories. Moreover, while a good deal of writing channels comfortably into the Aristotelian categories of science, poetic, and rhetoric and their subcategories, a good deal of it does not. Because Aristotelian theory focused upon fields of discourse as they existed in a primarily oral civilization, virtually no attention was given to discourse functions and situations that had primary affinities to the medium of writing: recordkeeping and administration; contracts, laws, and constitutions; information and official doctrine; intellectual and moral reflection. Such omissions as these do not really constitute a serious failure of ancient discourse theory; they reflect a civilization in which writing was not a fully elaborated and established medium. Most written genres had not yet completely flowered into the status of discourse performances, and the specialization of types was only beginning.

The dialogues of Plato make interesting test cases. One could draw up arguments for the dialogues as scientific, as poetic, or as types of rhetorical communication. Probably the best case can be made for science.[3] But argument over the matter would be essentially fruitless because we are dealing with writings produced under circumstances in which nothing approaching a mature elaboration of discourse genres in writing had occurred. The methods and language of the dialogues are too freewheeling by the standards of modern philosophical discourse; they are too concerned with deliberation and external standards of truth for literary art; and the demands upon readers are too rigorous for rhe-

---

3. Kinneavy, whose notion of an "exploratory" branch of scientific discourse is sound and provocative, places the Platonic dialogues into that category (96–105).

torical communication. It is perhaps best to regard them as experiments, wonderfully successful ones, in philosophical reasoning and communication, recognizing at the same time their literary and rhetorical qualities, and keeping in mind that the history of written discourse is one of increasing specialization and continuous experimentation.

A second area of Aristotelian theory that requires enrichment is its approach to meaning, and characteristic kinds of meaning, in discourse. Although Aristotelian rhetoric is not based in any systematic way upon a semantic theory, there is implicit in Aristotle and in most traditional rhetoric a set of common-sense assumptions about meaning that one commentator has aptly labeled "quasi-positivist." Traditional rhetoric, he notes, "seems to have assumed that hearers' responses to discourse are responses to the things talked about, and that obviously that discourse is understood (is meaningful) in those terms" (Sanders 114). This view of meaning, in which language is primarily an instrument for "referring" to things, accounts in large measure for the "probability scale" as a determinant of fields of discourse: some things, states, and relations are susceptible to more precise and rigorous forms of reference than some others.

These assumptions are not severely debilitating in Aristotle because they are squared with a practical understanding of the functioning of discourse in actual social settings. Nevertheless, the view of meaning-as-reference tends to obscure the fact that discourse is meaningful and successful not merely to the extent that it *refers to realities* correctly or effectively but also to the extent that it *performs actions* in an appropriate and satisfactory way.

Now there is a sense in which this distinction between reference and action bears upon all discourse and in which traditional theory is not in any special way deficient. A rhetorical performance which defends a public official against charges of improper conduct, for example, will be successful not merely to the degree that it is accurate or credible in its reference to actions and values but also to the extent that it adheres to certain civilities and makes effective use of the implicit opportunities for "defending" successfully. So far so good. But there are some instances of discourse in which the distinction between reference and action applies in a special way, and these are not comprehended adequately in classical theory. These are instances of discourse, both rhetorical and nonrhetorical, which exist *primarily* in the performance of certain administrative, civic, and ritual acts, and which are successful or unsuccessful almost entirely in terms of their appropriateness or functionality. Many of these, though not all, involve writing in a special or exclusive way.

The most useful discriminations about relations of action and reference in discourse are found in the branch of language philosophy known as "speech-act theory," from which I have already borrowed the terms "constative and performative" for the Motivational Axes, in chapter 3. J. L. Austin's *How To Do Things with Words* begins by positing a distinction between utterances that "say" something and those that "do" something. The *constative* utterance is one which "says," "reports," or "describes." It is formally separate from the action to which it refers, and it is normally either true or false, adequate or inadequate to facts, probabilities, or common understandings. The *performative* utterance, by contrast, is one in which "the uttering of the sentence is, or is a part of, the doing of an action which . . . would not normally be described as, or as 'just' saying something" (5). (This includes "actions" such as apologizing, granting, enacting, and so forth.) Such an utterance is not true or false (or convincing or unconvincing) in the ordinary sense but rather "happy or unhappy," appropriate or inappropriate, functional or disfunctional, according to its conformity (or lack of it) to the special conventions that govern such utterances.

An initial stumbling block for anyone wishing to examine the relevance of these concepts to discourse performances is that Austin himself rejected the distinction, claiming that whatever criteria seem to apply exclusively to one category also apply to the other. We can distinguish no formal features—either lexical, grammatical, or otherwise—which legitimate the distinction. Consequently, the distinction between performative and constative utterance is replaced in Austin's theory, and in refinements by Searle, with the doctrine of locutionary, illocutionary, and perlocutionary forces—categories in which every speech act participates simultaneously. The locutionary act—"performance of an act of saying something"—the illocutionary act—"performance of an act in saying something" (e.g. warning)—and the perlocutionary act— "performance of an act *through* saying something" (e.g. insulting)—are complementary dimensions of every speech act and essential components of its meaning. It is this complementariety, in fact, which creates the paradox of action and contemplation on which the Motivational Axes are partly based.

Recently, however, a number of philosophers and rhetoricians have argued that Austin too readily dismissed his own distinction (Black, Chisolm, Warnock). The drift of most of these arguments is that the two sets of distinctions—between constative and performative utterance on the one hand, and between the locutionary, illocutionary, and perlocutionary dimensions of utterance on the other—are not mutually exclusive. These arguments may be represented by G. J. Warnock's rejoinder to claims that all utterances are in some sense actions: "The fact that, if we choose to say so, all utterance is in that sense performative does not imply that there is not, and never was, a legitimate *subclass* of utterances called 'performatives,' to issue which is in a *special way* to do something . . ." (403).

Austin's original intuitions about constative and performative utterance are surely valid at some levels, and the insistence that such terms should have formal coordinates in language involves a failure to recognize the principle of asymmetry in language and discourse. The general relevance of speech-act theory to rhetorical theory is precisely that it broadens one's understanding of meaning in language, comprehending both language-as-reference and language-as-action. Of particular importance is the fact that *performative* and *constative* name important dimensions of extended discourse as well as different classes and dimensions of speech acts. Once again, though, we must be careful not to extrapolate too crudely from speech acts to discourse performances: The constative/performative distinction does not predict or typify aims of discourse. However, it does, along with other determinants, point and help to explain some of the omissions in Aristotelian theory.

Performatives play an important role in and typify important subclasses of the large category of nonrhetorical, nonaesthetic, and nonscientific writings which are here classified as "instrumental" discourse. This category—the only one of the four aims anticipated by the Motivational Axes which is not comprehended in classical theory—encompasses not only discourses which are commonly called "instruments"— contracts, decrees, charters, constitutions, and the like—but also many kinds of technical and operational information. The performative dimension is also a factor in the genus or subcategory of rhetorical discourse known traditionally as "epideictic" and here redefined as "rhetorical performative" discourse. These and other adjustments, to be detailed in the sections to follow, constitute not so much a rejection as a confirmation, refortification, and extension of Aristotelian discourse theory.[4]

III. THE AIMS OF DISCOURSE: INSTRUMENTAL, SCIENTIFIC, POETIC, AND RHETORICAL

The aims of discourse are "identified" by the Motivational Axes only in a philosophical and teleological sense: They rest, respectively, in operational, imaginative, formalistic, and ethical/pragmatic spheres of meaning and conceptualization. The criteria for practical identification and description lie in the situations of discourse itself: in the purposes and functions of discourse performances, in typical relationships of author and audience, in the occasions of discourse, in the conditions

4. For further discussion of these issues, see pp. 141–45.

that govern sucess or failure, and in norms and typicalities of language, form, and strategy. In identifying the aims we look for ways in which these matters converge in total discourse situations. Naturally, individual works very often depart in varying degrees from these states of convergence. The categories are not ideals; they are norms of activity. The aims of discourse, like other language and discourse categories, exist in relationships of continuum with each other, and their relations can be adequately comprehended in terms of departures from normal states of convergence in one or more respects. These terms can also help to indicate and explain particular instances of historical change, success or failure, experimentation, and abuse.

The working definitions below, partly functional, partly formal, partly ostensive, claim no greater immediate status than that of indicators. Full definitions emerge only in the extended discussion of situational and formal components that will follow.

Instrumental—The kind of discourse whose primary aim is the governance, guidance, control, or execution of human activities. It includes such specific products as contracts, constitutions, laws, technical reports, and manuals of operation.

Scientific—The kind of discourse whose primary aim is the discovery, construction, and organization of knowledge, particularly in those areas or subareas in which facts, classifications, and general laws can be verified by rational and empirical procedures, as opposed to the values and loyalties of communities. (Belief in rational investigation is a value, of course, but it is not a method of verification.) This category includes such specific genres as reports of historical, statistical, field or laboratory investigations; disputations about the validity or significance of such findings; theoretical treatises which posit general laws and principles governing events and phenomena; and philosophical treatises on the nature of reasoning and on the adequacy of the methods and principles of the various scientific disciplines.

Poetic—The kind of discourse whose primary aim is the construction of an object of enjoyment and reflection, using the materials and resources of language. Such objects usually involve forms of language and reference in a state of play, so that literal truth or probability is subordinated to a set of internal consistencies. Poems, stories, and novels are prominent modern instances.

Rhetorical—The kind of discourse whose primary aim is to influence the understanding and conduct of human affairs. It operates typically in matters of action that involve the well-being and destiny of communities (and of individuals within them); and in matters of value and understanding which involve the communal or competing values of communities. Rhetorical writing includes a broad range of types, from deliberative essays to popular information, to occasional and reflective pieces, to commercial promotions, to the public resolutions and declarations of competing groups within a community.

Distinctive Features of the Aims of Discourse

1. PURPOSE

Since purpose is the strongest of the defining features that have been identified, the purposes of the four aims are already indicated in the working definitions given above. However for the sake of consistency and clarity, they will bear repeating, embellishing, and qualifying here. Any single work of discourse may contain or exhibit a range of motives, of course—some of them explicit in the discourse, others implicit in the situation, others transparent only to a subset of the audience, and others immediately accessible only to the author. In writing a scholarly treatise, a professor may hope to make a contribution to knowledge, achieve wealth or fame or tenure, get even with his enemies, dispel feelings of inadequacy, and justify himself to his father-in-law, all at the same time. Even if we consider indicators of *communicative* purpose only, a writer may in a single article be evaluating a book or play, publicizing it, attempting to discredit or encourage certain political or cultural ideas, "making up" or "breaking up" with some group or constituency that constitutes a subset of the actual audience. Americans who write popular books on foreign policy are routinely accused of running for Secretary of State. These diverse elements of motivation are fascinating and they are of considerable importance to literary and rhetorical criticism.[5] Nevertheless, they should not impede the classification of aims. The purposes or motives that are crucial to an understanding of discourse types are those that are typically immediate and distinctive. Such purposes are primary, and fulfilling them is a necessary (though not sufficient) condition of success. Other motivations must exist in a state of harmony with (and at least ostensible subordination to) primary ones. Thus poetic may be spoiled by disharmonious attempts to propagandize or theorize; science by disharmonious participation in political or social debate; rhetoric by a disharmonious concern with scientific verification or beauty of form. Many individual discourses are of course splendidly harmonious in their complexity of motives, and some specific genres are defined by special complexities of motive. All of these occurrences help to illuminate relationships of continuum among the aims.

Instrumental: The principal motive is direction and control of human activities. To the extent that discourses amount to *recommendations* of the activities themselves, or recommendations of procedures in competition with other

5. Kenneth Burke has been a leader in establishing the importance of such motives. See esp. *A Grammar of Motives* and *A Rhetoric of Motives*.

procedures, they move in the direction of rhetoric. (The "annual reports" of large corporations notoriously mix instrumental with rhetorical motives.)

Scientific: The principal motive is the establishment and organization of knowledge. To the extent that it attempts to influence human action and opinion, or relies for verification upon communal values, as is often the case in the social sciences and the humanistic disciplines, it moves in the direction of rhetoric.

Poetic: The principal motive is the construction of an object of enjoyment and reflection. This motive is not strictly incompatible with the organization of meanings and references to experiences "outside" the art work, since language is intrinsically a structure of meanings. The discussion of the exact relations of these facets—of internal and external reference—is a perennial one in literary criticism, subject to different theoretical and ideological presuppositions. The classical and Enlightenment conceptions of poetic art as a medium of "instruction and delight" provides one set of terms for observing the continuum of poetic and rhetoric.

Rhetoric: The principal motive is the formation and information of opinion. To the extent that it seeks to establish stable and incontrovertible propositions of understanding, it moves in the direction of science; to the extent that it takes on the capability of *directing* human activities, as in the areas of information and certain types of resolution-making, it becomes instrumental; when the motives of formal beauty and enjoyment come into the picture, as very often happens in "familiar" and reflective writing, rhetoric takes a turn toward poetic.

2. SUBJECT OR FIELD

As we have already noted, the criterion of subject or field is an important one in classical theory. One determinant of this emphasis is the Platonic-Aristotelian probability scale, wherein different fields, because they are susceptible to varying degrees of investigative rigor, are linked to different methods and situations of discourse; another determinant is the relatively stable division of public discourse activity in a highly traditional, primarily oral, and pretechnological civilization.[6]

Contemporary civilization is radically different. While the aims of discourse have developed higher stages of differentiation and specialization in form and method, they have actually broadened their spheres of operation, virtually to the extent of constituting different "approaches," sometimes competing and sometimes complementary, to any subject or field. Practically all attempts to distinguish branches of discourse according to their "proper subjects" involve equivocations on purpose and method. The contention that fluctuations in the consumer price index are

6. Aristotle, for instance, could comfortably restrict the subjects of rhetorical deliberation to five topics: ways and means, war and peace, national defense, exports and imports, and legislation (*Rhetoric* 1359^b). *For a good discussion of the status and limitations of genres in traditional communities, see Kaufer, "Point of View in Rhetorical Situations."*

hardly fit subjects for poetry would be vulnerable on two counts: first, certainly more improbable literary events have occurred than a poem or story on the consumer price index; and second, the consumer price index is, strictly speaking, not a field or subject but in itself a scientific or technical way of talking about economic activity.

In spite of these complexities, and in spite of some equivocation, the component of field or subject remains a useful indicator of the aims, in at least two respects: first, with regard to *aspects* of subject matter; and second, with regard to the conventional or ideal relation of the discourse to its subject matter.

Aspects of Subject Matter

Although any subject is potentially the focus of poetic, scientific, or rhetorical treatment, it will be so only in certain aspects or dimensions of its reality, and these aspects constitute, in essence, special subject matters. (This consideration takes us back to the Motivational Axes and the demarcation of formalistic, operational, imaginative and ethical/pragmatic spheres or "arrests" of experience.) In early structural linguistics, for example, Leonard Bloomfield, attempting to impart rigor and empirical verifiability to statements about language, restricted the study of meaning to the very narrow, formalistic dimensions specified in *Linguistic Aspects of Science*; and this restriction constituted a concession that other aspects of meaning were not (or not yet) in his view amenable to scientific treatment.

The subjects of *scientific discourse* are those aspects of nature or experience whose regularities of form and occurrence can be discovered and verified by rational and empirical means. In areas involving human behavior or capabilities, the range of the subject can be a matter of philosophical debate, as it obviously is in linguistics and psychology.

The subject of *instrumental discourse* are those aspects of nature and experience amenable—by virtue of accumulated knowledge, by statute, or by custom—to practical control and supervision by means of discourse. Accumulated knowledge makes possible the construction of manuals to guide various technical operations; by statute a legislative body may write laws, and a government agency may write regulations; a group of philosopher-statesmen may compose a political constitution and then attempt—through rhetoric—to attain a consensus for its acceptance as instrumental discourse. In the case of information, a shift toward rhetoric occurs with subjects for which complete knowledge or authority does not exist and where values and group loyalties come into play. "How to Hang Sheet Rock" and "How to Win Friends and Influence People" are items of different status in this respect.

Poetic discourse does not make systematic restrictions of subject matter, but it does select those aspects of nature and experience that contribute most readily to the internal unities of an aesthetic object; and it does involve as a rule the direct fabrication of subject matter. Whereas science will typically offer exhaustive treatment of a highly restricted aspect of a subject, poetic will characteristically treat a narrow selection of particulars, for the sake of suggesting the whole. Biography is an illustrative genre: Where a dimension of a person's life is singled out for exhaustive treatment, and where that dimension is determined by the interests and methods of a particular scholarly discipline, the work moves in the direction of scientific discourse; where no such restriction is made, but where materials are drawn selectively and fashioned into a design of formal and thematic unities, the work moves in the direction of poetic. Rhetoric stands between these extremes.

The subjects of *rhetorical discourse* are those aspects of experience that involve questions of understanding and choice that cannot be settled by rational and empirical procedures alone or by administrative fiat alone. These are areas of broad and widespread interest within communities, and they call into play a competition of interests and values. Whereas scientific, instrumental, and poetic discourse all tend to restrict subject matter, rhetoric tends to open it up into the realm of human concern and choice. Unlike science, rhetoric is not identified with specific disciplines. Notes McKeon: "Rhetoric is not bound to a single subject matter but is universal; and the better one succeeds in establishing propositions proper to a subject matter, the more one departs from the proper concerns of rhetoric . . . and enters one of the special sciences concerned with definite subjects" (1947: 42).

This consideration calls attention to a special feature of rhetoric, namely its multiple lines of continuum with all the other aims of discourse. Perceptions of abuse or contamination in the other aims, and even abuses of rhetoric itself, are often labeled "rhetorical." This fact in turn calls attention to special relationships of continuum among various branches of scholarly discourse. The transition from the natural and mathematical sciences to the humanistic disciplines involves not merely the transition from rigid precision and control to the intelligent application of right reason, but also the transition from *laws of occurrence* to *norms of activity*, and hence, inevitably, the infusion of questions of value.

Relation of Discourse to Subject Matter

Reference is not the only dimension of discourse activity, and too exclusive a focus upon reference can be debilitating; nevertheless, differences in referential status among the aims can contribute to a larger set of definitions. In *scientific discourse*, the reality of immediate reference is (or is claimed to be) actual and literal; in *instrumental discourse* it is either actual and literal (as in the case of technical information) or *actualized* (as in the case of contracts and constitutions) by the discourse itself; in *rhetorical discourse*, reference is probabilistic and contingent (though it is a common rhetorical strategy to claim otherwise); in *poetic*, even where a selection is made from actual or probable reality, the reality of immediate reference is symbolic—not in the sense of necessarily involving the poetic device of symbolism, but in the larger sense explained eloquently by W. S. Howell: "[T]he words which make up the rhetorical utterance lead the reader to states of reality, whereas the words making up the poetical utterance lead the reader to things which stand by deputy for states of reality" (421).

3. AUTHOR-AUDIENCE RELATION

Every discourse situation involves an implicit set of relations between author and audience. Although these relationships are highly variable, we can identify two broad sets of distinctions which serve as determinants of rhetoric and the other aims.

First, it is significant that the greatest range of variability lies in the domain of rhetoric, whereas the author-audience relationship in the other aims is much less variable and more bound by convention. In scientific and instrumental discourse the relationship is typically static, governed by the norms and constraints of disciplines, by statute, or by the subject matter itself. In fact the dynamics of the relationship play virtually no role in the substance or success of the communication.

In poetic this relation does very often come into play, but usually in a spirit of play. Poetic allows for all sorts of projections of authorial presence and for audience manipulations; but in many cases these also are matters of convention, and in some instances involve outright fabrications, as in the cases of personae and "unreliable narrators." More importantly, whatever relationships emerge are ultimately less the constraining factors of a communicative enterprise than elements of the aesthetic unity itself. Even in cases where an author speaks in his own voice, there is an element of projection and fictionality which becomes part of an aesthetic equation. In some cases, it is perfectly proper to speak of the author as a character in his own work.

In rhetoric, the author-audience relation is dynamic and open-ended. It is not determined by convention or the exigencies of subject, nor is it fabricated; rather, it is discovered or established by a successful author and is developed or exploited as a strategy of persuasion. The traditional strategies of ethical and emotional appeal, whereby the author exploits preexisting reserves of authority and good-standing, or develops these resources in the process of the discourse itself, are founded on a dynamism that is unique to rhetorical discourse. Where the devices of literary projection and fabrication are employed in rhetoric (as they often are in writing but seldom in speechmaking), they are usually quite transparent, as in Swift's "A Modest Proposal."

The second way in which the author-audience relation is a special indicator of rhetorical discourse is the high premium that is placed upon the *accommodation* of language and matter to audience. This high degree of accommodation is determined, naturally, by the fact that rhetorical discourse cannot achieve its purposes without the understanding and approval of popular audiences. (Audiences are "popular" in the sense of being the general run of people rather than specialists, and also in the sense that, no matter what the particular audience, rhetoric appeals to the general rather than the specialized dimensions of understanding and intellect.)

The other aims of discourse obey special conventions which help to secure fidelity to fact (scientific and instrumental), completedness and legality of action (instrumental), and integrity of form (poetic). All of these place special burdens upon audiences and often lead to popular complaints about the impenetrability of scientific and instrumental jargon and the unapproachability of certain instances or traditions of poetic. Authors of scientific discourse in the humanistic disciplines often face the uneasy task of meeting the demands of rigor and of audience accommodation simultaneously.

James Kinneavy builds his entire theory of "persuasive discourse" on the principle of audience accommodation:

> Propaganda, science, literature, even expressive utterances are all determined for receptors of some sort. . . . But the last three, as it were, forget the audience and let the discourse speak for itself. . . . But in propaganda and similar kinds of discourse, the addressee is crucial and omnipresent, often explicitly. . . . Another way of putting this concept of different dominating components is to suggest that the receptor of the language process is contacted immediately in the other three uses of language. (59–60)

My own view differs from Kinneavy's only in regarding the high degree of audience accommodation as one of a variety of definers, rather than as the single defining principle. There are at least two practical deficiencies of Kinneavy's approach: First, as with any of the definers, there are important exceptions. There is a kind of popular instrumental discourse, for instance, consisting principally of "How To" productions, which achieves its purposes through conscious subordination of material integrity to popular capabilities of understanding. Second, the exclusive focus on audience caters too broadly to the identification of rhetoric with propaganda, at once conceding too much to the despisers of rhetoric and overlooking the essentially rhetorical character of a great deal of popular writing—chiefly political and cultural criticism—which underplays audience appeal in favor of the honest attempt to establish and communicate deeper understandings of current events.

4. CONDITIONS FOR SUCCESS

Success conditions are closely related to the author-audience relation. In scientific and in most instrumental discourse, conditions of acceptance are highly conventional, more-or-less openly established and agreed upon, and they typically ignore or downplay audience accommodation. In philosophy and the humanities, which form a continuum with rhetoric, audience appeal and accommodation very often are important factors, but it is a "universal audience" that is being appealed to (Perelman and Olbrechts-Tyteca 63–73). Disinterestedness, to use Arnold's term, is a general standard of such writing, and disciplinary norms usually weigh quite heavily, especially in the minds of the editors who accept, reject, and revise scholarly manuscripts.

With rhetorical discourse the situation is quite different. Conditions of acceptance are less conventional, less openly agreed to or explicitly understood, and they are appealed to in a more subtle, sometimes covert fashion by the author, who divines them out of a particular situation.

Poetic, as usual, presents a fascinating set of interrelations. Conditions of acceptance can be governed by convention, but in a way that is radically different from scientific and instrumental discourse, and with a much freer range of possibilities. As in rhetorical discourse, the approval of general audiences is usually sought in direct ways, but again there is a difference: Rhetoric succeeds with its immediate historical audience or it usually does not succeed at all. Poetic, whose success is largely based on beauty and integrity of form and thought, may not receive immediate approval, but it may be discovered and rediscovered by future audiences.

5. OCCASION AND CONTEXT

Context-sensitivity is a superordinate feature of all discourse activity, but it is also a special determinant of rhetoric. The other aims of discourse freeze, as it were, the element of immediate context, reaching out for contexts that are ultimate and enduring. The work of rhetoric, by contrast, typically comes into being as a direct response to context, taking its matter and its character from a specific situation. Lloyd Bitzer has defined the "rhetorical situation" as a "complex of persons, events, objects, and relations presenting an actual or potential exigence which can be completely or partially removed if discourse, introduced into the situation, can so constrain human decision or action as to bring about the significant modification of the exigence" (6).

As a norm of scientific discourse, the only significant element of context is what may be designated the "state of the question": What knowledge has been established as opposed to what remains unexplained or controversial? In rhetoric the "state of the question" exists alongside or is actually embedded in a context of social action, evaluation, or understanding. In instrumental discourse, individual works *are* often responses to various sorts of exigence, and they do respond in a certain way to immediate contexts: Technical information must be updated and corrected, contracts renegotiated, wills revised, and constitutions amended. However, the ideal in all of these cases is to prevent the occurrence of such exigences, to produce a document that can stand up to novel elements of situation.

In poetic, authors very often freeze out real-world or immediate contexts by creating fictional and imaginary ones, inducing a "willing suspension of disbelief." Even when works of literature respond in a direct way to immediate, temporal contexts, moving along the continuum toward rhetoric, they typically develop these contexts into a pattern of ultimate or traditional thematics, transcending whatever is immediate. To the extent that they fail to do so, they fail to endure as works of art.

6. LANGUAGE AND STRATEGY

Because readers necessarily experience words and sentences and paragraphs before they comprehend a whole work of discourse, considerations of language, style, and method often form the readiest indices to kinds of discourse. They are not the most reliable or powerful instruments, however, in spite of their usefulness in combination with the other criteria already discussed. Individual determinations can be influenced by prior expectations induced by such things as titles, places of publication, Library of Congress call numbers, even direct announcement (e.g., "In the Parking Garage—A Poem"); and individual determinations can be mistaken, at least initially, when made on the basis of language and form alone.

Readers may encounter meter, rhyme, or dramatic-narrative mode and conclude reliably that what they are reading is an attempt at literary art; encountering strict reasoning, frozen style, and specialized nomenclature, they will think science; and encountering unforbidding and relaxed prose, tones of opinionation, and value-laden vocabulary, they will think rhetoric. But such determinations are almost never completely isolated from other factors. In a magazine such as *New Yorker*, which provides very little in the way of announcement or contextual clues for its pieces, and which even reserves the names of authors until the end, it is entirely possible to read several hundred words of a prose piece without being completely sure whether one is reading a piece of deliberation, of information, or a short story.

Consideration of form alone, if that were possible, would lead to various sorts of confusion: between scientific and instrumental, scientific and rhetorical, instrumental and rhetorical, poetic and rhetorical discourse. And here—in the repeated appearances of rhetoric as a term of potential confusion—lies a fact of great importance: A defining feature of rhetorical discourse is the great variety of forms and strategies proper to it, whereas the other aims tend toward formalization and rigid convention. This wide range of forms and strategies has been, along with the partition of genres, the basic subject matter of rhetorical arts, taught independently of special disciplines or subject matters—a situation not nearly as possible in the case of scientific discourse.

Having registered these reservations about the ultimate reliability of formal criteria, one can proceed to enumerate some fairly reliable and provocative indications of language and method.

The methods of scientific discourse are those of empirical description, inductive and hypothetico-deductive reasoning, and (in the humanistic disciplines) practical reasoning. The "disposition" or linear arrangement of scientific discourse is usually determined either by exigencies of subject matter or by disciplinary convention. Language is chosen and edited specifically to attain the greatest degree of referentiality; metaphors, where used, are usually regarded as heuristic and mnemonic only. The fact that most scientific theories are at bottom metaphorical is a fascinating paradox, but it does not really impinge upon the character of scientific language.

The methods of instrumental discourse involve empirical description and practical reasoning, as well as the careful construction and arrangement of performative and directive statements, so as to insure the proper and efficient management of actions and processes. As in scientific discourse, language is chosen and edited specifically to delimit the range of meaning and implication in any given case.

The methods of rhetoric include practical reasoning (*logos*) plus a wide range of material (*ethos, pathos*), stylistic, and formal strategies, all of which are selected on the principle that favors persuasion or audience accommodation over exigencies of subject or the norms of disciplines. In developing and selecting strategies, the rhetorical author will characteristically appropriate and modify usages and conventions of scientific and poetic discourse, especially the latter. Metaphor and other forms of figurative speech are not at all unusual in rhetoric, and they are chosen principally for their persuasive impact. When William Jennings Bryan proclaimed that Labor would not be crucified on a cross of gold, he was arguing by analogy, engaging in wordplay, and stirring emotion simultaneously.

The methods of poetic lie chiefly in the orchestration and arrangement of "presentational" (chiefly narrative and dramatic) modes of discourse. Direct argumentation, where involved, is usually absorbed into or constricted by fictional constructs. Language is selected and arranged to call attention to the aesthetic construct, sometimes for sheer enjoyment but often at the same time as a way of emphasizing thematic developments. Metaphor and symbolism are critically important. Whereas scientific discourse seeks to supress or at least to neutralize metaphors, poetic exploits them for the fullest possible range of meaning and implication, restricted only by the contextual boundaries of a framing narrative or drama. Rhetoric, of course, exists somewhere between these extremes.

SUMMARY: THE PRINCIPLES AND NORMS OF RHETORIC

Purpose, Subject or Field, Author-Audience Relation, Conditions for Success, Occasion and Context, and Language and Strategy are interpenetrating features of any discourse performance. Out of their consideration emerge composite definitions of rhetoric and the other three aims of discourse. As a distillation and general summary of these features we may identify five basic principles and norms of rhetorical activity.

The first is the principle of *identification* (Burke's term), and it derives from considerations of purpose. Rhetoric is an art of identification not merely in its strategies, most of which involve techniques of association and dissociation (Perelman 415–49), but in its aims as well. Whether directly argumentative and persuasive or not, its ultimate function lies in the creation and fostering of consensus in communities.

The second principle is the principle of *contingency*, and it derives from considerations of subject. Rhetoric deals in a world of probabilities and uncertainties. The solutions it creates and the agreements and identifications that it fosters are temporary and fragile; if they survive over long periods of time, they do so largely through the continuing reinforcements of rhetorical activity.

The third principle is the principle of *exigence* (Bitzer's term), and it derives from considerations of occasion and context. Rhetoric usually arises out of and is already related to the immediate and long-range problems of communities.

The fourth principle is the principle of *accommodation*, and it derives from considerations of the final three areas of definition: author-audience relation, success conditions, and language and strategy. Donald C. Bryant has stated it eloquently: The rhetorical function is *"the function of adjusting ideas to people and people to ideas"* (413).

The fifth principle is the principle of *openness and centrality*, and it derives from a consideration of all six areas of definition. In each of these areas the other aims of discourse involve, in varying degrees, specializations and conventionalizations of discourse; the movement of rhetoric, by contrast, is in every case toward the common interests, the common capabilities, and the common norms and values of communities. It is fitting that the central strategies of rhetoric are known as "loci communes," commonplaces. In Zeno's metaphor, the method of rhetoric is the "open hand," as opposed to the "closed fist" of scientific demonstration. Rhetoric is involved in the most "open" range of subject matters, strategies, and contexts of all the aims of discourse; and surely one of its most prominent characteristics is the readiness with which it develops lines of continuum with the other aims. Since the other aims involve specializations of interest, method, and context, they invariably slide toward rhetoric as they become enmeshed (as they invariably do) in matters of contingency and value. Human beings are intrinsically creatures of will and choice, and this inescapable fact acts as a kind of centripetal force in discourse, as in all human activity.

The historical specialization of aims of discourse is in itself a *centrifugal* movement of great value and importance, born of the development of rational and technological civilizations, and at the same time fostering that development. "Civility" to a large extent must be measured by the degree to which science and instrumentality can be kept free from special interest; art and information from propaganda; and rhetoric itself from contaminating elements of vulgarity and ritual manipulation.[7] However, the single-minded pursuit and extension of any tendency of discourse or construction of reality leads to paradox, and there are clearly limits to the value of centrifugality (which is another name for specialization) as an ideal. Pushed to such extremes as scientism, art-for-art's sake, technocracy, and vulgar relativism and mobocracy, the centrifugal directions of discourse and culture become instruments of abuse, destructive of their own ends and of the community which language creates and serves. The field of discourse is not the only area in which the head of civilization can be misled into swallowing its tale.

7. See Kenneth Burke's penetrating analysis of Hitler's *Mein Kampf* in *The Philosophy of Literary Form*.

The consideration of "openness and centrality" opens discussion beyond the realm of the descriptive and compels the recognition that the principles of rhetoric are also values of rhetoric. They rest as presuppositions of rhetorical activity, and one discovers them in the process of understanding rhetoric as an aim of discourse. All of these considerations confirm and reinforce the placement of rhetoric in the "contextualist" or "ethical/pragmatic" dimension of the Motivational Axes. The relationship between rhetoric and the other aims is directly parallel to other relations in the Motivational Axes: to the relationship between contextualism and other world-hypotheses—formism, mechanism, and organicism; to the relationship between the statesman and other social character types—theorist, technician, and poet or prophet; and to the relationship between "ethical control" and other anthropological dimensions of religious experience—knowledge of God, control of nature, and revitalization. In each case we witness a dimension that is uniquely open to and dependent upon the claims of the other three, while insistent upon their limits, and while jealous of a proper territory of its own. Thus in each case we witness a contextualist or ethical/pragmatic dimension of activity and consciousness, operating as a centripetal force, with predilections toward diversity, pluralism, balance, civility, and the recognition of limits. These are norms of rhetoric, although obviously individual instances of rhetoric can and regularly do violate them. They are also norms of culture and of the liberal arts, in which rhetorical education has traditionally held a privileged place. As we now turn to an examination of specific varieties of written rhetorical discourse, we find further confirmation of rhetoric's unique placement and function among the aims. For the pattern of these varieties is also informed by the Motivational Axes, and it constitutes a mirror of the larger world of human discourse.

5. VARIETIES OF RHETORICAL WRITING

INTRODUCTION: RHETORICAL GENUS, MOTIVATIONAL AXES, AND THE AIMS OF DISCOURSE

The classical partition of rhetoric into deliberative, forensic, and epideictic branches seems patently inadequate to anyone faced with the task of comprehending the enormously varied world of modern rhetorical writing. As with the aims of discourse, however, a more comprehensive framework is supplied by the Motivational Axes, a broader perspective on fundamental dimensions of meaning, consciousness, and the functions of discourse than was available to classical theorists. The categories to be identified and defined here—of deliberative, informative, performative, and reflective/exploratory rhetoric—do in fact mirror in a remarkable way the larger world of discourse aims—of rhetorical, scientific, instrumental, and poetic discourse respectively. Just as the aims of discourse are anticipated and informed by the ethical/pragmatic, formalistic, operational, and imaginative dimensions of the Motivational Axes, so too are the genuses of rhetoric at a different level of application.

Some of the deficiencies and omissions of Aristotelian theory which apply to the aims of discourse apply likewise to the Aristotelian understanding of rhetorical genus.[1] First, the attachment to a world of oral discourse bound by distinct cultural forums makes forensic or legal discourse a separate genus in classical rhetoric, whereas for contemporary written rhetoric, forensic constitutes simply a special subject matter and direction of deliberation, very often encased in "instruments," such as appeals, briefs, opinions, and rulings. Second, as will be demonstrated shortly, an exclusively reference-based set of assumptions about meaning in language, resulting in an almost exclusive preoccupation with forms of proof (logical proof, ethical proof, emotional proof), obscures the "performative" nature of the category traditionally called "epideictic" and tends to broaden it into a catchall. The severest strains of all on traditional categories of rhetoric, however, have come about with the development, in writing, of ponderous amounts of informational litera-

---

1. See chapter 4, pp. 88-93.

ture, occurring in a wide variety of social, institutional, and literary contexts, and incorporating a very broad spectrum of social, political, literary, and commercial motivations unanticipated in the ancient world of speechmaking.

The world before print, before literacy as a norm of culture, and before the development of reading as a universal pastime, is a world of low-density communication. The occasions for (and consequently the types of) public discourse are defined by distinct cultural forums and events. Partly because rhetorical discourse is routinely and strictly channeled into such forums, genres of discourse are in traditional cultures perceived as universal and logically prior to actual instances (Kaufer 74–75). Both the scope and the range of communication are limited by technological circumstances, and they are also jealously guarded by authorities. The vast majority of people receive only the kind of— and the level of—information appropriate to their stations. They receive it orally and primarily as a form of teaching. The notion of the "free competition of ideas" is barely conceivable in such a world, and it is only marginally relevant to that world; it becomes an ideal worth fighting for only where there is the technological and social possibility for ideas to compete freely and extensively.

The modern world, by contrast with the ancient and medieval, is a world of high-density communication, which electronic and microchip technology have now extended to the point of saturation. Writing does not have to wait for distinct occasions, authors are not constrained by them, and dissemination of what they write is not limited by them.[2] In such a situation genres of discourse become less distinct. While preexistent genres and traditions of discourse continue to exercise constitutive influences, they are not perceived as universal and logically prior to actual instances, and they must now exist in creative tension with individualistic motives and novel forms of invention, inspired by novel situations. The spectrum of discourse tends to "fill out." The Motivational Axes constitute a more comprehensive and less culturally bound instrument for comprehending this new situation than do the ancient canons of speechmaking.

Informative Rhetoric

The question of how to handle information is the source of a good deal of dissatisfaction with traditional treatments of discourse, and the question of whether information belongs to rhetoric or not has been particularly vexing. Donald C. Bryant, in his landmark essay on the

2. There do exist various possibilities, constraints, and limitations in various social and political contexts, of course, and their relation to the range and substance of literary and rhetorical output is a a fascinating sociological and literary study.

functions and scope of rhetoric, brings information into the picture by making it a subcategory of epideictic, freely admitting that this makes epideictic a catchall, but claiming that Aristotle construed it that way from the beginning (405–6). This formulation is of course less than satisfactory, obscuring the differences among some rather distinct kinds of rhetoric and some distinct forms of information as well, at least in contemporary writing.[3] Edwin Black, in his provocative work *Rhetorical Criticism*, excludes information from rhetoric altogether, but he does not address the question of where information would fit in a comprehensive theory of discourse (11–13). James Kinneavy also banishes information from rhetoric, making it a genus of "reference discourse." This is a solution that works well for some forms of information but not for all: It overlooks the possibility of a properly *rhetorical* (as distinct from purely technical or scientific) information, and it distinctly implies that any "rhetorical" departure from strict norms of referentiality would involve contamination. There can be no doubt that a good deal of what passes for information is corrupt, but such a blunt instrument as Kinneavy proposes will not help us to define it or distinguish it from instances that are entirely proper within their contexts.[4]

What all of these formulations seem to overlook is the possibility that there are different sorts of information, serving different purposes and relating in different ways to the aims of discourse. Information is, after all, the broadest imaginable sort of discourse notion, and this fact in itself should provide a clue to its status: Information is the "stuff" of all the aims, particularly of scientific, instrumental, and rhetorical discourse, and it quite properly forms subcategories or genuses of each. (There is even a traditional kind of informational poetic, perhaps best exemplified by the late medieval and early Renaissance tradition of the courtesy book.) If we regard information in this way, as a common concern of all the aims, then the problem ceases to be one of finding a *place for* information among the aims; it becomes one of identifying the most important states of differentiation and specialization, and thereby designating different *kinds of* information among the aims.

There is a class of *scientific information* (exemplified by the specialized encyclopaedia article) which conveys knowledge; a class of *instru-*

3. Bryant may have been right in a way not intended. Ancient (as well as medieval) information, even technical information, is very often protreptic in nature—embedded in quasi-ceremonial "handbook" genres which combine practical with moral instruction. This tradition survives today in such instruments as the Boy Scout handbook.
4. Symptomatic is Kinneavy's analysis (135–41) of a particular essay by Stewart Alsop as a kind of information contaminated by bias and underhanded manipulation. In fact, taking into account the situation of publication and the normal functions and contexts (editorial and opinion pages) of columns such as Alsop's, there are no such difficulties as Kinneavy sees. The essay is clearly and openly a piece of deliberation, not information, and the bias and attempt at persuasion—although one might find them objectionable on ideological grounds (which Kinneavy surely does)—are perfectly proper to the essay and its kind.

mental information which guides practical operations (the shop manual, for instance); a class of *literary information* which is molded into a pleasing or provocative design (perhaps best exemplified in modern writing by popular biography); and a class of *rhetorical information* which appeals to popular audiences, informing and helping to shape opinion in matters of public decision-making. There are varying states of differentiation, of course, and there are lines of continuum, resulting in all sorts of mixed products. But the account of information provided by the "states-of-differentation" model (figure 10) is more inclusive and leads to fewer problems than any of the other solutions mentioned.

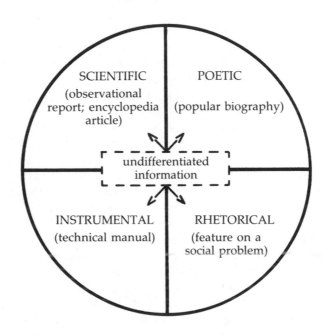

Figure 10. Information: states of differentiation

Performative Rhetoric (Epideictic)

With information established as a proper genus of rhetoric, it becomes possible to establish a more precise understanding of the category traditionally known as *epideictic*. The Aristotelian formula of "praise and blame" has always been less than adequate as a defining principle, since praising and blaming are the proper functions of deliberation as well as epideictic; and Aristotle's alignment of epideictic with "time-pre-sent," as opposed to the time-future of deliberation and the time-past of judicial discourse, has been soundly dismissed as an over-schematic con-trivance (Bryant 405; Burke, 1950: 71). Even when one adds the consider-ation that in epideictic these functions are fulfilled in the context of ceremonial or quasi-ceremonial occasions, the Aristotelian definers are not comprehensive enough to define the genus. The modern theorist Chaim Perelman gets closer to the mark in noting that, in contrast to deliberation, which seeks to gain or strengthen adherence to specific pro-positions, epideictic seeks to intensify adherence to traditional values already held by the audience (50). But even Perelman's idea faces the difficulty that while strengthening adherence to traditional values is almost always an *ultimate* motive of such individual productions as com-memorative essays, obituary editorials, public declarations, and the like, it is very seldom the principal or immediate motive.

As was the case with informative rhetoric, the difficulty here is traceable to a particular shortcoming of Aristotelian theory in general, in this case the failure to account for the "performative" dimension of language use and of discourse products. It is this dimension that most clearly identifies epideictic and explains the convergence of the other formal and situational features that help to define it (Beale). The most characteristic purpose of epideictic rhetoric lies not in substantiating theses or in communicating information, but rather in performing pub-lic acts of commemoration—such as saying welcome and bidding fare-well, declaring, pledging, and the many kinds of celebrating that require or inspire discourse. The distinction between "instrumental" and "rhetorical" applies to the performative motive as readily as to the informative: There is a kind of *instrumental* information that is highly conventional and guides practical operations, and also a kind of *rhetori-cal* information that informs opinion; likewise, there is a kind of *instru-mental* performative which is highly conventional and performs legal and business transactions, and also a kind of *rhetorical* performative which engages human values and loyalties.

In the world of speechmaking the paradigmatic example of epideictic is the public encomium, but the world of writing covers a broader range of possibilities, encompassing formal declarations such as the American Declaration of Independence at one end of the spectrum and private tes-timonials (such as religious-conversion narratives) at the other.

Reflective/Exploratory Rhetoric

In addition to deliberation, information, and epideictic, there is a fourth genus which, like the informative, owes its existence and character primarily to the phenomenon of writing and print. It is one of the earliest types of rhetorical *writing*, one that has been traditionally identified by the terms "essay" and "familiar essay." (I have adopted the term "reflective/exploratory" partly to help account for some modern developments in the tradition of familiar writing.) While this genus forms lines of continuum with the other branches of rhetoric and also with poetic, it is most clearly distinguished in contrast with deliberation: Whereas deliberative writing has developed historically in close alignment with deliberative speechmaking, often maintaining the strategies and even the partial illusion of the oral deliberative forum, reflective/exploratory writing has always had a tendency to make the most of the intrinsic privacy and individualism of the written medium. The result is a group of features commonly associated with the "familiar essay": the expression of private thoughts and feelings; the expounding of personal viewpoints, not so much with the hope of gaining adherence as of stimulating and disturbing thought; the pursuit of novel viewpoints, usually throwing to the winds the image of the responsible disputant; and the amateur exploration of delicate points of human psychology and behavior.

At a time when the boundaries between scientific and rhetorical deliberation were not so sharply drawn as they now are, reflective/exploratory discourse maintained closer alignments in the direction of information and deliberation, as exemplified perhaps in the essays of Francis Bacon. Modern encroachments of science into every area of human concern have pushed informal speculation much more deeply into the realm of personal expression, and the closely related development of romantic culture has at the same time placed a premium upon explorations of the self. But the intimate and individualistic orientation certainly predates romanticism and is really intrinsic to the type.

> The book was written in good faith, reader. It warns you from the outset that in it I have set myself no goal but a domestic and private one. I have had no thought of serving either you or my own glory. . . . I have dedicated it to the private convenience of my relatives and friends, so that when they have lost me (as soon they must), they may recover here some features of my habit and temperament, and by this means keep the knowledge they have had of me complete and alive.
>   If I had written to seek the world's favor, I should have bedecked myself better, and should present myself in a studied posture. I want to be seen here in my simple, natural, ordinary fashion, without straining or artifice; for it is myself that I portray. (Montaigne 2)

Montaigne's protestations to the contrary, this type of writing does encourage a good deal of artifice: as a means of sustaining interest through beauty and excitement of language; as a means of projecting character; and as a means of dramatizing the process of reflection itself. This element of artifice, and the complication of motives entailed in it, give reflective/exploratory rhetoric a strong line of continuum with poetic.

Theoretical Alignments of Rhetorical Genus

Like the classification of aims, the classification of rhetorical genus that emerges here is able to stand on its own as a comprehensive empirical account of what exists. Because it stands lower in the hierarchy of discourse categories, genus is a less stable construct, exhibiting more numerous and more fluid lines of continuum among types. Like the classification of aims, nevertheless, it is anticipated and confirmed by alignments with the ethical/pragmatic, operational, formalistic, and imaginative dimensions of the Motivational Axes.

The key to this set of alignments is the principle of openness and centrality already identified as unique to rhetorical discourse. Rhetoric is the central and least specialized art of human discourse, and other aims move in the direction of rhetoric as they engage human beings in matters of choice and value. By the same token, if rhetoric is the centripetal force of discourse activity, so is *deliberation* the centripetal force of rhetoric. By the same principle that the other aims of discourse tend to involve themselves in rhetoric—by involving themselves in matters of choice and value—so do the other kinds of rhetoric tend to involve themselves in deliberation—by involving themselves in particular causes or actions.

The theoretical alignments of rhetorical genus are dictated, then, by the following principle: *If deliberation is the paradigmatic "rhetorical" art, then the other branches of rhetoric distinguish themselves by movements of specialization toward the other aims of discourse.* Rhetorical information, by this account, involves a specialization in the direction of scientific discourse; performative (epideictic) rhetoric involves a specializtion toward instrumental discourse; and reflective/exploratory rhetoric involves a specialization toward poetic.

In specifying these alignments, we must issue the same sort of precautionary note as with the aims: They constitute a set of confirmatory and teleological relations, not descriptive ones. Individual instances of rhetorical information, for instance, may not be any more "scientific" in method or outlook than deliberation or other genuses of rhetoric. Moreover, there are other sources of theoretical and historical contact between specific genuses of rhetoric and the other aims of discourse. There is a line of continuum, for instance, from rhetorical to scientific deliberation, with scholarship in the humanities occupying a volatile middle ground; and there are strong historical connections between epideictic and poetic. Finally, it should be kept in mind that, while the deliberative, informative, performative, and reflective/exploratory branches of rhetoric reveal theoretical alignments with the higher categories of aims, they also retain strong lines of continuum among themselves. These last are indicated by the arrows in figure 11.

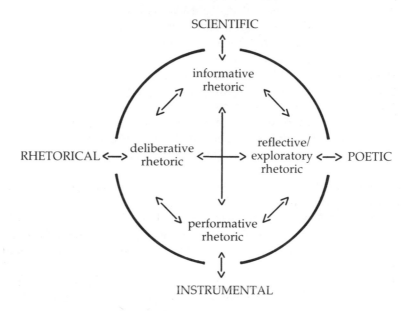

Figure 11. Theoretical alignments of rhetorical genus

In summary, the genuses of written rhetoric can be defined as follows:

Deliberative—the kind of rhetoric whose purpose is to support opinions or theses about specific problems of policy, value, or understanding in human communities.

Informative—the kind of rhetoric whose purpose is to form and inform public opinion through the nontechnical (and even entertaining) presentation of subject matter. It may incorporate a number of secondary or covert motives, such as promoting its subject or a certain attitude toward its subject.

Performative—the kind of rhetoric, traditionally known as epideictic, whose purpose is to perform various acts of declaration, celebration, or commemoration in a public arena, calling into play and reinforcing the values of a
  particular community.
Reflective/Exploratory—the kind of rhetoric whose purpose is to share, explore,
  and reflect upon human experiences, usually in a highly individualistic and
  entertaining way. It uses various presentational forms, sometimes borrowed from literary art, to relate personal experiences and reflections to
  general questions of understanding and value.

Wheels within Wheels—Variations within Variations

Neither the aims of discourse nor the genuses of rhetoric are natural or fixed categories; they are norms of action and consciousness,
historical developments, and channels of specialization for discourse
performances. An individual work of discourse succeeds partly by
conforming to the norms of a given rhetorical genre, partly by transcending them, sometimes even by flouting them. Any attempt to
define and describe a genre must freeze it in time, extrapolating a
static out of a dynamic reality. Beside such clean abstraction, the
world of actual products must seem varied and dappled indeed. In
such a world there exist a large number of items which conform to
pattern, a large number also whose novelties and innovations push
them along lines of continuum toward other patterns, and a smaller
number of strange mixtures—some more successful than others,
some completely idiosyncratic, others which will be quickly imitated,
entering into the general drift of things. The theory developed in
these chapters has no stake in suppressing these variations and novelties; its goal is to account for them—the specific conformity or non-
conformity of invididual performances and the specific ways in which
individual categories run together—in a more satisfactory, more provocative, and less reductive way than do competing theories. As a
critical instrument, the theory helps us to discover and explain both
the typicality and uniqueness of individual works.

The Motivational Axes constitute, in fact, a device for understanding variations, both in discourse and in ways of looking at experience.
And discourse, like consciousness itself, is a matter of wheels-within-
wheels, variations within variations. While my principal goal is to win
acceptance of the larger categories—the aims of discourse and the
genuses of rhetoric—I will attempt in a tentative way some account of
variation-within-type in the descriptive sections that follow. In suggesting these intermediate generic divisions between genus and de
facto genre, I make use of the following theoretical speculations:
Attempts to identify discourse categories at any level must take into

account a full range of features—subject, context, method, style, author-audience relationship, and so on. Nevertheless, the theoretical confirmation of rhetorical genus suggests two sorts of features that seem to weigh heavily enough to predict typical constellations of other features. The first of these is propositional status, which for unified and extended discourse performances may be determined either by identifying the status of the central proposition, or by asking, in general, what the entire performance "amounts to" (e.g., a policy statement, a manifesto, an apology, a warning, and so on). The most fundamental distinction of propositional status is the one between performative and constative utterance, which has already proved crucial in construction of the Motivational Axes and in the definitions of instrumental discourse and performative (epideictic) rhetoric. Other sorts of propositional distinctions may be useful at lower levels. Within deliberative rhetoric, for example, the familiar partition of policy, value, and interpretive propositions may provide the basis for a reasonably adequate subclassification; and a similar function for epideictic is conceivably performed by Austin's partition of the different classes of performative utterance (pp. 144–45 below).

A second and stronger factor, however, is the tendency of categories of discourse at every level to form lines of continuum with other categories. Rhetoric constitutes the richest field of activity in this respect, not only in its readier tendency to form lines of continuum with other aims of discourse, but also in the way its genuses mirror and form lines of continuum with the larger world of aims. It would be a mistake to insist upon clear-cut or fully articulated patterns of a similar nature and at every level. But these tendencies do exist and they help to clarify "directions" of variation within types of rhetoric. They also re-invoke the broad pattern of operational, formalistic, imaginative, and ethical/pragmatic dimensions specified by the Motivational Axes, revealing the thoroughly pervasive operation of these dimensions in human discourse.

Within each of the genuses of rhetoric, we find directions of variation that mirror the broader pattern of deliberative, performative, informative, and reflective/exploratory types, just as these mirror in turn the larger world of aims. Rhetorical information, for instance, can orient toward knowledge (the "base" informational position); toward problem-solving and decision-making (the realm of deliberation); toward entertainment and vicarious experience (the realm of reflective/exploratory, and beyond toward poetic); and, finally, toward celebration or commemoration of its subjects (the realm of epideictic). These speculations will be given a good deal of specification in the individual discussions of the basic classes of written rhetoric.

I. DELIBERATIVE RHETORIC

Deliberation is the branch of rhetoric that receives the most extensive treatments in textbooks, and about which there are fewest difficulties of recognition or definition. Its normal purpose is to support specific conclusions or opinions about questions of action, value, or understanding. It takes place in the context of public or institutional problem-solving, evaluation, and decision-making; and the normal aim of individual works is to make relatively well-defined and narrow contributions to these larger processes. Other branches of rhetoric, to the extent that they exhibit any such impulse, move in the direction of deliberation, and such an impulse often proves irresistible. In fact, in those cases where readers sense an abuse or contamination of discourse—a broken contract as it were—their indignation is usually directed at a perceived attempt to push informative, reflective/exploratory, or epideictic rhetoric toward deliberation. This is the basic, centripetal rhetorical genus. All matters are ultimately grist for its mill.

Of all the branches of written rhetoric, deliberation retains the closest affinities with the art of speechmaking, even though it represents in some respects a later historical development than other kinds of writing. (Only in the world of widespread literacy, cheap paper, and fast printing and distribution does the give and take of public written deliberation come fully into being.) The normal method of deliberation is argumentation, though not exclusively so, and in fact written deliberation will sometimes eschew direct argumentation altogether, relying upon narrative and dramatic modes of discourse that would pose great risks in the oral medium.

The Form of Deliberation

Nearly all classical rhetoricians recommend a scheme of argument—varying in different treatments from four to nine separate sections—which may be termed anticlimactic or deductive: After introducing the matter to be discussed, one puts forward directly the proposition to be proved, followed by arguments in its behalf, refutations of opposing arguments, and finally a concluding statement. The author of *Rhetorica ad Herennium*, who terms this kind of arrangement "ab institutione artis profectum," recognizes another sort, however, "ad casum temporis adcommodatum," wherein the speech is arranged according to the unique needs of a situation (III, ix, 16). Quintilian loosens the order by suggesting that the orator consider the possibility of refuting opposing arguments before advancing his own (VII, x). Not until Whately, however, do rhetoricians make fully explicit the advantages of an opposite kind of order, which may be termed climactic or investigative: "But when the Conclusion to be established is one likely to hurt the feelings and offend the prejudices of the hearers, it is essential to keep out of sight, as much as possible, the point to which we are tending, till the principles from which it is to be deduced shall have been clearly established" (142). Other possible values of investigative order are suspense and the illusion (if not always the fact) of dispassionate, evenhanded treatment. James Madison's "Federalist No. 10" is a celebrated example.

Most written deliberation, like most deliberative speech-making, follows one of these two methods. A third and utterly various set of possibilities, congenial more to writing than to speechmaking, lies in the area of special strategies of presentation, involving the creative appropriation of unaccustomed modes and genres, where things are not all they seem. This is the realm of formal and stylistic artifice, of masks and ironies and insinuations, varieties of feigning above and apart from the necessary conventions of straightforward written communication. A reader's sense that an individual performance using a special strategy of this sort constitutes a kind of deliberation will depend not upon external regularities of form and method but upon considerations of context, subject, and discernible intent. In some cases the author's motives are themselves complicated or compromised by the demands and opportunities of a special form, and we find ourselves with a discourse that is partly one thing, partly another; overtly one thing, covertly another; in its early stages one thing, in latter stages another. In almost every case the special strategy of presentation procures the possibility of startling or emotional impact, and the possibility of initiating, intensifying, or changing the course of reasoned debate; it does so at the expense, in the immediate moment, of reasoned debate itself.

For a transparent and reasonably uncomplicated example of such a strategy, witness the opening paragraphs of a short humorous essay by *Washington Post* columnist Art Buchwald:

> "The Committee to Abolish the Registration of Automobiles and the Licensing of Drivers" has just opened up a lobby in Washington and I was happy to visit with Roger Crash, their spokesman.
>
> Mr. Crash said, "We have formed this organization because the constitutional rights of all automobile drivers are at stake. There is no reason why anybody should not be allowed to own and drive an automobile in this country without his rights being infringed by local, state and Federal authorities."
>
> "Obviously you're against registration of vehicles, then?"

"We certainly are. Most people who drive should not be inconvenienced by some bureaucrat who wants to know what they intend to use a car for. There is a conspiracy in this country to get everyone to register their automobiles, so they eventually can be taken away from them."

"Who is behind the conspiracy?"

"The Communists. They know that America would collapse overnight if their automobiles were confiscated. This country is going through an hysterical period right now. They blame all the automobile deaths and accidents on the drivers. But you're not going to prevent accidents by asking people to register their vehicles. If somebody wants a car to kill somebody, he'll find it, no matter how many laws you have."

("A Crash Program for the Right to Drive,"
The Washington Post, June 27, 1968.
Reprinted by permission of Art Buchwald.)

At the time this essay appeared, there was before the U.S. Congress a bill requiring the registration of handguns. The bill was being fiercely opposed by the powerful National Rifle Association, whose spokesmen were maintaining that registration violated the Constitutional principle of the "right to bear arms." Buchwald's piece represents, first of all, the decisive role that *context* can play in determinations of generic status. While the essay contains no internal reference to firearms, to the National Rifle Association, or to the bill before Congress, its subject and status as policy deliberation were immediately discernible to most readers at the time.

The essay relies upon a "generic strategy," appropriating the form and style of the journalistic interview, in a humorous and satiric way, for deliberative purposes. From the standpoint of argumentation, the strategy amounts to an extended argument-by-analogy: Registration of firearms, which many consider threatening to basic freedoms, is really no different from registration of automobiles, which everyone takes for granted.

"A Crash Program for the Right to Drive" also illustrates the curiously indeterminate nature of de facto genres. One might expect such concrete, nameable, and widely acknowledged categories as "open letter," "book review," and "interview article" to exhibit a greater degree of functional determinacy than genuses and subgenuses, but this is very often not the case. Such terms tend to stand for rather loose convergences of subject, technique, and style which may be bent to informative, reflective, deliberative, or aesthetic purposes. (This seems to be true especially of Buchwald's de facto genre, that of the political humor or whimsy column.) This situation underscores once again the "openness," the fluid and dynamic nature of modern rhetorical writing and rhetorical categories in general. It also confirms a theoretical point established early in this book: The lower a category's position on the Discourse Hierarchy, the more susceptible it becomes to functional hierarchicalization—to play and metaphoric transfer, to appropriation to higher ends.

Types of Deliberation

Of the two keys to subclassification or directions of variation mentioned above—propositional status and lines of continuum that suggest mirrorings of the larger domain of rhetoric—the latter appear less effective in opening doors to deliberation than to the other genuses. It is true that lines of continuum exist between deliberation and other types of rhetoric; but most of the performances that exist conspicuously along lines of continuum seem to have begun at other points, so that the movement is *from* reflective/exploratory, informative, or performative rhetoric *toward* deliberation, and not the other way around. Undoubtedly this has to do with deliberation's status as the basic rhetorical genus, the one toward which the others gravitate. Mirrorings of the larger domain do exist, however, and with them the influence of the Motivational Axes. These can be used both to confirm and extend the more clearly discernible directions of variation suggested by propositional status.

The importance of propositional status in connection with deliberative and forensic discourse is acknowledged in the classical doctrine of *stasis* (or *status*),[5] and it is widely treated in modern textbooks on argumentation and debate. Although classifications of arguable propositions vary from source to source, the distinction between questions of policy, value, and interpretation is implicitly accepted in most treatments (Terris). (The category of "fact" is indistinguishable from interpretation in deliberative situations.) Naturally all three types appear (along with other sorts of utterance) in individual works of rhetoric; but every work constitutes a hierarchy of such propositions, and what is decisive is the nucleus or thesis proposition, or more generally what the entire piece "amounts to." An essay maintaining that television programs are not causes but reflections of cultural values "amounts to" an *interpretation*, although it may bear implications for value and policy—e.g., television is not culpable, nor should it be regulated on that account. An essay arguing that television news programs inherently distort the news amounts to an *evaluation*, even though it rests upon an element of interpretation and may have policy implications. Finally, an argument in favor of government control or management of television news amounts to a statement of *policy*.

5. On *status* see Dieter; Howell 1941: 36–45; and Húltzen.

These three types of statement serve as controlling propositions for three types of deliberation which (while sharing many features of form, strategy, and context) differ markedly in the types of issues relevant to each and in the ways in which individual lines of argument are marshaled to deal with them. *Policy deliberation* generally turns upon one or more of the following issues: the need for change, the causes of the problem, the workability of solutions, the feasibility of solutions, and the consideration of alternatives. *Values deliberation* involves a different set: the identification of value standards; the definition of standards; the relevance or relative importance of a standard to a given case; the measurement or assessment of individual acts or experiences against the standard; and the consideration of alternatives. *Interpretive deliberation* involves still another set: the establishment of facts, generaliztions, definitions, causes, and effects. Individual *topoi* (arguments *by definition, by comparison, ad hominem*, etc.) may apply in any of these types, but the ways in which they apply will be different, since they are in the service of different ends in each case.

Lines of Continuum

Do these three directions of variation form lines of continuum that reflect the larger world of rhetoric? They do, although in a less conspicuous way than will materialize with other genuses of rhetoric. Policy deliberation we may take as the paradigmatic deliberative type, just as deliberation itself is the paradigmatic rhetorical type; its line of continuum is toward deliberation itself, just as deliberation's line is toward rhetoric itself. Other types of rhetorical deliberation have a tendency to gravitate toward policy questions, and they take place in a wider context of policy considerations. (The question of the existence and extensiveness of the "black middle class," for instance, has a direct bearing upon social and economic policy, and the answer given is often influenced by this consideration.)[6] Values deliberation, on the other hand, often strikes a line of continuum toward reflective/exploratory rhetoric and the imaginative dimension. (See the essay by Ellen Goodman, with analysis, below.) And interpretive deliberation—involved with such questions as whether welfare programs have actually helped to decrease poverty, whether and to what extent the founding fathers actually believed in democracy, whether a space-based antiballistic mis-

6. Policy deliberation also involves the most comprehensive range of issues, and even at this level all the basic motivational directions are apparent: The need for change and the moral or political acceptability of solutions point toward the contextual or ethical/pragmatic dimension; "causes of the problem" is an interpretive, even sometimes a scientific question and points toward the formalistic dimension; feasibility and workability belong to the operational dimension; and the consideration of alternatives involves an imaginative projection of the future as well as a creative consideration of possibilities.

sile system would increase national security—takes a turn toward the formalistic dimension, involving a greater recourse to scientific information and close-fisted dialectic than other types of deliberation.

Instrumental Deliberation

The application of the Motivational Axes to these types reveals one conspicuous blank space in traditional accounts and helps us to account for a fourth type of rhetorical deliberation: the "instrumental," which forms a line of continuum toward instrumental discourse and the operational dimension. Significantly, this is a type of deliberation that occurs only in writing; it is usually either a direct function of institutions or sponsored by institutions; it is often composed by committees; and the final product usually has a more or less "official" character. It is usually called either a "report" or a "decision." Typical examples are commission reports (National Commission on Crime, Advisory Commission on Substance Abuse, etc.); recommendation-reports forwarded by individuals and committees within corporations and bureaucracies; "pastoral letters" and other semiofficial publications which take stands on public issues in behalf of institutions; product evaluations by consumer agencies (*Consumer Reports*); majority decisions of the Supreme Court; and other legal instruments (depositions by experts, for instance) which embody arguments on specific cases.

Three features in particular determine the leaning of this type of deliberation toward the operational dimensions of discourse: First, instrumental deliberation shares with both instrumental discourse and epideictic rhetoric an institutional context, often as a matter of explicit provenence. Second, it shares a "performative" quality and status. Unlike direct examples of instrumental discourse or epideictic rhetoric, operational deliberation is often highly controversial and directly surrounded by deliberation of all types; but the very fact that a particular "report" or "decision" or "letter" is the focus of all this deliberation indicates that it "carries weight" of a special kind. (So important is this factor that choice of the operational "direction" has become an important rhetorical strategy in the competition between organizations and interest groups: Not only are the arguments now enshrined in a quasi-official status; the very publication of the arguments can be turned into a public event, gathering public attention far beyond what is possible under ordinary circumstances.) Finally, this type of deliberation shares with instrumental discourse (though not with epideictic) a predilection for formal rigidities. The disposition of arguments is often controlled by strict conventions related to particular fields or institutions, and the style may have either a highly "official" quality (larded with performatives such as "we resolve," "we therefore commit ourselves," and so on) or a highly technical quality (larded with statistics and accompanied by charts and diagrams). The discourse may even proceed in rather procrustean fashion from one conventional rubric to another: Background, Analysis, Recommendation, Costs, Returns.

Rhetorical and Scientific Deliberation

Deliberation is a genus of scientific as well as of rhetorical discourse, and it is clear that scientific and rhetorical deliberation exist in a state of continuum. The differences between them involve the whole range of significant features—purpose, subject, context, strategy, author-audience relation, success-conditions, and style—but the first three of these seem to determine the others. To the extent that the purpose is exclusively that of establishing knowledge, in a disinterested context, about a subject which admits of rational discovery and characterization separable from communal or metaphysical values, the other features of scientific discourse usually follow. To whatever extent these highly specialized conditions are not possible or desirable, the discourse leans toward rhetoric—a leaning which is sometimes taken for granted, as in the humanistic disciplines, and other times experienced as a "loosening" of scientific rigor.

The extent to which various subject matters are amenable to scientific treatment (insofar as that term implies application of scientific method) is itself a matter of philosophical and rhetorical debate. It is clear, however, that some disciplines, particularly those that Aristotle referred to as practical and productive (including rhetoric itself), depend less upon rigid discovery procedures than upon the application of right reason to human products and behavior. Discourse whose aim is to establish knowledge in such an area is nonetheless "scientific discourse," even though its form and style may be indistinguishable from rhetoric, and even though its author may be animated by a desire to see the subject—and the values which rest as presuppositions of the subject—prosper and prevail.

Examples and Analyses

This section and each of the three to follow (on informative, performative, and reflective/exploratory rhetoric) are concluded with short examples accompanied by commentary. One could not possibly hope to illustrate the entire range of any particular genus in the space available here; nor have these examples been chosen for their sterling quality. Their purpose, rather, is to tie down a sense of of the genus, to indicate something of the range of formal and motivational possibility within the genus, and to illustrate some special points that have been made in the preceding discussions. They may be passed over by readers more interested in proceeding with the inventory of basic rhetorical types.

Deliberative Example 1: Vernon E. Jordan, Jr., "The Truth about the Black Middle Class," *Newsweek*, July 8, 1974. Reprinted by permission.

Recent reports of the existence of a vast black middle class remind me of daring explorers emerging from the hidden depths of a strange, newly discovered world bearing tales of an exotic new phenomenon. The media seem to have discoverd, finally, black families that are intact, black men who are working, black housewives tending backyard gardens and black youngsters who aren't sniffing coke or mugging old ladies.

And out of this "discovery" a new black stereotype is beginning to emerge. Immaculately dressed, cocktail in hand, the new black stereotype comes off as a sleek, sophisticated professional light-years away from the ghetto experience. As I turn the pages of glossy photos of these idealized, fortunate few, I get the feeling that this new black image is all too comforting to Americans weary of the struggle against poverty and racism.

But this stereotype is no more real than was the old image of the angry, fire-breathing militant. And it may be just as damaging to black people, for whom equal opportunity is still a theory and for whom a national effort to bring about a more equitable distribution of the fruits of an affluent society is still a necessity. After all, who can argue the need for welfare reform, for guaranteed jobs, for integrated schools and better housing, when the supposed beneficiaries are looking out at us from the pages of national magazines, smiling at the camera between sips from their Martinis?

Ballyhoo

The "new" black middle class has been seen recently in prime time on a CBS News documentary; it has adorned the cover of The New York Times Magazine, and it has been the subject of a Time cover story. But its much ballyhooed emergence is more representative of wishful thinking than of reality. And important as it is for the dedication and hard work of countless black families finally to receive recognition, the image being pushed so hard may be counter-productive in the long run.

The fact is that the black middle class of 1974, like that of earlier years, is a minority within the black community. In 1974, as in 1964, 1954 and in the decades stretching into the distant past, the social and economic reality of the majority of black people has been poverty and marginal status in the wings of our society.

The black middle class traditionally included a handful of professionals and a far larger number of working people who, had they been white, would be solidly "working class." The inclusion of Pullman porters, post-office clerks and other typical members of the old black black middle class was due less to their incomes—which were well below those of whites— than to their relative immunity from the hazards of marginal employment that dogged most blacks. They were "middle class" relative to other black people, not to the society at large.

Despite all the publicity, despite all the photos of yacht-club cocktail parties, that is where the so-called black middle class stands today. The CBS broadcast included a handyman and a postal worker. Had they been white they would be considered working class, but since they were black and defied media-fostered stereotypes, they were given the middle-class label.

Income

Well, is it true that the black community is edging into the middle class? Let's look at income, the handiest guide and certainly the most generally agreed-upon measurement. What income level amounts to middle-class status? Median family income is often used, since that places a family at the exact midpoint in our society. In 1972 the median family income of whites amounted to $11,549, but black median family income was a mere $6,864.

That won't work. Let's use another guide. The Bureau of Labor Statistics says it takes an urban family of four $12,600 to maintain an "intermediate" living standard. Using that measure, the average black family not only is *not* middle class, but it earns far less than the "lower, non-poverty" level of $8,200. Four out of five black familes earn less than the "intermediate" standard.

What about collar color? Occupational status is often considered a guide to middle-class status, and this is an area in which blacks have made tremendous gains, breaking into occupations unheard of for non-whites only a decade ago. When you look at the official occupation charts, there is a double space to separate higher-status from lower-status jobs such as laborer, operative and service worker. That gap is more than a typographical device. It is an indicator of racial separation as well, for the majority of working whites hold jobs above that line, while the majority of blacks are still confined to the low-pay, low-status jobs below it. At the top of the job pinnacle, in the elite categories of the professions and business, the disparity is most glaring, with one out of four whites in such middle-class jobs in contrast to every tenth black worker.

Tenuous Gains

Yes, there are black doctors, dentists and lawyers, but let no one be fooled into thinking they are typical—those professions include only 2 per cent blacks. Yes, there are black families that are stable, who work, often at more than one job, and who own cars and homes. And yes, they are representative of the masses of black people who work the longest hours at the hardest jobs for the least pay in order to put some meat on the table and clothes on their backs. This should be emphasized in every way possible in order to remind this forgetting nation that there is a dimension of black reality that has never been given its due.

But this should not blind us to the realization that even with such superhuman efforts, the vast majority of blacks are still far from middle-class status. Let us not forget that the gains won are tenuous ones, easily shaken from our grasp by an energy crisis, a recession, a rampant inflation or nonenforcement of hard-won civil-rights laws.

And never let us fall victim to the illusion that the limited gains so bitterly wrenched from an unwilling nation have materially changed the conditions of life for the overwhelming majority of black people—conditions still typified by discrimination, economic insecurity and general living conditions inferior to those enjoyed by the majority of our white fellow citizens.

COMMENTARY

Vernon Jordan's essay is a classic instance of rhetorical deliberation—in subject, form, and strategy. The essay argues a proposition of understanding—namely that the "new" image of the middle-class black person is distorted and misleading—which has direct and explicitly recognized implications (par. 3) for public policy. The form of the essay is anticlimactic (classical), moving from an introduction in which a definite thesis is stated (par. 1–3), to a confirmation which advances several arguments in behalf of the thesis (par. 4–10), to a "refutation" which concedes something to the opposition but overwhelms the point with broader considerations (par. 11–12), and finally to a conclusion.

The initial paragraph serves at once to introduce the topic, to slip in an argument from comparison (one that is *ad hominem* in its effect), and to establish a tone of buoyant indignation, directed not at the error of the image, which the essay will seek to explain and document, but at its glibness and self-serving nature. The tone is justified not only by the substantive concerns of the discourse but by contextual circumstances as well: *Newsweek's* "My Turn" section, in which this essay originally appeared, encourages a posture of "speaking out."

The principal issue of the essay, the one toward which Jordan directs four separate arguments in the confirmation section, is one of definition, specifically of the term "middle class." In par. 6, Jordan challenges the implicit contradictions in media definitions of middle class, claiming that certain occupations labeled "working class" for whites are considered "middle class" for blacks. In succeeding paragraphs Jordan calls forth three objective criteria of middle-classness—income, living standard, and collar-color—citing statistical evidence in each case to show that the vast majority of black citizens fall outside the definition.

In a general sense, Jordan's entire essay is a refutation. His "refutation" section takes the form of a concession—"Yes, there are black doctors . . ."—which serves the dual purpose of validating earlier claims, showing the reader that the author is aware of the obvious, and finally of setting up the counterpunch, the larger appeal to general standards of equality and fairness which conclude the essay. This piece of discourse also follows another classical strategy, using the penultimate concession or refutation as a springboard for an eloquent peroration. In this and other ways (including tone and style), Jordan's essay demonstrates the close functional and formal ties that can exist between written and oral rhetoric. The fact that the essay is far shorter than most speeches dare be serves as a reminder of the real gulf between the two.

Deliberative Example 2: Ellen Goodman, "Participants, Not Patients," *The Boston Globe* and other newspapers, May 1976. Reprinted by permission from *Close to Home* (New York: Simon and Schuster, 1979).

Ten years ago, when Marilyn was twenty-six, she became pregnant with her first child in a midwestern university town. She was excited and anxious when she went to the clinic to ask the doctor what he thought about natural childbirth.

His answer was pretty succinct. She remembers it vividly, and, in truth, bitterly. He said, "I think about natural childbirth the way I think about natural appendectomy." So when Marilyn's son "was delivered by the doctor" (that's the way she talks about it), her role was simple: She was a patient. Her son came into the world upside down and howling at the cold bright light of the operating room. He was, first of all, a patient.

About a year ago, Marilyn's father died. He was, of course, in a hospital, in the cardiac unit of what's called "a major metropolitan teaching hospital." He, too, was a patient, a good one, who took his medicine on time, without complaint. He died during the day shift.

During the months that followed, Marilyn's mother said, over and over, until it became her mantra, "Well, he had the best of care, didn't he? We did everything we could." Since then, Marilyn has been thinking about it, all of it. It seems to come together, these bits and pieces of her life.

She thought about her hospitalized delivery when she read Suzanne Arms's *Immaculate Deception*, a book that reported on the ways in which medicine—with the best intentions, mind you—has turned maternity into an illness and childbirth into a medical crisis.

She thought about her son's birth when she heard the gentle French obstetrician, Dr. Frederick Leboyer, say that he believes infants should have a "birth without violence," a quiet, warm, bathed entry into the world of the family.

And, of course—how could she help it?—she thought about her father's death during the horrendous Karen Ann Quinlan case. The thing that impressed her about the Quinlan case wasn't whether the girl was legally alive or dead but that she was, she is, indisputably a medical patient. Her existence is a question of medical technology.

So it's not surprising that, this month, when she read a quote from Ivan Illich, the former priest and sociologist, in *Psychology Today*, she memorized it. "Death that was once viewed as a call from God, and later as a natural event, has become an untimely event that is the outcome of our technical failure to treat a disease."

Marilyn has joined a growing number of Americans concerned about the effect of medical technology on our lives. Not the lack of technology—the intrusion of it. Our well-being is now thought of as a medical question, and the stages of our lives are marked by passages from the pediatrician to the obstetrician to the geriatrician. Through them we avoid pain and treat death pathologically.

Have we given up birth and death to medicine? If they are abnormal, certifiable sicknesses and we send them to the hospital to be dealt with, don't we also lose our emotional involvement with each other and with the critical moments of our lives? If we become passive and patient and seek only the absence of pain, aren't we missing the passages of life instead of experiencing them? What does it do to us when we treat death as a technical error? When someone dies, will we sue for malpractice?

Marilyn is not the type to rail against doctors. She is not for dismantling hospitals and closing down medical schools. She doesn't want to give birth in a rice paddy or have a natural appendectomy. She uses Novocain at the dentist's. But she thinks, as many do, that we have to distinguish between a disease and a process of life. We all are born and die of "natural causes."

She would like the medical establishment to concentrate more on helping us do this in our own time and our own beds. She would like them to use their technology more judiciously, more skeptically. After all, with all the fetal monitors in the obstetrics wards, we are still eighteenth in infant mortality in the world. With all the fancy cardiac units, there is new evidence that home care may be just as effective.

Right now, she says the patients and the doctors conspire in a medical delivery system whereby the patient delivers himself or herself up to be "cured" from life and death. She wants to remind us to be participants, not patients. More and more she has been thinking, just thinking, mind you, that the important questions about the way we live and die aren't medical ones at all.

COMMENTARY

In her syndicated column for the *Boston Globe*, Ellen Goodman has established a reputation for an unusual melding of the public and private worlds, exploring the personal and domestic ramifications of public policy, and conversely the political and cultural implications of trends in behavior and sensibility. In accomplishing this melding (usually avoiding the shrillness and sentimentality that often accompany such attempts), Goodman typically eschews direct argumentation, prefers narrative and dramatic presentational modes, and cultivates a familiar style. Such strategies often push her rhetoric far along the continuum toward (and sometimes completely into) reflective/exploratory rhetoric. For all her courting of familiar style and postures, nevertheless, a goodly number of her columns are deliberative, aiming at timely interpretations and evaluations of the passing scene, spilling over at times into direct political advocacy. (On regular columnizing as a modern influence on reflective/exploratory rhetoric, see further below, pp. 156–59.)

What distinguishes the deliberation of "Participants, Not Patients" is the burden placed upon strategies other than those of argumentation. The overall strategy may be characterized as a radical extension of the familiar introductory gambit of the focusing-event, or what Whately termed "introduction narrative." Whereas in normal deliberation the focusing narrative is an appendage to the argument proper, usually followed by a discursive presentation of issues and arguments, in the present case it has swallowed up the whole, becoming the frame for an argument that is developed implicitly within.

Once this circumstance is understood, the essay submits readily enough to conventional analysis. It posits a thesis of value, attributing a variety of health-care problems to a prevailing mind-set among physicians and hospital administrators, as well as among the public at large. Marilyn's various experiences (Is Marilyn a real, a composite, or a fictional character?) serve as arguments-by-example, demonstrations of the consequences of the prevailing attitude. Moreover, Marilyn's reflections on her experiences, as "reported" by Goodman (par. 11–13), amount to a recommendation.

The essay is transparently deliberative in other ways. In par. 9–10, Goodman drops all pretense and modulates into a discursive presentation of the public problem under examination; she picks up the veil again in par. 11, but even here Marilyn's attitude amounts to a clarifying concession, which gives the essay a semblance, ironically, of classical order.

It is remarkable that, in contrast to the essay by Vernon Jordan (above), "Participants, Not Patients" would be entirely unsuitable as a speech. In its present mode and highly abbreviated form, it would seem mawkishly overdramatic and artifical in a situation with the author and audience face-to-face in the same room; and to extend it much beyond its present length would render the presentational strategy insupportably tiresome. Jordan's essay could be easily extended without changing its essential character (and his essay may in fact be a distillation of an oral address), but any workable extension of Goodman's essay would encase it in discursiveness, reestablishing the normal contours of deliberation, putting the focusing narrative back into its place as an appendage, and thus dismantling the literary device that makes the essay work.

II. INFORMATIVE RHETORIC

Some of the difficulties that both the concept and reality of "information" pose for discourse theory have already been handled in the introductory section of this chapter. The identification of information as a genus of rhetoric rests upon two qualifying principles: first, that while information is "in everything," as a kind of unconditioned vortex of discourse (see figure 10, p. 110), there are classes and subclasses of writing that may be properly designed "informational," where the information is not appropriated to the specific ends of another established class (deliberation, for instance); and second, that not all of these classes are rhetorical: Some are scientific, some are instrumental, and possibly others are aesthetic. *Rhetorical* information has the aim of forming and informing public opinion, through the nontechnical (and even entertaining) presentation of subject matter. Rhetorical information incorporates, depends upon, and implies generalizations about its subject matter, but it does not argue or directly seek to establish the validity of these generalizations. It may, however, incorporate a number of secondary or covert persuasive motives, such as promotimg its subject matter, or contributing to the subject's public reputation.

In comparison to information in the other aims, rhetorical information is distinguished by timeliness, by its accommodation to popular audiences, and by its lack of specialization, either in style or content. From the standpoint of any of the other aims, rhetorical information must inevitably be perceived as compromised, ephemeral, and vulgar— sacrificing factual, theoretical, operational, and aesthetic integrity to the needs and whims of the moment and the literary marketplace. Rhetorical information is also distinguished by its service to institutional and ideological agendas. Authors and editors do have reasons for choosing certain subjects over others, and questions of bias are relative to context, audience, and place of publication. Literally thousands of institutional and special interest publications all over the world publish informative articles that further interest in and cater to the interests of the institutions and organizations that sponsor them. In many cases a high percentage of these articles are written by free-lancers who (with the aid of various special-interest publications of their own) have studied the expectations and needs of particular "markets" as intensely as they have the subjects about which they write.

Another characteristic of the work of rhetorical information is that it often exists in ideological as well as commercial competition with other works of rhetorical information. Different kinds of advice—about such things as financial investments, rearing children, attaining professional success or personal contentment—reflect competing approaches to these subjects. In various specialized forums the proponents of these different views engage each other in academic or rhetorical deliberation. Meanwhile, at the stage where deliberation is yet inconclusive (and may likely remain so), they publish works of advice and practical instruction for laymen. Their motives for doing so are invariably mixed, but in some cases the work of rhetorical information may be designed to feed back eventually into the process of deliberation. The fact that a coherent and comprehensive body of practical instruction may be constructed as an extrapolation of theory may in itself stand as an argument for the theory. And the practical success of the information with its intended audience may provide an even stronger argument.

Questions about bias and objectivity permeate discussions of informative rhetoric, and they surround it in actual practice as well, through printed rejoinders (routinely styled as "letters" or "responses") and counterarticles. Fascinating as such questions can be, they are not resolvable in the abstract. Framing generalizations, unifying tone, and unifying metaphor are required not merely by the needs of specific audiences or by the covert motives of authors and publishers but also by the demands of coherence and readability in discourse itself. What distinguishes informative from deliberative rhetoric is not at all the absence of such devices but rather their lack of argumentative function (within context) and the characteristic relationships that they form with the facts and information being presented. In deliberation it is normal for facts and information and testimony to be arranged in support of theses, as part of a general argumentative design. For informative rhetoric, the pattern is normally reversed: Generalizations and conclusions support and are drawn incidentally out of the facts and information, lending coherence and unity, and providing entrance and satisfying closure to the discourse.[7] (As a way of catching interest or underscoring the significance of whatever information is being presented, writers will often open with disjunctive verbal formulas of the type *X However Y*: "For years in the field of arms deployment the subject of X has been taboo; however, with the introduction of Y, the administration has come out of the closet." These gambits create the momentary illusion of an argumentative pattern, sometimes putting a "spin" on the information through tone and choice of metaphor, while the discourse itself has no deliberative thesis.)

In summary, discourse remains in the informative corner as long as generalizations and conclusions retain the following characteristics:

1. Their chief function is to frame the subject matter and to create interest and closure.
2. They "grow out of" or seem justified by balanced assessment of the information. (This is the opposite of the deliberative procedure, whereby facts, descriptions, and quotations are selected narrowly to lend support to propositions.)
3. They are not *under the circumstances* controversial or *in effect* engaged in controversy or advocacy.

7. A similar relationship between argumentation and information is posited by Brandt, *The Rhetoric of Argumentation* 260–80.

The variables that lend considerable elasticity to the third criterion above are chiefly those of subject and audience. Sports and entertainment writers, for example, regularly engage in a style of flambuoyant generalizing and evaluating that would be shockingly inappropriate for informative articles on government or foreign policy. A similar pattern of opportunity and constraint is provided by the relative narrowness or broadness of audiences. Information pitched directly at an ideologically homogeneous group, or a group animated by similar commitments in a particular area (members of the Humane Society, for instance) can successfully make use of generalizations, controlling metaphors, and projected attitudes that would spoil the discourse in broader, more heterogeneous settings. A good deal of what may be legitimately termed bias is less the result of conniving and bad faith than is normally perceived. Since the degree of tolerable generalizing, concluding, or attitudinizing varies from situation to situation, all sorts of miscalculations are possible. Moreover, authors may choose framing generalizations injudiciously—through haste, sloth, inherent bad taste, the desire to entertain or titillate their audiences, or the desire to call attention to themselves. This problem seems to be aggravated in news-magazine reporting, which sometimes combines glittering framing and attitudinizing with brevity and thinness of reporting. This results in a proportion of (sometimes flippant) generalizaing to hard matter that readers occasionally find intolerable.

Lines of Continuum

Information is the most volatile of the rhetorical genuses, distinguished at least partly by a certain indeterminacy of function and setting, and the most varied in method or style. The various lines of continuum that it forms with other kinds of discourse are thus to some degree lines of formal and functional specialization. At least two of the nonrhetorical aims of discourse, instrumental and scientific, have informative genuses, and rhetorical information forms lines of continuum with these in ways already suggested. More instructive for the present are lines of continuum with the other genuses of rhetoric itself: deliberative, reflective/exploratory, and performative.

As in all other cases of rhetoric, deliberation is the lodestone and the object of first attention. One potential meeting place, that of suasory advice and instruction, has already been touched upon. However, among the various paths on which information and deliberation can meet, clearly the broadest lies in the exposition of public problems. From the standpoint of deliberation, this exposition is the initial and often most troublesome stage of the problem-solving process. Debate founders, solutions go unproposed and untested, unless the existence of a problem is broadly acknowledged in a community and its causes understood. Information thus feeds into the process in a direct way. Looking at the situation from the other perspective, that of informative discourse, it is apparent that writers must choose what to write about and editors must choose what to publish, implicitly making decisions about what areas of potential deliberation to foster. Most journalists acknowledge and welcome the agenda-setting role and "social respon-sibility" outlook that such a role implies (Gerald; Shaw; Siebert, et al.). The focus on problems takes an even stronger (and sometimes nastier) turn toward deliberation in the genre of "investigative reporting," whose products sometime amount to outright indictments of their targets[8] and hence become almost entirely deliberative in orientation, while maintaining the formal posture of reportage.

Information establishes a line of continuum with reflective/explora-tory rhetoric as the author relinquishes the role of reporter, expert, or authority figure and begins to assume the role of sensitive conscious-ness through which events and experiences are projected to the reader. Such a transformation may occur in conjunction with a shift in subject matter, away from the area of public evaluation and problem-solving and toward the area of vicarious experience and entertainment. These shifts will typically be accompanied by movements toward the kind of expressive language characteristic of reflective/exploratory writing, or by literary techniques, involving narrative or dramatic modes, symbol-ism, plot, and characterization. One de facto genre that moves along this continuum is the "personal report" or "editorial correspondence"; another is the travelogue article; another is the "profile" or interview article that aims at a sensitive portrayal and assessment of the subject.

Finally, information looks in the direction of epideictic or performa-tive rhetoric in feature articles or promotional pieces that adopt a celebrative stance toward their subjects, resulting in highly positive publicity for the individuals, groups, or activities involved. In some cases, these performances lack only the institutional or occasional/com-memorative contexts that would push them completely over into epideictic.

Types of Information

The principal types of rhetorical information are informed by the Motivational Axes and are fairly well indicated in the lines of contin-uum just mentioned. The first and principal type is *reportorial* and includes the news article as well as the "news analysis," which offers coherent but relatively uncontroversial accounts of causes and implica-

8. For a lively account of such activities and the motives and attitudes connected with them, see Jessica Mitford's *Poison Penmanship*.

tions. A second type, looking toward deliberation, is *suasory* and includes problem-reports, investigative pieces, advisory articles, and some reviews,[9] as well as clearly biased reports pitched at sympathetic audiences. A third type is *experiential*, forming a line of continuum with reflective/exploratory rhetoric and the imaginative dimension. It includes personal reports, "letters," profiles, and travelogues, in which the sensibilities of the author stand as an important mediating factor. (Many examples of "new journalism," with their startling personal and quasi-literary intrusions into reportorial settings, amount to experiential informative rhetoric.) A fourth type, finally, is *celebrative*, along the continuum toward epideictic. Its standard vehicles are feature articles, profiles, "human interest" stories, and promotional pieces of the sort already mentioned.

Examples and Analyses

Contemporary civilization is awash in rhetorical information, and its extraordinary variety could not possibly be represented here, although the range of variation I believe is circumscribed by the analysis of basic types. The two examples below represent *suasory* and *experiential* subcategories of rhetorical information.

Informative Example 1: Kenneth Y. Tomlinson, "You'll Be a Hooker or Else!" *Reader's Digest*, February, 1981. Reprinted with permission from the February 1981 *Reader's Digest*. Copyright © 1981 by The Reader's Digest Assn., Inc.

> At 18, Teri DeLoache was attractive, an excellent student, a children's-hospital volunteer. Her life, however, was hardly out of a fairy tale. At night, while other teen-agers slept, whe was a waitress, working the grave-yard shift in a doughnut shop in Oakland, Calif. The hours were long and the working conditions poor.
>
> For Teri DeLoache, who had grown up in Oakland's toughest public-housing projects, waitressing was a means to an end. She was determined to get an education. Someday, she told herself, she was going to be somebody.
>
> Then, shortly after her first semester in college, her life and plans were thrown into turmoil. The restaurant's manager accused her of stealing and fired her. Teri knew she was innocent. Two days later, accompanied by a fellow waitress who would vouch for her character, whe went to Local 28 of the Hotel and Restaurant Employees and Bartenders International Union to file a grievance. Surely the union would help clear her name and perhaps through its hiring hall find her another job.

9. Although some reviews of books and artistic productions are straightforwardly deliberative in character, many are basically informative pieces, sometimes laced with mildly positive or negative characterizations of an incidental nature.

Ray Lane, the 52-year-old East Bay boss of Local 28, heard Teri's story, then said that he was late for an appointment. He told Teri to meet him next day at a nearby restaurant to discuss job possibilities.

Her ordeal began as soon as they were seated. "You don't want to be a waitress," he said firmly. "With a body like yours, you could be making big money."

Teri listened incredulously as Lane listed the jobs he had available: prostitute at a Washington convention for $300 plus expenses; topless waitress on bus junkets to Reno for $500 a weekend and any money she could make turning tricks; model in a San Francisco porno studio; and—for really big bucks—performing sexual acts with animals at a private Las Vegas club. Or, she could have an office job with Local 28 if she became Lane's mistress.

To each offer Teri said no, pleading that she only wanted a waitress job so she could continue her education. But she dared not walk out; everyone knew Local 28's hiring hall controlled the desirable waitress jobs in the East Bay, and Ray Lane was Local 28. Lane punctuated his offers with references to his political power and his connections with organized crime, and described in vulgar terms what her sexual relationship with him would have to be.

When Teri DeLoache finally got back to her apartment, she burst into tears. The date was February 17, 1976—and the worst was yet to come.

Later that week Teri found a $2.57-an-hour night-shift job at a mid-city Sambo's. Technically, she had circumvented Local 28's hiring hall. In reality, the hours were considered undesirable and these jobs frequently were filled with walk-in help. Nonetheless, Teri had to fork over monthly dues to Lane's union, and Lane came by the restaurant from time to time to see if she had changed her mind about his "jobs." To Teri he was saying, in effect, "You'll be a hooker—or else." She was polite but firm in her refusals.

Then Teri met Karin Seritis, another waitress working her way though college who had also encountered Ray Lane. "He tried to force me into prostitution and pornography," Karin told Teri.

To other colleagues Karin complained about paying union dues to Lane. *And* she complained to her Local 28 business agent about Lane's sexual harassment. Lane had a way of dealing with girls who didn't shut their mouths. He personally ordered the restaurant manager to fire Karin. It was legal; like Teri, Karin *had* circumvented the hiring hall.

Karin erupted in blind rage. Lane, she vowed, had not heard the end of this. Within days after her termination, Karin wrote to the union's international headquarters outlining her experiences with the boss of Local 28. Then she filed a formal complaint with the National Labor Relations Board (NLRB). But NLRB officials explained they could do little more than try to get back her job; from the international union she received no reply.

Then one night a Local 28 bartender appeared with a message: "Lane's got underworld connections, and he's talking about a bad accident on the freeway." Karin withdrew the complaints.

However, in the days that followed, Karin came to realize that she could not turn her back on Lane's activities. She decided to sue Lane and his union.

Meanwhile, Teri DeLoache had returned to Oakland from Long Beach, where she had had a summer-waitress job on the docked *Queen Mary*. She hoped the time away had solved her problems with Lane. But when she went to the hiring hall, Lane again said she could work only if she played his game.

By chance, Teri ran into Karin Seritis, who asked her to join in the lawsuit. It was the last thing Teri wanted to do. It would be their word against Lane's, and they were nobodies. But maybe the pressure generated by their lawsuit would stop Lane and save other young women from their experience.

In November 1976, they filed suit. Again, the same bartender confronted Karin with death threats. The telephones rang at all hours with threatening calls. At one point, Karin considered suicide. Teri lived with constant fear of death, haunted by nightmares. She lost 25 pounds.

In March 1977, the National Right to Work Legal Defense Foundation, Inc., after examining Teri, Karin and the issues involved, agreed to assume the cost and management of their case. They were no longer just two brave young women tilting at legal windmills.

James Wilhoit, a scholarly Virginia attorney, was selected to direct the litigation. He recognized that cracking the shady world of Ray Lane and Local 28 would be a herculean investigative task and turned to a most uncommon private investigator, Joan Brachmann of the West Coast based firm of Krout and Schneider. With the appearance of the warm Jewish grandmother that she was, Brachmann found few doors closed to her.

In the next months investigative file folders became file cabinets jammed with reports. It was learned that Ray Lane was in fact Raymond Robert Rosenthal, an ex-con who had served time for armed robbery. His takeover of Local 28, as well as chunks of his life, were shrouded in mystery. So, too, were his close relationships with leaders of the Hotel and Restaurant Workers International, a union which U.S. Justice Department investigators say is "completely dominated by men who either have strong ties to, or are members of, the organized-crime syndicate."

Brachmann went into the case with professional skepticism. But as she knocked on the doors of waitresses and former waitresses, the evidence fell into place. The same stories were told repeatedly by women Lane had sought to victimize.

Many were relieved that someone finally had mustered the courage to challenge Ray Lane. One woman, the sole breadwinner for two children, had gone to Lane desperate for a job. Once she had agreed to be his mistress, Lane placed her in a comfortable position at a Bay Area race-track. But there was a limit to what she would do—even for the sake of her children. Suddenly, she was out of a job. Would she testify? Yes, she would.

There were, of course, numerous dead ends. Brachmann followed the trails of women as far as Florida and Washington, D.C., before they dropped from sight. Other women changed their stories when they realized they would be required to appear in court.

One woman, a former gospel singer, had found employment as an organizer for Lane's union. Brachmann suspected Lane had used the woman for more than organizing. But now she was married. Her parents were church leaders, and she wanted no notoriety from the Lane case in her new life. A few days before the trial began, however, she telephoned Wilhoit. She had told her family about Lane, and felt it was her responsibility to testify. On union trips to Los Angeles and Palm Springs, Lane had coerced her to have intercourse or lose her job.

As the National Right to Work Legal Defense Foundation pursued its investigation of Lane, so too did the Justice Department's Organized Crime Strike Force. Indicted in 1978 on 30 counts of embezzlement, racketerring and obstruction of justice, Lane copped a plea to one charge of embezzlement. He was sentenced to two years in prison, with all but six months suspended, and fined $5000. (As required by law, he had to resign his union job.)

For attorney Wilhoit and detective Brachmann, the four-day civil trial last February was anti-climactic. The real work of assembling the case had come to an end. For Teri and Karin the trial was an unforgettable experience. They told their stories not knowing if they would be believed. They watched with gratitude as woman after woman testified against Ray Lane. They listened as an eminent psychiatrist described the trauma they had endured.

On March 10, California's Superior Court Judge Robert H. Kroninger handed down his decision. He ordered the union to pay them $75,000 each and both Lane and the union to pay Teri an additional $75,000. Although the case is on appeal, many legal authorities believe the finding will turn out to be a landmark decision both in terms of women's rights and the legal responsibilities of unions that enjoy the right of exclusive representation.

Today, Karin Seritis is back in college studying to be a structural engineer. Teri DeLoache is both a student and a buyer for a drugstore chain. The two women remain intensely ambitious, determined that one day they will do something extraordinary in life.

In fact, they already have.

COMMENTARY

A good deal of suasory information is directed at insiders, contains overtly evaluative language, and is larded with signals of group allegience. While the audience of this piece is an identifiable one—the predominately middle-class, conservative, over-thirty readership of *Reader's Digest*—the appeal of the piece is not specifically to insiders, and there are few such signals. The immediate appeal of the piece is aesthetic—of the somewhat sensationalist human-interest variety— with a narrative that is captivating and well-crafted in its own right. The suasory status of the piece lies not in its assumptions of allegiance but

in its implicit service to a broad political outlook that is consistently projected by the *Reader's Digest* organization. Composed as a special entry
(that is, not condensed from some other publication) by an associate
editor of the magazine, the article supports in an implicit way the magazine's probusiness, antilabor political stance. It is deliberately bad press
for labor unions, good press for the National Right to Work Legal
Defense Foundation, whose exertions in behalf of the two victimized
waitresses are described at great length.

Although the author supplies virtually no direct commentary,
allowing the chilling story to speak for itself to a large extent, he does
employ a form of narrative with enough discursive clues to draw distinct lines between good and evil in the case. The union boss and his
auxiliaries are presented in ways that inspire amazed indignation and
reinforce gangster stereotypes. On the other side, the Right to Work
Foundation's lawyer is described as a "scholarly Virginian attorney,"
while the private investigator on the case is almost too good to be true:
a "warm Jewish grandmother." And the penultimate paragraph
presents discursively the political significance of the story and the lawsuit, speculating that the judge's ruling "will turn out to be a landmark
decision both in terms of women's rights and the legal responsibilities
of unions that enjoy the rights of exclusive representation."

Informative Example 2: Mollie Panter-Downes, "Letter from London," *The New
Yorker*, June 8, 1981. Reprinted by permission.

                                                                    MAY 28
The at first incredulous shock and despair at the shooting of Pope John
Paul, and the relief when the more hopeful bulletins answered the prayers
of people of every denomination or none, seems to tie up confusedly in the
thoughts of some citizens with their despair over the continuous outrage of
Ulster, on which a healthier prognosis would indeed seem a miracle. The
Guardian reprinted the Pope's blunt words to the ecstatic Drogheda crowds
in 1979, so that they could be read with sad, ironic hindsight: "Violence
destroys what it claims to defend—the dignity, the life, the freedom of
human beings. . . . Let none concerned with Ireland have any illusions
about the nature and the menace of political violence." After the latest brutal murder, this time of the five young British soldiers blown up a fortnight
ago in South Armagh, the bitter public mood toward the catalogue of
losses, military and civilian, seems to be hardening. There is no doubt that
even those who are angrily against Mrs. Thatcher and her Government are
for once behind her in her refusal to be pressured into giving political status to the hunger strikers. The Opposition in Parliament—barring a handful of left-wing Labour Members, now joined by the maverick Tony
Wedgwood Benn, who loses no useful opportunity to show Michael Foot,
his leader, that he is not following—are so far unbudging in their support,
saying no to turning the Maze Prison into a licensed I.R.A. club on terms

that would surely encourage more recruitment to it. The emotional anti-British sentiments in American and European papers caused surprise and much irritation therefore. Not that there is not plenty of muddled emotion here on the subject. According to a recent opinion poll, large numbers of British, while backing Margaret Thatcher on the hunger-strikers issue, would yet be profoundly thankful if they could wake up one morning to find out that this nightmare of a mostly unknown province, for which they have to shell out in taxes, and to which they must send their sons to be killed trying to keep the peace, had been lifted off their chests into the large Irish air. More down-to-earth and historically better-informed realists, who understand that there is not the ghost of a moral or honorable chance of any weakening of the Government's obligation to its citizens over the water, can only hope desperately that there will be more talking between London and Dublin in the House of Commons when it gets back from recess, and between all the parties everywhere, which might turn up a new initiative in the present awful deadlock.

It is no wonder that a good deal of anxious speculation is going on about London's festive nuptial event in July. It seems a very long time to all since the celebrations of the Queen's Silver Jubilee, when she rode to St. Paul's visible and apparently vulnerable inside a state coach designed to display her like a glass showcase. The royal wedding will doubtless be managed with the same lofty insouciance as far as the crowds will be able to see, but people discussing the risky possibilities sound as uneasy as the I.R.A. would certainly like them to be. Meanwhile, the bride-to-be continues to win glowing opinions from people who have watched her making the not very onerous public appearances with her fiance that are obvious warm-up exercises for a life that will often have to include such things. She has already added a new dimension of gaiety to the usual calm style of royal occasions. On a recent stroll along a line of waving children and beaming mothers, she accepted the standard limp flowers from a few of the little girls and then reached over suddenly and tugged a surprised little boy's hat smartly down over his nose, to shrieks of delighted laughter from all. She looks so dazzlingly young that people feel protective about her when they think about the unceasing job she is taking on. They seem to be absolutely confident, though, that she will do it in her own way, and that it will be just right.

. . . .

The weather is continuing bad news. This has been the meanest, most dispiriting spring that anyone can remember, delivering snowstorms, claps of thunder, strong gales, and, during May, buckets of rain. The whole of the country is like a sopping green sponge. The Bank Holiday sports were washed out, and so are the farmers' fields, in which the seeds are rotting. Shopkeepers, already worried to death, are looking glumly at stocks of summery gear while the customers splash by crossly under their umbrellas. The cold and the wet have been seemingly relished, though, by nature in London and suburban gardens. The azalea patch in Kensington Gardens has treated passengers on tops of buses to a mad Fauve riot of color, and the chestnut trees in the great royal parks have been a sight to see in the exceptional opulence of their loaded pink and white candelabra.

COMMENTARY

Here is an example of *experiential* information, in this case a combination of observations, reflections, and opinions amounting to a rendering of the atmosphere, the general feel of a place at a certain moment. Not merely the generic veil of the "letter" but also the leisurely pace, laconic tone, and high degree of personal reflection signal that here is information projected through the sensibility of the author—in this case a sensibility and intellect appropriately congenial, or at least understandable and acceptable, to the customary audience of *New Yorker*. (My own excision of several middle paragraphs does not detract from the sense of unhurriedness, and the sense of episodic drifting would also be there in any case.) This discourse has no particular proposition to establish or issue to explore; the various details and explanations and reactions reflect the interests (even whims) of the author as well as her literary sense of how to project a general atmosphere.

In many instances of experiential information, the author is even more of a direct presence, a character in his or her own first-person account of things, in a more directly expressive mode than we find here, and expressing opinions more directly and openly. The following excerpt is from a much longer piece in the same specific genre:

> There is a sense of loss here. It has come over the city as a kind of quickening sadness, like one of those early spring evenings that suddenly light the blackened stones of Parliament and the Embankment with streaks of gold. Everybody has an explanation for it. People talk about 'the decline'—which is the fashionable phrase lately—as if the country's distress were a moment in some historical aesthetic, something to survive and savor. . . . It is as if Londoners were grieving for themselves, for the decency they have always held, as an article of faith, to be a particularly English quality, for the civility, the fairness of mind and spirit, that they believe is finally what sets them apart from millions of smarmy and disreputable Europeans waiting just across the channel to corrupt them. They seem to be suffering from a loss of faith in the British character. . . . (Jane Kramer, "A Reporter in Europe—London," *The New Yorker* May 11, 1981)

Even though the "Letter from London," which stands as our primary example, does not contain such overt subjectivity as this quotation displays, signs of the author's reflective and evaluative presence are detectible in various places:

Not that there is not plenty of muddled emotion here on the subject . . . (par. 1)

It is no wonder that a good deal of anxious speculation is going on . . . (par. 2)

This has been the meanest, most dispiriting spring that anyone can remember . . . (final par.)

These elements, along with the organization and tone of the piece, place it in the experiential quadrant of the informational compass, but they do not push it over into reflective/exploratory rhetoric. The author stands as trusted agent of observation and reflection, and the audience's gaze is fixed on the experience as projected through her, rather than on her response to the experience.

III. PERFORMATIVE RHETORIC (EPIDEICTIC)

Just as there is a kind of *instrumental* information, which is highly conventional and guides practical operations, and also a kind of *rhetorical* information, which operates in a broader sphere and informs general opinion, so there is a kind of *instrumental* performative discourse, which is highly conventional and performs legal and business transactions, and also a kind *rhetorical* performative, which engages human values and loyalties. This is the rhetorical category traditionally known as epideictic. Its usual purpose is neither to substantiate theses nor to communicate information but to perform public acts of commemoration, declaration, celebration, recognition, among others, in connection with the functions and values of public institutions. Adapting once again the language of J. L. Austin, we may define the work of performative or epideictic rhetoric as the unified act of rhetoric which does not merely say, argue, or allege something about the world of social action, but which constitutes (in a way usually determined by the conventions or customs of a community) a significant social action in itself. To a remarkable extent, it participates in the reality to which it refers.[10] Prominent *de facto* genres include the following: the obituary editorial or essay; the anniversary or commemoration essay; the "appreciation," focused either on individuals, institutions, or accomplishments such as art works; the book preface or dedicatory essay; the "testimony," particulary in religious contexts; and in modern times, the political manifesto or declaration.

10. For an extended definition and defense of the category along these lines, see Beale. On traditional epideictic see Burgess, Buchheit, and Chase.

Historically, epideictic has identifying associations with public ceremony, with stylistic display, and with literary art. While these associations persist, particularly for oral rhetoric, the development of literate
culture has modified them, and they have become particularly weak
definers of written epideictic. The separation of writing from immediate
contexts-of-situation is the most important factor in this development,
affecting the form and content of individual performances, and more
important, the character and range of the genus itself.

A great deal of written epideictic is quasi-ceremonial in character,
and many printed pieces are in fact speeches edited for publication. But
written epideictic is always at most occasional, never actually embedded in ceremony; its audiences are potentially broader, its subjects and
strategies less directed by the actual moment. And like most modern
rhetorical writing, while employing a wide range of stylistic and organizational strategies, it studiously avoids the kind of stylistic ornament
and flambuoyance associated with traditional oral epideictic.

The emancipation from ceremony has also broadened the range of
the genus, into subjects and situations for which the forums of oral discourse are inaccessible or nonexistent. This emancipation is partially
evident, from classical times onward, in the literature of occasions and
in the appropriation of epideictic genres to literary art (Burgess, Hardison). Traditional literary epideictic, however, retains very close ties to
speechmaking; today we witness a great outpouring of epideictic prose,
in thousands of institutional, special-interest, or in-house publications,
which exist not merely to provide information about but also to pro-
mote the causes of their subjects and institutions. The abundance of
these writings goes hand in hand with the enormous increase in the
density of written communication in modern times.

Cicero comes close to identifying the social function of epideictic,
noting that this type of rhetoric "does not establish propositions that
are doubtful but amplifies statements that are certain" (*Partitiones
Oratoriae* xxi, 71). This function has in modern theory been re-empha-
sized by Perelman:

> Unlike the demonstration of a geometrical theorem, which establishes once
> and for all a logical connection between speculative truths, the argumenta-
> tion in epideictic discourse sets out to increase the intensity of adherence to
> certain values, which might not be contested when considered on their
> own but may nevertheless not prevail against other values that might come
> into conflict with them. (51)

This observation explains why epideictic, even when distinctly
argumentative in method, has the effect of intensifying or reaffirming
propositions rather than of establishing them. This feature, often dis-

cernible more readily from the context of a work than from its form or style, perhaps more than any other specifies the "performative" quality of the genus.

In homogeneous and authoritarian cultures, as well as in the modern totalitarian state, performative rhetoric tends to be the special property of a political or intellectual elite. (It also tends to engulf other branches of rhetoric: One sees this most clearly in the insistence of dictators and dictatorial bureaucracies that all communication reaffirm the cause and continue the struggle.) But in modern times rhetorical performative discourse has come to play a role in the conflict and competition among political and social movements, where a dominant strategy has become not so much to argue the superiority of certain ideas or policies as to demonstrate and reaffirm the force, legitimacy, or solidarity of the movement. In such instances, particularly those involving the publication of resolutions and declarations by interest groups and professional organizations, performative rhetoric seeks to intensify and enlarge the support for propositions within the membership of a specific group, but it also hopes to affect a larger audience by throwing the prestige of the entire group behind the proposition. Such instances form a line of continuum with "operational deliberation," feeding into the processes of deliberation much more directly than does traditional epideictic.

The American Declaration of Independence is a notable example of modern performative rhetoric in writing. It is often represented in composition textbooks under the heading of "argumentation," and it does well illustrate the method of syllogistic reasoning. It is not deliberative, however. The purpose of the Declaration is not to argue that the colonies ought to declare their independence but rather to assert their independence. Its arguments do not participate in a process of deliberation or problem-solving; they have the status of justifying clauses in a resolution.[11] As such, they have both persuasive and directive purposes: They attempt to inspire and solidify colonial support for the declaration and they seek the support of all rational people and nations. They are also addressed to posterity, setting forth the political principles on which the new nation must be founded. Any future government must adhere to these principles.

J. L. Austin remarks that the success of performative utterance is less dependent upon its truth or reference value than upon valididating conditions within the communicative situation itself, particularly the relationships of status between interlocutors (14–15). (The person who

---

11. Kinneavy also calls attention to the nondeliberative character of the Declaration (409–18). He overlooks its performative nature, however, and misses entirely the connection with epideictic. Kinneavy regards the Declaration as an example of "expressive discourse," a category I have rejected.

pronounces two people "man and wife" must have the authority to do so, for instance, and he must do so under the appropriate conditions.) It follows that author/audience relations are particularly important to epideictic, and it is no accident that the authorship of performative rhetoric is often authoritative. There are important exceptions, of course, but even where no special relationship is apparent, the discourse often stands as the voice or record of the institution of publication, which stands for certain values or interests and has some prestigious standing in a community.

Types of Performative Rhetoric

Propositional status provides an interesting though weak partition of some epideictic types. Although Austin rejects *per se* the notion of performative speech acts, he does provide a useful subclassification of "illocutions," the performative dimensions of speech acts (152–59). It is possible to discover in these types the nuclei or central propositional elements of some easily recognizable genres. These are here arranged to form a continuum from subjective to objective focus.

Behabitives. This category involves "reaction to other people's behavior," and it includes such acts as apologizing, thanking, condoling, welcoming, bidding farewell, and congratulating. In these we recognize the the nuclei of various occasional genres, such as obituary essays, welcoming, valedictory and congratulatory editorials, and commemorative essays.

Commissives. These "commit the speaker to a certain course of action," and they include promising, undertaking, contracting, pledging, and swearing. The most common form of commissive discourse is not rhetorical but instrumental: the legal contract. Commissives do play an important role in the written counterparts to acceptance speeches, maiden addresses, and the like. In resolutions passed by delegate assemblies of various professional organizations and interest groups, commissives are often made on *behalf* of an audience. ("We pledge our continued support for . . .")

Exercitives. These involve the "decision that something is to be so, as opposed to a judgment that it is to be so"; they include such acts as appointing, dismissing, naming, enacting, and dedicating. Exercitives play a greater role in instrumental discourse (laws, regulations) and in oral than in written epideictic, but they do form the nuclei of written declarations such as the Declaration of Independence.

Verdictives. These "consist in the delivering of a finding, official or unofficial, upon evidence or reasons as to value or fact," including such acts as finding, ranking, acquitting, and convicting. These are non-starters for epideictic; they are almost exclusively the nuclei of either instrumental discourse or instrumental rhetorical deliberation (above 121–22).

Expositives. These are "used in acts of exposition involving the expounding of views, the conducting of arguments, clarifying of usages and of references"; they include such acts as conceding, urging, defying, agreeing, and testifying. We must tread carefully here, because this category includes precisely the kinds of utterance that Austin originally classed as nonperformative. But there is really no difficulty with regard to the role of these utterances in performative rhetorical acts. The key to the role of expositives—we might term them *quasi-informative* or *quasi-deliberative* nuclei—in performative rhetoric is that they "signify something quite apart from the general representation of ideas to the mind of the audience" (Chase 296). They have a public, celebrative, or commemorative character, and in some cases an official or authoritative status within a community. They typically do not break new ground: They remind, reiterate, reinforce, and amplify. Some "expositive" genres of epideictic include the "appreciation" article, the inspirational or testimonial narrative, and in specifically religious contexts, the "devotion" and the moral/theological "lesson."

Lines of Continuum and the Motivational Axes

The partition suggested by Austin's propositional analysis is illuminating enough, but taken by itself it forms a less than satisfactory theory because it does not bring fully into play the situational determinants of discourse. A more comprehensive view, once again, may be suggested by the Motivational Axes, as we examine of lines of continuum toward other rhetorical genuses, with an eye toward the ways in which the single genus mirrors the rhetorical world at large.

A type which immediately suggests itself is the *celebrative*, and it should be considered the paradigmatic performative type (in the same way that deliberation is the basic rhetorical type or that reportorial is the basic informative type), since it is most clearly and directly involved in public acts of commemoration. Its placement is in the direction of performative rhetoric itself, looking toward the operational dimension of the Motivational Axes.

The second type, *suasory*, forms a direct line of continuum with deliberation, and it has two distinct varieties: The first is the kind of political resolution or declaration already mentioned, usually a document of multiple authorship, claiming to be the voice of an entire community or constituency; the second is the essay of single authorship which seizes an occasion—usually an anniversary or holiday—to attempt to rekindle an audience in behalf of some broad cultural premise. Such discourse uses argumentation to "increase the intensity of adherence to certain values, which might not be contested when considered on their own but may nevertheless not prevail against other values that might come into contact with them" (Perelman 51). Familiar topics of suasory epideictic include such values as freedom of the press, free enterprise, courage, and discipline, and all sorts of civic virtues in which audiences are implored to "keep the faith."

A third type of performative rhetoric, forming a line of continuum with rhetorical information, is the *instructive*. This type usually deals with a matter of interpretation or value, and its author is usually cast in the role of mentor, spiritual leader, or savant. The purpose of instructive performative rhetoric is to interpret and reinforce the value, importance, or true significance of a thing. Examples include the moral/theological "lesson," the religious meditation or devotion, the "appreciation" essay, and the "What I Believe" or "What We Stand For" essay.

The last type of rhetorical performative is the *experiential*, which forms a direct line of continuum with reflective/exploratory rhetoric and is often indistinguishable from it in form. What most often distinguishes the two—especially in the most prominent genre of experiential performative, the testimonial narrative—is that in performative rhetoric, points of interpretation and reflection are suggested and controlled by the established concepts and traditions of a particular community, usually a particular religious tradition. In reflective/exploratory rhetoric, by contrast, these points of interpretation are more original, even private and idiosyncratic.

Examples and Analyses

Most performative types are easily recognizable, either by subject, form, or context. The two examples below represent somewhat difficult cases, and they illustrate how the print medium places strains on traditional categories while at the same time gathering substance and support from them.

Performative Example 1: Anthony Lewis, "We Gather Together," *New York Times*, November 26, 1981. Copyright © 1978/81 by The New York Times Company. Reprinted by permission.

Thanksgiving Day, as history and symbol, throws some curious light on a myth of our day: that American greatness came from free enterprise, from individual rather than community effort, and that a return to individualism can solve our current problems. That myth informs Ronald Reagan's whole political program, and a lot of people believe it. But it is a myth.

The Pilgrims who landed at Plymouth Harbor in 1620 were a community in the deepest sense. Those in charge were a group of separatist religious believers, moved by their faith to seek a place where they could live in their own way together, undisturbed by outsiders.

Their survival in the new land depended on joint struggle, and on the help of friendly Indians. Half the colonists died during their first terrible winter. When Governor William Bradford declared a thanksgiving to celebrate their first harvest in 1621, Indians shared the feast.

Individualism in the political sense was there at the beginning. In the Mayflower Compact, drafted on the way across the Atlantic, the company agreed that their settlement would be governed by majority rule. There was no divine right or inherited rank; every man had an equal vote.

The development of this country has been shaped, from that beginning, by a mix of individualism and community enterprise: at times more of one than the other, then swinging back. It was an America of pioneers and frontiersmen—but also, by some of our earliest political decisions, of public roads and a national postal system. It was a country of Horatio Alger and Henry Ford—but also of public schools and public libraries.

One of the distinctive aspects of American culture was and is an expression of community. That is the existence of myriad civic organizations: the educational, business, professional and philanthropic groups that have such an influence on the society. We are so used to these collective enterprises that we do not usually realize how American they are: how much more numerous and significant, for example, than they are in European countries.

Since the 1930's we have looked increasingly to government to meet community needs. That is the trend that President Reagan says he wants to stop, and he has a point—especially about the concentration of responsibility in Washington. Liberals, too, ought to recognize that we sometimes go too far in relying on the Federal Government to solve local problems. The point was made 50 years ago by that great liberal, Louis Brandeis.

But it does not follow that national programs are automatically bad, that ending Federal regulations will always free the people's creative energies, or still less that individual enterprise can solve all of today's social and economic problems. Those are not just myths but pernicious ones.

Like it or not, the United States is a nation now—much more so than before the 1930's, with a national economy and a highly mobile population. We need a national monetary policy, a Federal system of unemployment insurance, a Social Security system.

Nor can we escape the consequences as a nation if we ignore social evils here or there. We learned in the 1950's and 1960's that the country as a whole was damaged when black citizens were not allowed to vote in Mississippi, and it would be a disaster if the national commitment against racial discrimination were weakened now. And the same for the food stamp program, by which the richest country on earth protects its poor and weak from hunger: a highly efficient way to meet a community responsibility.

The most misguided notion in the current political rhetoric, and the most dangerous, may be the idea that relaxing Federal environmental standards will help the economy. And it is not just an idea. The Environmental Protection Agency is eliminating wholesale the rules that protect our air and land and water.

It is the very essence of an industrial world's environmental problems that they cannot be met by individual or local action. What happens in one place affects others. Poison in Chesapeake Bay or the Hudson River touches the striped bass fishermen of New England. Sulfur fumes coming from the smokestacks of the Middle West poison the lakes of New York State and Canada with acid rain.

When we speak of the environment these days, we are most often talking about health. It is not just a question of esthetics when the E.P.A. undoes just about all the restraints on toxic waste dumping—as it has done in the alst 10 months. It is not just some "environmental extremists" who will suffer if the E.P.A. budget is cut in half from its 1981 fiscal year level, as the Reagan budget-cutters are trying to do.

There are community values that can be preserved only by action of the community. And Americans really do understand that. In a recent poll 61 percent said they would keep present clean-air laws even if some factories must close. Thanksgiving is a good time to remember that America is not synonymous with individual greed.

COMMENTARY

Perilously perhaps, this example of *suasory* epideictic moves farther along the continuum toward deliberation than most occasional and commemorative pieces. It does have the form of deliberative rhetoric and a rather combative tone, but other significant features keep it in the territory of performative rhetoric. It is, first of all, unmistakably occasional: Both its subject and theme are drawn directly from the traditions of the Thanksgiving holiday, and although the piece makes explicit reference to contemporary political struggles, it is clearly inspired by the holiday itself rather than any particular focusing event in the political world. More importantly, its thesis involves no particular point of policy, evaluation, or interpretation but rather a matter of broad cultural and political consensus—the value of community enterprise—and this is precisely the sort of proposition that belongs to epideictic: one that "might not be contested when considered on its own but may nevertheless not prevail against other values . . ." The purpose of the article is to stress this value and to remind readers that it is central to the idea of America, rooted in its earliest and deepest traditions.

The combative tone of the piece and its movement toward deliberation are due not merely to Lewis' insistence upon pointing to specific ramifications of public policy but also to the broader historical context: It was written at a time when current political rhetoric had placed the contrary values of public and private enterprise in sharper-than-usual conflict, and when the current government seemed ideologically committed to the latter. It is notable also that this particular message is delivered by one of America's leading spokesmen for the liberal statist point of view, and in the newspaper known as a leading supporter of that point of view. The debate represented here is of the sort that is never fully resolved, because there is truth and broad consensus for both individualistic and community values, even as different political persuasions emphasize one over the other and, more importantly, define such things as "community enterprise" and "private enterprise," in different ways. It is not inconceivable that on this very Thanksgiving Day, a similar essay might have appeared in a right-of-center publication, extolling "community values," and blaming the party of Anthony Lewis for an excessive preoccupation with individual rights.

A final point. This essay well represents the effects of one of the powerful features of written discourse—the emancipation from direct ceremony and immediate contexts-of-situation. This is secular written epideictic, with no particular institutional focus other than the nation, well suited (at least in its opening paragraphs) to a very broad readership, as opposed to a specific and physically present audience. The essay also represents a possible liability of the emancipation from direct ceremony, for Lewis here strays more easily into the byways of partisan policy debate than might have been his inclination upon a distinct ceremonial occasion and in the presence of a live audience. Even if we take that audience to be the party of the likeminded, which it cannot entirely be, Lewis' departures from thematic generality and also from the quasi-ceremonial tone of thanksgiving and community spirit established at the beginning are potential spoilers of the discourse.

Performative Example 2: Frederic Morton, "Kristallnacht," *New York Times*, November 10, 1978. Reprinted by permission of the Sterling Lord Agency, Inc. Copyright © 1978 by Frederic Morton.

Forty years ago—on Nov. 9–10, 1938—the Nazis attacked Jews, Jewish-owned property, and synagogues throughout Germany and Austria. The action was in retaliation for the assassination of Ernst Vom Roth, third secretary of the German Embassy in Paris, by Herschel Grynszpan, the son of Polish Jews who lived in Germany until their deportation to the Polish-German frontier a month earlier. The death and destruction marked a turning point in the treatment of Jews and accelerated their emigration. As the Nazis swept through the Jews' lives, arresting and sending victims to Buchenwald, Sachsenshausen and Dachau, they left in the streets a trail of broken windows. Hence, Kristallnacht—"Crystal Night." [Editor]

The day began with a thudding through my pillow. Jolts waked me. Then, like an alarm clock, the doorbell rang. It was six in the morning. My father, my mother, my little brother and I all met in the foyer, all in our robes. We did not know yet exactly what. But we *knew*. We were Jews in Vienna in 1938. Everything in our lives, including our beds, stood on a cliff.

My father opened the door on Frau Eckel, the janitress.

"They are down there . . . they are throwing things." She turned away. Went on with her morning sweep. Her broom trembled.

We looked down into the courtyard. Pink-cheeked storm troopers chatted and whistled. Chopped-up furniture flew through the window. The troopers fielded the pieces sportively, piled them into heaps. One hummed something from "The Merry Widow."

"Franz! Run somewhere!" my mother said to my father.

By that time we'd gone to the window facing the street. At the house entrance two storm troopers lit cigarettes for each other. Their comrades were smashing the synagogue on the floor below us, tossing out a debris of Torahs and pews.

"Oh, my God!" my mother said.

Something overwhelming wanted to melt down my eyes. I couldn't let it. All this might not be real as long as real tears did not touch my face. A crazy last-resort bargain with fate.

"All right," my father said. "Meanwhile we get dressed."

Meanwhile meant *until they come up here.* No other Jews lived in the building. It had no back door. But as long as I could keep my tears down, I could keep *them* down. While they were destroying down there, they would not come up here. As long as the shaking of the floor continued, the axe blows, the sledgehammer thuds, we might live.

I had gym for my first class. I laced on my sneakers. I knew I never would see school that morning. I didn't care that I knew. I only cared not to cry. I tried to pour my entire mind into the lacing of my sneakers.

We met in the living room. We saw each other dressed with a normality made grotesque by the crashing of the perdition downstairs. It stopped. The shaking and the thudding stopped. Silence. A different sound. Heavy, booted steps ascending. I relaced my sneakers.

My father had put on his hat. "Everybody come close to me," he said. "My two sons, you put your hands on top of your heads."

We put our hands on top of our heads, as hats. My father put his arms around all our shoulders, my mother's, my brother's, mine.

"*Shema Yisroel,*" my father said. "Repeat after me: *Shema Yisroel Adonoy Elohenu Adonay Echod. . . .*" ["Hear, O Israel: the Lord our God, the Lord is One. . . ."]

The doorbell rang. Once. Ever since *the Anschluss,* we'd rung our doorbell twice in quick succession to signal that this was a harmless ringing, not the dreaded one. Now the dreaded ring had come.

"Hansi, you go," my father said.

"No!" my mother said.

"Hansi is the only one they might not hurt on sight," my father said. "Hansi, go."

My brother, a tiny blond eight-year-old, an Aryan-looking doll, went.

A minute later he returned. Behind him towered some 10 storm troopers with heavy pickaxes. They were young and bright-faced with excitement. Ten bridegrooms on their wedding day. One had freckles. How could a freckle-faced man kill us? The freckles kept me from crying.

"House search," the leader said. "Don't move."

We all stood against the wall, except my father. He placed himself, hat still on, a foot in front of us.

They yanked out every drawer in every one of our chests and cupboards, and tossed each in the air. They let the cutlery jangle across the floor, the clothes scatter, and stepped over the mess to fling the next drawer. Their exuberance was amazing. Amazing, that none of them raised an axe to split our skulls.

"We might be back," the leader said. On the way out he threw our mother-of-pearl ashtray over his shoulder, like confetti. We did not speak or move or breathe until we heard their boots against the pavement.

"I am going to the office," my father said. "Breitel might help."

Breitel, the Reich commissar in my father's costume-jewelry factory, was a "good" Nazi. Once he'd said we should come to him if there was trouble. My father left. My mother was crying, with relief, with terror; she cradled against herself my little stunned brother. I turned away from her. I swore I would do something other than cry.

I began to pick up my clothes, when the doorbell rang again. It was my father.

"I have two minutes."

"*What?*" my mother said. But she knew. His eyes had become glass.

"There was another crew waiting for me downstairs. They gave me two minutes."

Now I broke down. Now my father was the only one not crying. His eyes were blue glass, relentlessly dry. His kiss felt stubbly. He had not shaved this morning. After one more embrace with my mother he marched to the door, turned on his heel, called out.

"*Fritz!*"

I went to him, sobbing.

"*Stop!*"

I couldn't stop.

Harshly his hands came down on my shoulders.

"If I don't come back—avenge me!"

He was gone. The fury of his fingers stung. It burned into my skin a sense of continuity against all odds. I stopped.

Four months later he rang our doorbell twice, skull shaven, skeletal, released from Dachau, somehow alive.

Forty years later, today, he is practicing the tango with my mother in Miami Beach. My little brother Hansi is chairman of the political science department at Queens College. I am a writer in America with an American family. We are atypically lucky. But to this day we all ring our American doorbells twice.

COMMENTARY

Here is an example of *experiential* epideictic fixed to a specific occasion: the anniversary of the event described, "Kristallnacht." The necessity of the editor's note signals a substantial difference between

this and the kind of occasional setting enjoyed by Anthony Lewis'
Thanksgiving essay above. Here is an occasion which, already well-
known to many, requires historical introduction for the essay's broad
readership; and in fact one of the purposes of the piece is undoubtedly to broaden as well as perpetuate memory of the event. Though
many readers will have found a good deal of information in the piece,
it is not informative rhetoric. It is delivered from the perspective of a
uniquely qualified author, and it is charged with the communication
of value. On the other hand, while it has some of the literaryness and
expressive, individualistic perspective of reflective/exploratory rhetoric, it has not the texture and development (which would require considerable extension) of a reflective/exploratory essay. The occasion
frames the piece and serves as its raison d'être in its present form and
setting.

Although the narrative is not tightly thematic, the article's dominant impressions are of the chilling contrast between the boyish
appearance and the gruesome purposes of the Kristallnacht storm-
troopers, as well as the contrast between the family's situation in
Germany forty years ago and in America today. The reader experiences these events from the perspective of the author's childhood,
and the experience is in itself a repudiation of certain values and a
reaffirmation of others.

IV. REFLECTIVE/EXPLORATORY RHETORIC

The definition of reflective/exploratory rhetoric may be recapitu-
lated in the following features:

1. the general purpose, not so much to persuade or inform as to stimulate and
   entertain an audience, while sharing and reflecting upon experience;
2. an informal, conversational, intimate, and often rambling style;
3. the cultivation of individuality, in both style and viewpoint;
4. a frequent use of narrative and dramatic modes, in ways that approach
   poetic.

Considering the relations of rhetoric to the larger aims of discourse, the
fundamental alignments of reflective/exploratory are theoretically with
the imaginative dimension and historically with the tradition of belles
lettres. This relation is borne out not merely in the cultivation of style
but also in the appropriation of themes and conceptual patterns characteristic of literary art, especially lyric and occasional poetry.

The lineage of reflective/exploratory rhetoric is basically that of the
familiar essay, and the history of that genre reveals developments that

help to account for the variety that exists in contemporary writing.[12] The "essais" of Montaigne have direct antecedents in the "leçon" or informal moral disquisition. In Montaigne's case, however, they are highly individualized, original, and searching, rather than conventional; rambling and idiosyncratic, rather than correct and formal. They are instructive and persuasive, and at the same time highly personal and playful explorations of truth and value. This instructive and persuasive element is retained to a certain degree by eighteenth century periodical essayists, but the subsequent history of the genre, at least through the nineteenth and early twentieth centuries, has involved a substantial degree of specialization in the direction of literature or belles lettres—a movement that parallels the specializations of other genres as well. The flowering of the personal, experiential, literary essay, conspicuously distinct now from both scientific discourse and rhetorical deliberation, is a reflection of this development as well as of literary romanticism.

While the romantic tradition continues in the twentieth century (more strongly in the essay, actually, than in poetry), modernity has occasioned some developments away from subjectivity and the expression of personality, and toward exploration upon distinct fields of subject matter. In contrast to the romantic essayist (Lamb, Hazlitt, Stevenson), who depended upon the persona of the general man-of-letters and cultivated sensibility, the twentieth century essayist is more likely to draw upon specialized knowledge or experience in science, politics, or one of the professions.[13]

The most recent twentieth-century development, fostered in part by the contemporary flourishing of the regularly appearing "op-ed" column, is the movement toward subjects of contemporary news interest—subjects that are also matters of contemporary information and deliberation. Whereas the traditional familiar essayist ventures not very far beyond the generalized areas of "manners and morals" and armchair psychology, addressing a leisured audience assumed to have literary predilections, the contemporary journalist-essayist writes for a much broader, more hurried audience, catering to subjects already on the reader's mind, usually suggested by information or deliberation in the same issue of the same magazine or newspaper. Particular instances of this sort are not by any means the exclusive province of the regularly-appearing column, but that forum does provide a special opportunity for building the personal dimension crucial to the genre: a regular space

12. On the history and character of the familiar essay see Bryan and Crane, Law, Lukacs, Marr, Thompson, and Whitmore.
13. While a modern essayist like E. B. White remains firmly in the romantic tradition, modern developments toward less personalized reflection within distinct subject areas are repesented by such writers as Loren Eisley and Lewis Thomas (science); George Orwell and Joan Didion (journalism, social commentary); George Will and Ellen Goodman (politics and contemporary social issues.

wherein the author becomes known as a personality, develops a distinctive persona, cultivates a distinctive literary style, and establishes clear identifications with certain subjects, interests, or persuasions. Many of the author's columns will be deliberative or informative, but the general situation makes it possible and even desirable to work in an occasional reflective/exploratory or performative item.

Conceptual Patterns

Neither classical nor modern systems of rhetorical invention comprehend very well the intellectual designs of most reflective/exploratory writing, for they are really more akin to literary art. Like poems and short stories, reflective/exploratory essays often derive their success and interest from surprising or entertaining syntheses and disjunctions—provocative analogies, elevations of the lowly, defamiliarizations of the commonplace, familiarizations of the out-of-the-way and bizarre, depreciations of common wisdom. The tradition of the familiar essay reveals three particularly congenial conceptual patterns: the paradoxical, the enigmatic, and the emblematic.

Paradoxes are wonderful reflective instruments, startling writers and readers into discoveries of new truths and rediscoveries of old ones. The course of paradoxical reflection is the creation and resolution of emotional or intellectual conflict, and the startling perception of reality in the coalescence of opposites. It is not difficult to see the application of paradoxical reflection to some of the traditional subjects of the familiar essay: The retelling of personal experiences builds to the discovery of paradoxical insights in the resolution of emotional conflict; in "character" essays, either of the sentimental or satiric type, we discover paradoxical features of personality, or we discover the essential unity behind seemingly contradictory features; the "reversals" or overturnings of commonplace wisdom so common to the genre are for the most part elaborations of paradoxical insights. (In fact "paradox" in older usage names a type of essay that argues a contrary opinion.) And there is a distinctly paradoxical quality in another traditional theme—the celebration or elevation of commonplace things and incidents.

Closely related to the paradox is the *enigma*—the situation that resists explanation and is out of line with the orderly flow of things. An essay based upon an enigma usually states or reveals the situation in which the enigma became apparent, and then it attempts to resolve it and reflect upon its significance. The best reflections are those that uncover enigmas that few people have thought of before, leading to new and surprising insights.

The *emblem*, finally, is the object, scene, or action which symbolizes or suggests some larger idea or experience. In reflective/exploratory rhetoric, as in literary art, emblems are powerful intellectual devices because they are integral to the way the mind absorbs, interprets, and retains experience. They are also powerful agents of memory and reminiscence, attaching thoughts and feelings to sensory images.

All of these devices figure prominently in one of the most universally admired (and probably the most anthologized) of modern essays, George Orwell's "Shooting an Elephant." The essay opens with the exposition of an enigma. In his state of youthful ignorance and confusion Orwell hated imperialism but had no sympathy, either, for its victims: "With one part of my mind I thought of the British Raj as an unbreakable tyranny. . . ; with another part I thought that the greatest joy in the world would be to drive a bayonet into a Buddhist priest's guts." The burden of the rest of the essay becomes to resolve, or at least to explain, this contradictory feeling. The narrative proceeds to its epiphany, where the narrator discovers a paradox in the moment of shooting the elephant: "I perceived in this moment that when the white man turns tyrant it is his freedom he destroys." The earlier enigma is resolved here: The simultaneous hatred of oppressor and oppressed is explained by the fact that the oppressor *is* the oppressed. Finally, as the essay moves to its conclusion, it develops an emblem out of the actual shooting of the elephant. The excruciatingly slow death of the elephant, caused in part by the incompetence of the executioner (Orwell himself), suggests something also about the dilemmas of imperialism: There is no fast and easy way out of it, even though one may have the best of intentions. The extrication is slow, painful, and disastrous.

Types of Reflective/Exploratory Rhetoric

Rhetoric by its very nature involves a propensity for novelty and innovation; and nowhere is this propensity more conspicuous than with reflective/exploratory rhetoric, where play, innovation, and idiosyncracy of both form and attitude are bywords. The continuing traditions of the familiar essay, nevertheless, taken with modern developments, create a picture in which the genus is "filled out" along lines of continuum that suggest the larger realms of discourse and, in turn, the experiential dimensions of the Motivational Axes.

The central or paradigmatic reflective/exploratory type, contributing most directly to the larger continuum between rhetoric and poetic, is the *lyrical* or *experiential*. It consists of personal experiences and reflections, very often cast in narrative or dramatic mode, developing moral and psychological insights from memories of concrete experience. A second type, forming a line of continuum with informative rhetoric, is the *instructive*, which conveys a good deal of knowledge or seasoned wisdom about a subject, while actually engaging in irregular or even whimsical speculation about it. The essays of Montaigne fit most readily into this category, retaining something of the teacherly stance of the prose "leçon." In modern times instructive reflection is usually composed by authorities or experts in particular fields. Essays written out of specialized disciplines by scientist-essayists like Loren Eiseley and Lewis Thomas also illustrate this direction of variation.

A third type is *celebrative*. It forms a direct line of continuum with epideictic, and it sometimes resembles epideictic in form. It differs in three crucial respects: (1) The subject, although it or he or she may be widely known, is not treated as part of a traditional or institutional sort of celebration, and it does not have the communal importance associated with the subjects of epideictic. (2) The author's viewpoint is a personal one and does not involve the viewpoint of some larger constituency or organization. (3) The discourse itself plays no role in the preservation or intensification of institutional commitments or values. The sentimental essay on a fascinating or personally influential character is an easily recognizable example of this type.

The fourth variety of reflective/exploratory rhetoric, coming full circle and forming a line of continuum with deliberation, is *suasory*. Like the instructive category, suasory reflection has traditional as well as distinctively modern varieties. The traditional sort consists of essays which may use argumentation to support distinct points of view, but which, because of the nature of the subject, or because of eccentric treatment, fall outside the regular public processes of deliberation. Topics generally fall in the category of "manners and morals"—matters somewhat removed from the arena of public or institutional debate. A traditional type of thesis is the "paradox" (Thompson 94–105), which cleverly overturns popular or conventional wisdom on a subject, urging such notions as the virtue of laziness, the consolations of consignment to drudgery, the superior morality of egotism, when practiced by the right sorts of people.

The distinctively modern variety of suasory reflection is one already given some notice—the essay which focuses on topics of immediate social interest and controversy, but using strategies of reflection rather than of deliberation, and conveying a distinctly personal attitude. Because the other three types are so distinctive and easily recognizable to readers of this book, only this last *suasory* variety will be treated by way of example and commentary.

Reflective/Exploratory Example: Edwin M. Yoder, Jr., "On 'Reds': The Age of Political Innocence," © *The Washington Post*, January 4, 1982. Reprinted by permission.

WASHINGTON—It is Warren Beatty's good fortune, I suppose, that his big movie "Reds" is a hit of this season of repression in Poland. The hero, played by Beatty himself, is John Reed, the young American journalist who witnessed and chronicled the Bolshevik seizure of power in 1917.

Those who see the movie with Poland in mind will probably marvel at Reed's giddy infatuation with what he believed to be a "workers" revolution. Events in Poland since the rise of Solidarity, and especially since Dec. 13, leave no doubt that the communist oligarchs cannot abide a genuine workers' movement.

Reed, the Harvard-educated provincial from Portland, Oregon, eagerly devoured Marxist theories about the connection between capitalism and war. In an early scene we see him pertly telling the Liberal Club of Portland that World War I, soon to be the grave of Czarist Russia, is about "profits." He probably thought so, as many did.

That glib theory about the war was to enjoy a long, sinister influence. It followed, and Reed also believed, that the war could not survive worker power. National conflict would melt away once the stronger bond of international class solidarity was cemented.

That was the primal hope of 19th century socialists. And in 1917 the hope remained sufficiently plausible to stir great and innocent illusions.

Even if a democratic workers' state had been Lenin's real objective, the belief that it would stymie international conflict was pure moonshine. But it was the most useful, the most exploitable, of the elements of the old Russia's weariness. The war seemed to millions of ordinary Europeans self-destructive and fruitless.

Looking back now, through the medium of Beatty's film, it is astonishing that a theory of war so false to history and human nature would be credited, let alone become a rallying cry that revolutionized a vast people. Yet is was; and it did.

But we must remember that the theory did not, at the time, seem so implausible. That is why "Reds" in effect is a tale not only of lost illusions but of the lost possibility of illusions. Millions of young Europeans were, by 1917, dying in the stalemated trench warfare of the Western front. Yet an unearthly hopefulness remained the dominant mood. War's consuming fires would purge the dross of selfishness; then the merely postponed march of progress would resume.

The cataclysm of 1914–18 was thought of, not as the curtain-raiser of succeeding horrors but as a temporary aberration; a sort of historical mistake. Other attendant illusions were possible, including the myth of international worker solidarity. None foresaw that 22 years later Stalin would join Hitler to carve up Poland. Or that 42 years after that, Stalin's heirs would still be operating at Poland's expense.

"Reds" reminds us how open-ended the world's political horizons seemed 60-odd years ago, even though at the outbreak of war Lord Grey had seen the lights going out all over Europe. The narrowing of horizons is perhaps the saddest of all the consequences that were to flow from the upheaval Reed witnessed and celebrated in his book, *Ten Days That Shook The World*.

The world was shaken all right, but not as Reed supposed. Of all the evil deeds for which Lenin and his heirs are answerable, not the least is that they introduced an entirely new cynicism about political ideals.

Even the powerful credulity of a John Reed would wither in its knowledge now.

Poland's present agony, though not the first lesson in this bitter legacy, is a telling measure of it. Workers, heroized in communist theory, are
now clearly a menace to its survival. This lesson has replaced for us the
hopes of a historically innocent young journalist who delighted in the
smashing of a weary, discredited ancient regime.

Lenin's coup d'etat differed in few important essentials from other vio-
lent and self-serving power grabs. It was different, even unique at the time,
in its brazen manipulation of humane instincts and ideals for narrow
purposes.

Indeed, the official lies issuing from Poland now only emphasize that
the legacy of cynicism lives on, long surviving the death of political
innocence.

COMMENTARY

Here is an example of the modern type of journalistic suasory
reflection which we have associated with regular columnizing, and
which normally focuses on contemporary events being reported and
deliberated about in the same publication in which the column appears.
Edwin M. Yoder, Jr., a journalist who was trained as an academic histo-
rian, has a reputation for a somewhat deeper background in history,
philosophy, and literature than most political columnists. In keeping
with his background, his characteristic subjects are those which at some
point involve issues of historical interpretation. Though most of his columns are deliberative, some are reflective/exploratory, not so much crit-
icizing or evaluating events as reflecting upon their cultural or historical
significance.

The central tactic of this column on Warren Beatty's movie *Reds* is
not that of the deliberative but rather of the familiar essayist: not a thesis supported but a connection drawn—in this case between the idealis-
tic attitude toward the Bolshevik revolution depicted in the popular film
and the sober revolution against communism being played out in
Poland at the time of the essay. The conspicuous conceptual pattern of
the piece is not a dialectical or argumentative topos but, as so often
happens, a playing with the coalescence of (or tension between) opposites—between the heady idealism and euphoria depicted in the film
and the stark realities of the brutal repression that have been the legacy
of the revolution it portrays.

The author makes no attempt to suppress his own opinions about
"that glib theory about the war" or about the nature and consequences
of Bolshevism—in fact, these opinions form the basis of his reflections.
Yet the essay is not fundamentally an attempt to intensify support for
these opinions, nor is it an attempt to make any particular aesthetic or

political evaluation of the film. It does, however, project an attitude of some importance, in the form of a meditation on the stark contrast between illusion and reality suggested (to him) by the film. The central point of the essay—that "Reds" is "in effect . . . a tale not only of lost illusions but of the lost possibility of illusions"—is not a thesis, nor even a conclusion, but rather a "resolution" of the intellectual dissonance occasioned by this particular reflection on particular discrepancies between appearance and reality. It is "literary" in this respect, while at the same time it constitutes a commentary on contemporary world politics.

CONCLUSION: RHETORIC, MOTIVATIONAL AXES, AND THE LANGUAGE ARTS

The study of what human beings do with discourse occupies a place somewhere between linguistics and the sociology of knowledge. This is not at all a comfortable middle position but rather a dizzying height, with infinitely receding realities on either side of the unresolvable and energizing dichotomy of form and meaning. What places one in this position is the universal condition of symbolization, the simultaneously denotative and constitutive function of language in the construction of reality; what provides a foothold is the fact of infinitely receding *patterns* of reality on either side.

In the liberal arts tradition, this middle position between linguistics and philosophy has been held by the study of rhetoric, energized from time to time by the perception that the ground on which it stood constituted a centrally important educational, philsophical, and political territory. One can study the traditions of rhetoric without sharing this perception but not without understanding it. There are many roads to it, and it has been reasserted in modern times by such critics as Burke, Weaver, Perelman, Booth, Corbett, and Kinneavy, from a variety of academic, historical, and cultural perspectives. The theory of discourse presented here provides the basis for another such reassertion, from the perspective of discourse itself.

On the side of formal structures, the receding patterns of reality are constituted in the superordinate features of asymmetry, hierarchy, continuum, and context-sensitivity. These features are discovered and described in chapter 1. They operate at every observable level, from phonology and grammar to the articulation of unified discourse performances in distinct cultural settings. These are not merely powerful critical instruments for understanding the operations of discourse; they also provide the basis for the stabilization and placement of such elusive concepts as aim, genre, strategy, and mode in a "Hierarchy of Discourse Categories."

The very articulation of this formalistic framework, however, reveals the need for a broader, semiotic framework for the understanding and placement of *meanings* and motivations in discourse. In chapter 3, such a framework is provided by the Motivational Axes, a semiotic "grammar of motives" that identifies a series of *primary* concepts naming fundamental antinomies of "meaning" at several different levels. At the most basic level the poles of the Motivational Axes articulate two sets of tensions that inhere in the meaning of speech acts: between constative and performative dimensions, on the one side, and between literal and tropological dimensions on the other. Expressed in terms of dialectical relations, these poles articulate dichotomies at another level: between description vs. classification and analysis vs. synthesis. (At this same level can be placed the Viconian/Burkean "master tropes" of metonymy, metaphor, synechdoche, and irony.) At a higher level we encounter the philosophical tensions of empiricism vs. formalism and realism vs. relativism.

This semiotic framework generates "ratios" or secondary concepts which constitute directions of specialization, motivational placements of human "makings" where language is a central factor. The map thus created has several different levels of application, and the aims of discourse occupy a middle position between—but also exist in theoretical alignment with—its linguistic and philosophical placements. The instrumental, scientific, poetic, and rhetorical aims of discourse align on one side with the operational, formalisitic, imaginative, and ethical/ pragmatic dimensions of speech acts; and on the other side with mechanism, formism, organicism, and contextualism as world hypotheses. All of these relations are represented in figure 12, which is reproduced here (with slight variation) from the first chapter. The unique standing of rhetoric in this scheme—its centrality as an aim of discouse which mirrors and draws upon the other aims, and in addition the special social and philosophical significance of its alignments with contextualism—have emerged at various points in this study, and they cast an interesting theoretical light upon the historical drama of rhetorical studies.

The science of rhetoric developed out of (and continues to develop within) a struggle over the problematic relation of language to truth. Accordingly, there are both ancient and modern schools of rhetoric, language, and philosophy that lean toward extreme positions of two fundamental types: One extreme (Plato, General Semantics, positivitist language philosophy) would resolve the struggle by reconstructing rhetorical discourse so as to align it with "truth," generally ignoring the problem of how to enforce the unnatural discipline that such a reconstruction would impose; the other extreme (sophism, deconstructionism) regards the relationship between language and reality as in all cases hopelessly arbitrary, thus licensing both rhetoric and poetic to construct their own truths in whatever ways

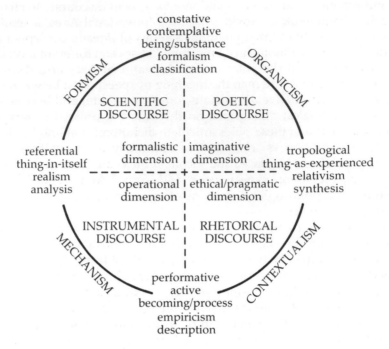

Figure 12. Theoretical alignments of the aims of discourse

they can manage.[1] Both of these extremes constitute absolutisms that leave little room for a rhetorical theory or practice both internally consistent and responsible to the moral and phenomenal world outside of language. The central tradition of rhetoric, by contrast, has sought to avoid these extremes, both by qualifying the epistemelogical claims on either side and by demarcating different spheres of application, in which different sorts of "knowledge" are available, and to which different canons of proof and substantiation apply. The Isocratean tradition dealt with this struggle in a practical, atheoretical way, by pulling back from extreme positions of all kinds and by injecting an element of cultural moralism (extralinguistic notions of right action, allegience to the "best that has been thought and said") into its cultivation of rhetoric. Aristotle dealt with the problem philosophically, constructing a hierarchy of epistemelogical situations, in which questions of truth and value are susceptible to different treatments at different levels.

1. For the relationship between ancient sophistry and modern deconstructionism, see Harris, "Toward an Ecological Criticism: Contextual versus Unconditioned Literary Criticism: Contextual versus Unconditioned Literary Theory."

The perspective provided by the central rhetorical tradition is useful because it is schooled in the risks of absolutism on the one side and relativism on the other, and it has a knack for sensing reductionisms, for resisting epistemelogical exclusivities. It has acquired this knack in the process of defining itself, of claiming its own territory. Rhetoric is the least specialized art of discourse; it is in fact the central art of discourse, reflecting in its own subsystem of aims all the larger aims (rhetorical, scientific, instrumental, poetic). As such, rhetoric has a stake in all perspectives and all modes of discourse. The other aims of discourse are historical specializations which achieve success by restricting both scope and method. They are centrifugal forces, both of language and culture. Rhetoric is the centripetal force. Both linguistically and culturally, it has a vested interest in openness and variety, in a pluralism of ways of living and of seeing the world. The other aims tend toward specializations both of language and of viewpoint, and their practitioners have a tendency to tend solely to their particular constructions of reality, their own particular ways of arresting experience. Rhetoric, by contrast, generates arrests of experience that have a stake in other perspectives as well.

Plato attempted to absorb rhetoric into the up-there out-there there framework of philosophical realism, for use in a Republic which would tolerate neither sophistry nor poetry; just as his enemies the sophists (by his construction) wished to absorb it into the down-here in-here framework of pragmatic relativism. The General Semanticists of a generation ago wished to absorb it into the out-there, down-here framework of scientific positivism. But rhetoric resists such exclusivisms, even when they attempt to pin it down in its own "natural" habitat, as in the case of sophistry. There is a great irony in this circumstance, for the arrests of experience, the constructions of reality produced by rhetoric are inevitably less brilliant, less durable, and in many senses less "true" than those produced by other aims of discourse. At at the same time it is rhetoric itself which sometimes provides a strong antidote to exclusive reductions, and therefore the strongest hold on the complete reality of situations, by preserving the mysteries, by flushing out the dilemmas behind a good deal of practical, technical, and scientific discourse. It was the sophists who discovered and sometimes made cynical use of the insight that behind most practical and scientific difficulties are dilemmas of an unresolvable nature. Plato was offended both by the cynical use *and* the insight itself; Isocrates was offended principally by the cynical use, and it is his tradition of rhetoric that has rightly prevailed.

The Motivational Axes is itself a contextualist framework inspired by the attempt to define and claim a territory for rhetoric. In the process of staking that claim it has uncovered the enormous cultural significance of the openness and centrality of rhetoric as an aim of discourse. It remains now to delve into some particularities close at hand, applying the Motivational Axes to some specific dimensions of literature, literacy, and the teaching of rhetoric.

APPROACHES TO TEXTS

The Motivational Axes constitute a guide not to reality but to the meanings of texts, which are themselves approaches to reality. The various arts of language and criticism approach texts both as realities to be explored and as guides to other realities. It is a complicated situation, and the Motivational Axes can provide some assistance in sorting it out.

Occasionally we can derive unexpected guidance in such a project from the re-appreciation of older canons of judgment. Though outmoded in a practical sense, older systems may nevertheless display a comprehensive wisdom that modern constructs lack. The medieval interpretive scheme of literal, allegorical, tropological, and anagogical meanings is rightly regarded as a fantastical scholastic curiosity when considered in the light of practical criticism. The system has been shown, nevertheless, to have a more general relevance to the interests of criticism (Frye 115–38), and from our point of view it is clear that its components do reach out toward each of the four motivational directions—respectively, the operational, formalistic, imaginative, and ethical/pragmatic.

The medieval scheme first comprehends a general distinction between "practical" meanings (literal and tropological) and "theoretical" meanings (the allegorical and anagogical). This division is supplemented by an implicit distinction that gets as close as the medieval mind can get to our distinction between referential and tropological dimensions of language use. Literal and allegorical constitute down-to-earth and spiritual (lower and upper) variants of "direct reference." (The bridegroom of the *Canticle* serves both as historical character and as a "type" of another historical character, Christ.) Tropological and anagogical readings, by contrast, are extrapolations from these forms of reference, to the present-tense, pragmatic sphere of right action; and to the future-tense, imaginative sphere of "last things."

This examination of a creed outworn reveals a pattern of relationships bearing upon our larger project: The tropological (ethical/pragmatic) reading occupies a special position with regard to maintaining an equilibrium among possible readings in general. Although medieval commentators were very concerned about "orthodox" readings, they were not very much concerned about "correct" readings, not at least in the senses supplied by modern philology and "higher criticism." Orthodoxy consists in the general conformity of readings to established points of doctrine, and also in maintaining a proper balance among *types of readings*, with each given its proper due. Denial of the literal carries overtones of gnosticism and Manicheanism, while denial of the tropological carries overtones of antinomianism. Heresy, both theological and critical, may in fact be defined as the attempt to elevate certain forms of partial truth to the exclusion or distortion of others.[2]

What is interesting is that the tropological and ethical/pragmatic sphere plays a special role in holding on to the "orthodox" equilibrium of partial truths: The moral reading is potentially the most various and the most dangerous because the various forms of "direct reference" are very poor guides, in themselves, to right action. One discovers the proper ethical reading by sorting it out against other readings, which must also be considered and weighed as possibilities. For example, the fact of Abraham's multiple wives must obviously be consigned, *as a fact of the narrative*, to the historical sphere, not the moral. It would be monstrous, likewise, to extrapolate from the beginning of *Pilgrim's Progress* the lesson that one is required to abandon one's family responsibilities and leave home in order to follow Christ. As facts of the narrative, these elements must be consigned to the imaginative sphere: The love of God is morally prior to the love of one's family, and the experience of conversion can involve a form of estrangement from the recalcitrant world, of which one's family may be a part. An additional and broader check on wayward readings, and one that more explicitly assigns a role to the ethical/pragmatic sphere, is the hoary principle that, since all readings of scripture are finite reductions of an infinite wisdom, multiple readings are acceptable as long as they express and conform to the "law of charity" (Augustine III. x–xviii).

The medieval canons of interpretation stand as a model of how any system of reading, and therefore any human science that aims at comprehensiveness, tends to fill out along lines anticipated by the Motivational Axes. These "fillings out" can be reflected under a variety of critical banners and contexts, and the various modern specializations of literary study and traditions of reading also can be construed as placements in this semiotic model. Northrop Frye's "polemical" distinction between criticism as knowledge and criticism as evaluation (3–29) corresponds to our referential/tropological axis, delineating descriptive vs. evaluative ("out-there" vs. "in-here") tendencies of reading and writing. To this distinction we can add another, along the constative-performative axis, delineating formalistic versus empirical tendencies.

2. "The subject-matter of both faith and heresy is . . . the deposit of the faith, that is, the sum total of truths revealed in Scripture and Tradition as proposed to our belief by the Church. The believer accepts the whole deposit as proposed by the Church; the heretic accepts only such parts of it as commend themselves to his own approval" (J. Wilhelm, "Heresy" 256).

This points on the one hand to criticism focused on the "system" of literature (formalism, structuralism), and on the other to criticism devoted to the meanings and unities of individual works (practical criticism).

This broad system of placements has a number of levels and contexts of application, ranging from different approaches to literature, different types of theory, different schools of criticism, different tendencies within schools. In connection with traditions of reading, for instance, the neoclassical approach epitomized in such phrases as "instruct and delight" is a "contextualist," ethical/pragmatic theory, while the kinds of theory that Meyer Abrams somewhat reductively labels "expressive" are better characterized as "organicist": They focus not so uniformly upon on expression as upon art as a system of imaginative unities. Marxist approaches, by contrast, are mechanistic in orientation, focusing on literature as the effect of economic and social causes.

A thorough examination of these placements would carry this discussion far afield and is really the subject of another book; however, without getting bogged down in consideration of different critical schools, we can construct from the Motivational Axes a broad map which delineates major components of (and major traditions in) literary history and criticism: These are philology, literary theory, cultural criticism, and practical criticism; and they relate to the operational, formalistic, imaginative, and ethical/pragmatic spheres, respectively.

Philology is concerned with the language, authorship, provenence, and immediate historical surroundings of texts; it shares with literary theory a focus on literature itself as the immediate object of systematic study, and with practical criticism a focus on individual texts or groups of texts. Literary theory, in turn, shares with cultural criticism a focus on broad patterns and relationships of which individual texts form examples. Cultural criticism and practical criticism share a concern with the value and significance of literary works, but with a difference: Practical criticism makes the individual work (or tradition of works) the focus of study and is concerned to work outward from consideration of the work as an aesthetic unity, whereas cultural criticism exhibits more of a tendency to use the individual work as a springboard for consideration of a broad set of issues and problems that could be discussed without explicit reference to the work.

Because these components represent different dimensions of the reality of literary art works, they are all relevant to and typically form components of "readings"—both literary histories and commentaries on individual texts—while constituting at the same time directions of specialization within the field of literature. As directions of specialization each has its proper sphere and a world of work to do there. Each has operational, formalistic, imaginative, and ethical/pragmatic dimensions within itself, and each can be conceived in broader or narrower terms, accordingly. The least likely to close off into a world of its own, however, is practical criticism, for it forms a meeting ground for the other three, and it cannot do its work without taking them into account. Different traditions of practical criticism itself, moreover, reveal leanings toward the different spheres of conceptualization—toward philological and historical concerns; toward formalism; toward the cultural and political contexts of literature; and toward public reading, interpretation, evaluation, and appreciation—the intrinsic concerns of practical criticism. In this respect the position of practical criticism vis-à-vis the other traditions and components of literary study is precisely that of rhetoric vis-à-vis the other aims of discourse. It is the form of reading that is most open to different spheres of contextual reality, and it embodies in its own traditions the larger world of reading itself. Like rhetoric also, it acts as a centripetal force: Its contextualist predilection for the "rich concrete event, in which features interpenetrate," has the ability to recall criticism from some of the extremities (critical heresies) that the various branches can fall into: from the occasional pedantries of philology; the occasional abstract reductions of theory; the occasional distortions and ideological bodysnatchings of cultural criticism;[3] and the occasional vulgarities and absurdities of public reading, interpretation, and reviewing.

THE VALUES OF LITERACY

If we turn from the disciplines of literary criticism to the broader context of the values of the language arts in general, we discover a different but congruent set of relationships. Like the component disciplines of literary criticism, the various educational approaches to literacy, as well as the historical rationales and defenses of literary education, reveal orientations toward the operational, formalistic, imaginative, or ethical/pragmatic dimensions of the field. Any program or set of reflections on literacy will tend to "fill out" along all four directions, but

---

3. The most deliberately and frankly articulated version of contemporary "cultural criticism" is Marxism, which interestingly enough has attempted to appropriate the name and tradition of "rhetoric" in its own apologia (Eagleton 1981: 101–13; and 1983: 194–217). There is something apt in such an appropriation, because Marxists want to direct criticism away from the subjectivism and radical skepticism of the contemporary avant garde and toward a readier engagement of cultural and political values, a traditional concern of rhetorical humanism. Antithetical to rhetoric and the rhetorical tradition, however, are the Marxist tendency to absolutism, the tendency to treat competing readings of experience and of texts as examples of false consciousness, and the total conflation of rhetoric and poetic as aims of discourse. Marxism derives its energy more from the prophetic and imaginative dimension of the Motivational Axes than from the ethical/pragmatic, where lies the impulse to rhetoric and rhetorical criticism.

by the same token any particular view will likely reveal a primary affinity to one of them.

1. In the operational dimension we find an orientation toward "functional literacy"—reading and writing as essential skills for living and working in society. The traditional art of language related to this sphere is grammar.

2. In the formalistic sphere we find an orientation toward reasoning, conceptualization, and creative thinking. The rationale for this orientation lies not simply in the awareness that writing is the repository of learning but also in the insight that the operations of literacy activate structures of cognition that *produce* knowledge and insight (D'Angelo 1975; Ong 1971; Emig). The traditionally related art of language is dialectic.

3. In the imaginative dimension we find an orientation toward "culture" in the Arnoldian sense—awareness and internalization of the "best that has been thought and said," and cultivation of the qualities of mind and sensibility that attend such an awareness. The related art of language is the study of literature.

4. Finally, in the ethical/pragmatic dimension, we find an orientation toward civic participation and leadership—the effective discussion and promulgation of ideas and values. The related art of language is, of course, rhetoric. This is the orientation that makes the most extensive use of and has the most active interest in preserving the integrity of the other three. Historically, it is most conspicuously represented by the orientation of classical and Renaissance humanism, which envisions a program of linguistic, philosophical, and literary studies heavily invested in rhetoric, and aimed at producing the well-rounded individual, the integrated sensibility of the citizen and statesman. This is a sensibility that is schooled in a variety of sciences, in all the arts of language and communication, and in the art of perceiving and attempting to balance the inevitable dichotomies of value that enter into human situations. It is no accident that the tensions between active and contemplative life and between scientific and popular understanding are frequent topics and underlying themes of humanist literature, for these are the ineradicable tensions of humanism itself.

Components of Literacy

These observations can be given a sharper focus by shifting them from the *values* and *arts* of literacy to the *components* of literacy. In the operational dimension we observe *processes* of language—the actual motor skills and hand-eye coordination that go into reading and writing, as well as the conventions of linguistic encoding and decoding in the written medium. The work of Mina Shaughnessy in the area of "basic writing" has touched upon the underdevelopment of these skills, rather than deficiencies of intelligence or language development per se, as factors in the "errors" committed by students in remedial writing courses. As Shaughnessy herself realizes, however, there is a broader range of linguistic and conceptual skills that inform and encompass these processes; and this realization points us to the formalistic dimension and what may be termed *principles of language*. In their application to literacy these include not merely principles of grammar and the logic of discourse (the lore of coherence), but also of logic and conceptualiztion (both dialectical and imaginative)—the entire range of processes that Frank D'Angelo has brought together under the heading of "conceptual rhetoric."

These two dimensions taken together form material and conceptual versions of what may be termed "formal literacy," while the imaginative and ethical/pragmatic dimensions anticipate versions of "cultural literacy." In the imaginative dimension we may place the *knowledge and experience of literature* (in the broadest sense) as a contextual component of literacy; and in the ethical/pragmatic dimension there is *cultural knowledge* as a contextual component of literacy. There is obviously as rich an interplay between the "upper" and "lower" (or contemplative and active) variants of cultural literacy as between those of formal literacy.

Traditions in the teaching of English in America reveal fluctuations back and forth between these orientations.[4] While tremendous outpourings of research in linguistics and the processes of disourse have tended to shift the balance toward "formal literacy" in recent decades, a good deal of this research has also come to recognize the importance of contextual and extra-textual frames of reference in reading and writing processes. Sentences are understood from the "outside" as much as from the "inside"; texts are comprehended from the "top down" as well as the "bottom up." (Dillon, Hirsch 1980, Wanner). What these studies reveal is that even the analysis of forms and processes themselves must eventually come around to the awareness of ever-expanding circles of context, and they call renewed attention to knowledge in the subject disciplines, knowledge of literature, and cultural knowledge. They should also call renewed attention to the value of rhetoric. For these recognitions are logical extensions of the principle of context-sensitivity which operates at all levels of linguistic activity, and they dovetail with the special "contextualist" roles and placements of rhetoric and rhetorical literature that have been identified in both theoretical and historical

4. These movements are recorded in great detail by Applebee, *Tradition and Reform in the Teaching of English: A History.*

terms.[5] The tradition of rhetoric constitutes a moderate formalism, balanced and enriched by the awareness that its efficacy is partly dependent upon its submergence within a broader program of liberal learning.

RHETORIC AND WRITTEN COMPOSITION

In the field of composition studies we can identify placements that parallel those for the study and teaching of literacy in general. We identify a "functional," practical orientation in the operational sphere; an "intellectual" or academic orientation in the formalistic sphere (writing as an instrument of conceptualization and learning); an "aesthetic" orientation (most often combined with an emphasis on self-expression and self-realization) in the imaginative sphere; and a "civic" orientation toward rhetoric and public discourse in the ethical/pragmatic sphere. These orientations reflect important insights about the nature and value of written communication, and programs that aim at comprehensiveness inevitably seek to capture something from each. They also reflect the different emphases and informing rationales of different programs. In fact, a recent typology of "theories of composition" (Berlin) identifies traditions that correspond exactly to these dimensions: the "current-traditional" modes-of-discourse framework (narration, description, exposition, persuasion) is operational and mechanistic in orientation; the tradition of "new rhetorics," focused primarily on heuristics and cognitive processes, is formalistic in orientation; romantic-expressive theories are imaginative and organicist in orientation; and neoclassical theories are ethical/pragmatic or contextualist in orientation.[6]

A point that is not widely appreciated emerges from reflection on these placements: The preponderance of theoretical attention in the field of composition studies has tended to focus on "new rhetorics" in the battle against the "current-traditional" modes-of-discourse paradigm. But both of these "theories" constitute variations of "formal literacy" as a matter of fundamental orientation; they both concentrate on forms and processes, throwing into shadows the rhetorical contexts in which forms, processes, literary traditions, and cultural knowledge

5. There is an obvious sense in which formal literacy is more "basic": one must be taught directly how to read and write. However, this proposition cannot be accepted without extensive qualification, even at very rudimentary levels of application. Many individuals have acquired the skills of formal literacy indirectly, with very little direct training, motivated by fascination with a particular subject or by a general desire for knowledge. By contrast, in the field of written composition, there is a tradition of negative results in studies on the direct teaching of grammar, usage, and mechanics.
6. In classifying these "theories," Berlin does not use a model corresponding to the Motivational Axes. He identifies them as historical traditions, and then evaluates them by the criterion of "epistemological adequacy." I believe that the guidance provided by the Motivational Axes could lead to a more illuminating view of these traditions and also toward a correction, in favor of the classical tradition, of Berlin's evaluations.

come together in discourse performances. In contrast to both of these modern orientations, the great tradition of rhetoric stands as a centrist language art, capable of absorbing a variety of insights from every relevant sphere and of relating them to rhetorical situations.

In a passage directed at the pitfalls of an exclusive orientation toward form, George Dillon concludes:

> The view that uncertainty at the foundation imperils the whole discourse seems to depend on the fallacious assumption that sentences are perceived botoom-to-top, then the paragraph is constructed out of them, and so on. But sentences usually are not processed outside of a discourse except in psycholinguistic laboratories and English classrooms. Normally, the discourse context gives top-down guidance in the perception of sentences. . . . This point is widely recognized today, though its consequences have not been fully digested (6).

One of the reasons that the consequences of this have not been fully digested is that scholars and teachers in the field of English have tended to relegate rhetoric to the operational and formalistic dimensions, failing to incorporate into their teaching and study the kind of sophistication about aims and genres and traditions that they normally bring to literary art works. The top-down guidance that Dillon refers to is partially *inside* the rhetorical text but partially *outside* the text, in the situation, the system of "exigences" to which the text is a response, and just as importantly, in the traditions of texts that respond to similar situations. This is the kind of knowledge specified by a pragmatic or contextual theory of rhetoric, focused on the "rich, concrete event, in which features interpenetrate." The importance of such a theory is bound up in the importance of rhetorical discourse and rhetorical education themselves as forms of culture.

WORKS CITED

Abrams, M. H. *The Mirror and the Lamp*. New York: Oxford U. P., 1953.

Applebee, Arthur N. *Tradition and Reform in the Teaching of English: A History*. Urbana, Ill.: NCTE, 1974.

Aristotle. *Nichomachean Ethics*. Trans. W. D. Ross. *The Basic Works of Aristotle*. Ed. Richard McKeon. New York: Random House, 1941.

Politics. Trans. Benjamin Jowett. Oxford: Clarendon P., 1905.

——. *Rhetoric*. Trans. Lane Cooper. New York: Appleton-Century-Crofts, 1932.

Augustine. *On Christian Doctrine*. Trans. D. W. Robertson, Jr. Indianapolis: Bobbs-Merrill, 1958.

Austin, J. L. *How To Do Things With Words*. Cambridge, Mass.: Harvard U. P., 1962.

Bain, Alexander. *English Composition and Rhetoric: A Manual*. American ed., revised. New York: D. Appleton & Co., 1867.

Beale, Walter H. "Rhetorical Performative Discourse: A New Theory of Epideictic." Philosophy and Rhetoric 11 (1978):221–45.

Berlin, James. "Contemporary Theories of Invention in the Rhetorical Tradition." CE 44 (Dec. 1982): 765–77.

Bernstein, Basil. "Elaborated and Restricted Codes." *The Ethnography of Communication*. Ed. J. Gumperz and Dell Hymes. [American Antropologist 66 (1964)]. 55–69.

Bitzer, Lloyd. "The Rhetorical Situation." *Philosophy and Rhetoric* 1 (1968): 1–14.

Black, Edwin. *Rhetorical Criticism: A Study in Method*. New York: Macmillan; rpt. Madison: U. of Wisconsin P., 1978.

Black, Max. *Critical Thinking: An Introduction to Logic and Scientific Method*. 2nd ed. New York: Prentice-Hall, 1952.

——. "Austin on Performatives." *Symposium on J. L. Austin*. Ed. Ted Honderich. New York: Humanities Press, 1969. 401–11.

Bloomfield, Leonard. *Linguistic Aspects of Science*. International Encyclopedia of Unified Science, Vol. I, no.4. Chicago: U. of Chicago P., 1939.

Booth, Wayne C. *The Rhetoric of Fiction*. Chicago: U. of Chicago P., 1961.

——. *Modern Dogma and the Rhetoric of Assent*. Notre Dame, Ind.: Notre Dame U. P., 1974.

Bormann, Ernest G. "Generalizing About Significant Form: Science and Humanism Compared and Contrasted." *Form and Genre: Shaping Rhetorical Action*. Ed. Karilyn Kohrs Campbell and Kathleen Hall Jamieson. Falls Church, Va.: Speech Communication Assoc., 1978. 51–74.

Brandt, William J. *The Rhetoric of Argumentation*. Indianapolis: Bobbs-Merrill, 1970.

Brinton, Alan. "William James and the Epistemic View of Rhetoric." QJS 68 (1982): 158–69.

Britton, James, et al. *The Development of Writing Abilities (11–18)*. London: Macmillan, 1975.

Bryan, William F., and R. S. Crane. *The English Familiar Essay*. Boston: Ginn, 1916.

Bryant, Donald C. "Rhetoric: Its Function and Scope." QJS 39 (1953): 401–24.

Buchheit, Vinzenz. *Untersuchungen zur Theorie des Genos Epideiktikon von Georgias bis Aristoteles*. München: Max Huber Verlag, 1960.

Buchwald, Art. "A Crash Program for the Right to Drive." *The Washington Post* June 1968: A25.

Burgess, Theodore C. *Epideictic Literature*. Studies in Classical Philology, no. 3. Chicago: U. of Chicago P., 1902.

Burke, Kenneth. *A Grammar of Motives*. New York: Prentice-Hall, 1945; rpt. Berkeley and Los Angeles: U. of California P., 1969.

———. *A Rhetoric of Motives*. New York: Prentice-Hall, 1950; rpt. Berkeley and Los Angeles: U. of California P., 1969.

———. *Language as Symbolic Action: Essays on Life, Literature, and Method*. Berkeley: U. of Cal. P., 1966.

———. *The Philosophy of Literary Form*. 2nd ed. Baton Rouge, La: L. S. U. P., 1967.

Cairns, William B. *The Forms of Discourse*. Boston: Ginn & Co., 1896.

Campbell, Karlyn Kohrs, and Kathleen Hall Jamieson. *Form and Genre: Shaping Rhetorical Action*. Falls Church, Va.: Speech Communication Assoc., 1978.

Carlisle, O. A. "Solzhenitsyn's Invisible Audience." *Newsweek* 24 July 1978: 13.

Cassirer, Ernst. *Language and Myth*. Trans. Susanne K. Langer. Harper and Row, 1946.

———. *The Logic of the Humanities*. Trans. Clarence Smith Howe. New Haven: Yale U. P.: 1961.

Carothers, J. C. "Culture, Psychiatry, and the Written Word." *Psychiatry* 22 (1959): 307–20.

Chase, J. Richard. "The Classical Conception of Epideictic." QJS 47 (1961): 293–300.

Chisolm, Roderick M. "Austin's Philosophical Papers." *Symposium on J. L. Austin*. Ed. Ted Honderich. New York: Humanities P., 1969. 101–26.

Chomsky, Noam. *Aspects of the Theory of Syntax*. Cambridge, Mass.: M. I. T. Press, 1965.

Cicero. *Partitiones Oratoriae*. Trans. Horace Rackham. Cambridge, Mass.: Harvard U. P. 1942.

Conners, Robert J. "The Rise and Fall of the Modes of Discourse." CCC 32 (Dec. 1981): 444–55.

Croasman, Earl, and Richard A. Cherwitz. "Beyond Rhetorical Relativism." QJS 68 (1982): 1–16.

Cushman, Donald P., and Phillip K. Tompkins. "A Theory of Rhetoric for Contemporary Society." *Philosophy and Rhetoric* 13 (1980): 43–67.

D'Angelo, Frank. *A Conceptual Theory of Rhetoric.* Cambridge, Mass.: Winthrop, 1975.

———. "Modes of Discourse." *Teaching Composition: 10 Bibliographical Essays.* Ed. Gary Tate. Fort Worth, Texas: T. C. U. Press, 1976. 111–36.

Dieter, Otto A. L. "Stasis." SM 17 (1950): 345–69.

Dillon, George. *Constructing Texts: Elements of a Theory of Composition and Style.* Bloomington: Indiana U. P., 1981.

Eagleton, Terry. *Walter Benjamin, or Towards a Revolutionary Criticism.* London: Verso Editions, 1981.

———. *Literary Theory: An Introduction.* Minneapolis: U. of Minnesota P., 1983.

Edman, Irwin. *Four Ways of Philosophy.* New York: Henry Holt & Co., 1937.

Emig, Janet. "Writing as a Mode of Learning." CCC 28 (1977): 122–28.

Frye, Northrop. *Anatomy of Criticism: Four Essays.* Princeton: Princeton U. P.: 1957).

Fulkerson. Richardson P. "Kinneavy on Rhetorical and Persuasive Discourse: A Critique." CCC 35 (Feb 1984): 43–56.

Genung, John F. *The Practical Elements of Rhetoric.* Boston: Ginn & Co., 1886.

———. *Outlines of Rhetoric.* Boston: Ginn & Co., 1893.

Gerald, James E. *The Social Responsibility of the Press.* Minneapolis: U. of Minnesota P., 1963.

Goodman, Ellen. "Genius is More than Genes." The Boston Globe 6 March 1980: 13.

———. "Participants, Not Patients." *Close to Home.* New York: Simon and Schuster, 1979: 246–47.

Grassi, Ernesto. *Rhetoric as Philosophy: The Humanist Tradition.* University Park, Pa.: U. of Pa. P., 1980.

Halliday, M. A. K., Angus McIntosh, and Peter Strevens. *The Linguistic Sciences and Language Teaching.* Bloomington, Ill.: Indiana U. P., 1964.

Halloran, S. M. "On the End of Rhetoric, Classical and Modern." CE 36 (Feb. 1975): 621–31.

Hardison, O. B. *The Enduring Monument: A Study of the Idea of Praise in Renaissance Literary Theory and Practice.* Chapel Hill: U. of N. C. Press, 1962.

Harrell, Jackson, and Wil A. Linkugel. "On Rhetorical Genre: An Organizing Perspective." *Philosophy and Rhetoric* 11 (1978): 262–81.

Harris, Wendell V. "Toward an Ecological Criticism: Contextual versus Unconditioned Literary Theory." CE 48 (Feb. 1986): 116–131.

Hemingway, Ernest. "Indian Camp." *The Short Stories of Ernest Hemingway.* New York: Charles Scribner's Sons, 1953. 91–95.

Hernadi, Paul. *Beyond Genre: New Directions in Literary Classification.* Ithaca: Cornell U. P., 1972.

Hirsch, E. D., Jr. *The Philosophy of Composition.* Chicago: U. of Chicago P., 1977.

———. "Culture and Literacy." Journal of Basic Writing 3 (Fall/Winter 1980). 27–47.

———. "Cultural Literacy." American Scholar 52 (1983): 159–69

Hocking, William Ernest. *Types of Philosophy.* 3rd ed. New York: Charles Scribner's Sons, 1959.

Hodson, C. A., et al. "Effects of a Prolactin-Secreting Pituitary Tumor on Hypothamlmic, Gonadotripic and Testicular Function in Male Rats." *Neuroendocrinology* 30 (1980): 7–10.

Howell, Wilber Samuel. *The Rhetoric of Alcuin and Charlemagne.* Princeton: Princeton U. P., 1941.

————. "Literature as an Enterprise in Communication." QJS 33 (1947): 417–26.

Hultzen, Lee S. "Status in Deliberative Analysis." *The Rhetorical Idiom: Essays in Rhetoric, Oratory, Language and Drama Presented to Herbert August Wichelns.* Ithaca, N. Y.: Cornell U. P., 1958. 97–123.

Hymes, Dell. "The Ethnography of Speaking." *Readings in the Sociology of Language.* Ed. Joshua A. Fishman. The Hague: Mouton, 1968. 99–138.

Jakobson, Roman. "Linguistics and Poetics." *Style in Language.* Ed. Thomas Sebeok. Cambridge, Mass.: M. I. T. Press, 1960. 350–77.

James, William. *The Varieties of Religious Experience: A Study in Human Nature.* [1902] New York: Modern Library, 1936.

————. *The Will to Believe and other Essays in Popular Philosophy.* New York: Dover, 1960.

Jaynes, Julian. *The Origin of Consciousness in the Breakdown of the Bicameral Mind.* Boston: Houghton Mifflin, 1977.

Jordan, Vernon E., Jr. "The Truth about the Black Middle Class." *Newsweek,* 8 July 1974: 11.

Kaufer, David S. "Point of View in Rhetorical Situations: Classical and Romantic Contrasts and Contemporary Implications." QJS 65 (1979): 171–86.

Kinneavy, James E. *A Theory of Discourse.* Englewood Cliffs, N. J.: Prentice-Hall, 1971; rpt. New York: W. W. Norton, 1980.

Kinneavy, James E., John Q. Cope, and J. W. Campbell. *Writing—Basic Modes of Organization.* Dubuque, Iowa: Kendal/Hunt, 1976.

Kramer, Jane. "A Reporter in Europe—London." *The New Yorker* May 11, 1981: 91–124.

Körner, Stephen. *Categorial Frameworks.* Oxford: Basil Blackwell, 1974.

Langer, Suzanne K. *Philosophy in a New Key: A Study in the Symbolism of Reason, Rite, and Art.* Cambridge, Mass.: Harvard U. P., 1957.

Law, Marie Hamilton. *The English Familiar Essay in the Early Nineteenth Century.* Philadelphia: U. of Pennsylvania Diss., 1934.

Lessing, Doris. "One Off the Short List." *A Man and Two Women.* New York: Simon and Schuster, 1963. 9–37.

Lewis, Anthony. "We Gather Together." *The New York Times* 26 Nov. 1981: 19.

Longacre, R. E. *An Anatomy of Speech Notions.* Lisse: Peter DeRidder, 1976.

Lukacs, Georg. "On the Nature and Form of the Essay." *Nature and Form.* Trans. Anna Bostock. Cambridge, Mass.: MIT Press, 1974. 1–18.

McKeon, Richard. "Aristotle's Conception of Language and the Arts of Language." *Classical Philology* 41 (1946): 193–206; 42 (1947): 21–50.

————. "Philosophical Differences and the Issues of Freedom." *Ethics* 61 (1951): 105–35.

Mantle, Mickey. *The Quality of Courage: True Stories of Heroism and Bravery.* New York: Bantam, 1965.

Marr, George S. *The Periodical Essayists of the Eighteenth Century.* New York: D. Appleton, 1924.

Mathes, J. C. "The Design of Advanced Writing Courses: A Taxonomy of Communication Acts." *Proceedings of the Inaugural Conference of the University of Maryland Junior Writing Program.* Ed. Michael Marcuse and Susan Kleiman. College Park, Md.: U. of Maryland, 1981). 39–57.

Mitford, Jessica. *Poison Penmanship: The Gentle Art of Muckraking.* New York: Knopf, 1979.

Montague, William. Pepperell. *The Ways of Knowing, or The Methods of Philosophy.* London: George Allen & Unwin; New York: Macmillan, 1925.

Montaigne, Miguel de. *The Complete Works of Montaigne: Essays, Travels, Journal, Letters.* Trans. Donald M. Frame. Stanford, Cal.: Stanford U. P., 1958.

Niebuhr, Reinhold. *Leaves from the Notebook of a Tamed Cynic.* Chicago: Willett, Clark, and Colby, 1929.

———. *The Nature and Destiny of Man: A Christian Interpretation.* 2 vols. New York: Charles Scribner's Sons, 1942.

Norton, Frederic. "Kristallnacht." *The New York Times* 10 Nov. 1978: 31.

Novak, Michael. " 'Story' and Experience." *Religion as Story.* Ed. James B. Wiggins. New York: Harper & Row, 1975. 175–97.

Oakeshott, Michael Joseph. *Experience and its Modes.* Cambridge: Cambridge U. P.: 1933; 1966.

Ong, Walter J. "The Province of Rhetoric and Poetic." *The Modern Schoolman* (Jan. 1942); rpt. The Province of Rhetoric. Ed. Joseph Schwartz and John C. Rycenga. New York: Ronald, 1965. 48–55.

———. *Rhetoric, Romance, and Technology.* Ithaca, N. Y.: Cornell U. P., 1971.

———. "The Writer's Audience Is Always a Fiction." *PMLA* 90 (1975): 9–22. .

———. *Interfaces of the Word: Studies in the Evolution of Consciousness and Culture.* Ithaca, N. Y.: Cornell U. P., 1977.

Panter-Downes, Mollie. "Letter from London." *The New Yorker* 8 June 1981: 134–37.

Pepper, Stephen. *World Hypotheses: A Study in Evidence:* Berkeley and Los Angeles: U. of Cal. P., 1961.

Perelman, Chaim, and L. Olbrechts-Tyteca. *The New Rhetoric: A Treatise on Argumentation.* Trans. John Wilkinson and Purcell Weaver. Notre Dame, Ind.: Notre Dame U. P., 1969.

Pike, Kenneth. *Language in Relation to a Unified Theory of the Structure of Human Behavior.* 2nd ed. The Hague: Mouton, 1967.

Pitkin, Willis. "Hierarchies and the Discourse Hierarchy." *CE* 38 (March, 1977): 648–59.

———. "X/Y: Some Basic Strategies of Discourse." *CE* 38 (March 1977): 660–72.

Postman, Neil. *Amusing Ourselves to Death: Public Discourse in the Age of Show Business.* New York: Viking, 1985.

Quintilian. *The Institutio Oratoria of Quintilian.* Trans. H. E. Butler. 4 vols. New York: G. P. Putnam's Sons, 1921–22.

Rhetorica Ad Herennium. Trans. Harry Caplan. Cambridge: Harvard U. P., 1954.

Ross, John Robert. "The Category Squish: Endstation Hauptwort." *Papers from the 8th Regional Meeting, Chicago Linguistic Society.* Ed. Paul M. Peranteau,

Judith N. Levi, and Gloria C. Phares. Chicago: Chicago Linguistic Society, 1972. 316–28.

Sanders, Robert E. "Utterances, Actions, and Rhetorical Inquiry." *Philosophy and Rhetoric* 11 (1978). 114–33.

Sapir, Edward. *Language: An Introduction to the Study of Speech*. New York: Harcourt Brace, 1921.

Searle, John R. *Speech Acts: An Essay in the Philosophy of Language*. Cambridge: Cambridge U. P., 1969.

Shaughnessy, Mina P. *Errors and Expectations: A Guide for the Teacher of Basic Writing*. New York: Oxford U. P., 1977.

Shaw, Donald L., et al. *The Emergence of American Political Issues: The Agenda-Setting Function of the Press*. St. Paul, Minn.: West Publ. Co., 1977.

Siebert, Fredrick S., Theodore Peterson, and Wilber Schramm. *Four Theories of the Press: The Authoritarian, Libertarian, Social Responsibility, and Soviet Communist Concepts of What the Press Should Be and Do*. Urbana, Ill.: U. of Illinois P., 1963.

Simons, Herbert. "Genre-alizing About Rhetoric: A Scientific Approach." *Form and Genre: Shaping Rhetorical Action*. Falls Church, Va.: Speech Communication Assoc., 1978. 33–50.

Singleton, Mary Ann. *Divorce as a New Beginning*. New York: Dell, 1977.

Solzhenitsyn, Aleksandr. "A World Split Apart": Commencement Address Delivered at Harvard University, June 8, 1978. Trans. Irina Ilovayskaya Alberti. New York: Harper and Row, 1978.

Steiner, George. "A Future Literacy." *The Atlantic Monthly* August 1971: 40–44.

Terris, Walter F. "The Classification of the Argumentative Proposition." QJS 49 (1963): 266–73.

Thompson, Elbert N. S. *The Seventeenth-Century English Essay*. New York: Haskell House, 1967 [1926.

Tomlinson, Kenneth Y. "You'll Be a Hooker or Else!" *Reader's Digest* Feb. 1981: 147–50.

Wallace, Anthony F. C. *Religion: An Anthropological View*. New York: Random House, 1966.

Wallace, Karl R. *Understanding Discourse: The Speech Act and Rhetorical Action*. Baton Rouge, La: L. S. U., 1970.

Wanner, Eric. "Do We Understand Sentences from the Outside-In or from the Inside-Out?" *Language as a Human Problem*. Ed. Einer Haugen and Morton Bloomfield. New York: W. W. Norton, 1974. 165–86.

Warnock, G. J. "Some Types of Performative Utterance." *Essays on J. L. Austin*. Oxford: Clarendon P., 1973. 69–89.

Watson, Robert. " 'The Car Thief' is for All Ages." *Greensboro Daily News* 25 Jan. 1980: A5.

————. "Mediamartyrdom: The Greensboro Shootout." *Harpers* March 1980: 95–101.

Weaver, Richard. *Ideas Have Consequences*. Chicago: U. of Chicago P., 1948.

————. "The Spaciousness of Old Rhetoric." *The Ethics of Rhetoric*. Chicago: Henry Regnery, 1953. 164–87.

Whately, Richard. *Elements of Rhetoric*. Ed. Douglas Ehninger. Carbondale, Ill.: Southern Illinois U. P., 1963.

White, Haydon. *Metahistory: The Historical Imagination in Nineteenth-Century Europe*. Baltimore: Johns Hopkins U. P., 1973.

Whitmore, C. E. "The Field of the Essay." PMLA 36 (1921): 551–64.

Wilhelm, J. "Heresy." *The Catholic Encyclopedia*.

Williams, Joseph. "Linguistic Responsibility." CE 39 (Sept. 1977): 8–17.

Yoder, Edwin M. "On 'Reds': The Age of Political Innocence." Copyright *The Washington Post*, week of 4 Jan. 1982.

Young, Richard, Alton Becker, and Kenneth Pike, *Rhetoric, Discovery, and Change*. New York: Harcourt, Brace, and World, 1970.

Young, Richard. "Paradigms and Problems: Needed Research in Rhetorical Invention." *Research in Composing*. Ed. Charles R. Cooper and Lee Odell (Urbana, Ill.: NCTE, 1978). 210–16.

INDEX

Abrams, M. H., 57, 166
Accommodation, as principle of rhetoric, 105
Administrative rhetoric, 22
Aggregative contact, 48
Aims of discourse, 63–66, 81–107; as historical specializations, 105, 163
Alsop, Stewart, 109n
Analogy, argument by, 104, 119
Anticlimatic order, 117–18, 126
Applebee, Arthur N., 169n
Aristotelian theory, omissions and shortcomings in, 88–93, 111
Aristotle, 9, 13, 70, 75, 77, 109, 123, 161; approach to discourse, 8; division of genres, 6–7, 107–8; *Nicomachean Ethics*, 13; *Politics*, 79; *Rhetoric*, 51, 81–82, 96n; *Topica*, 35n; treatment of epideictic, 111
Arnold, Matthew, 101
Arrangement, 52, 117–18, 126
Asymmetry, as structural feature, 17–21, 76, 93, 160
Austin, J. L., 10, 11, 16, 57, 91–93, 116, 141, 143-45
Author-audience relation, as distinctive feature of aims, 99–101

Bain, Alexander, 35
Beale, W. H., 111, 141
Becker, Alton, 44, 78
Berlin, James, 78, 170
Bernstein, Basil, 84-85

Biography, popular, as informational poetic, 110
Bitzer, Lloyd, 101–2
Black, Edwin, 52, 108, 109
Black, Max, 52, 92
Bloomfield, Leonard, 97
Booth, Wayne C., 160
Bormann, Ernest, 3
Boy Scout handbook, 109
Brinton, Alan, 77n
Britton, James, 14
Bryan, William F., 153n
Bryan, William Jennings, 104
Bryant, Donald C., 105, 108-9, 111
Buchheit, Vinzenz, 141n
Buchwald, Art, 118–19
Burgess, Theodore C., 141n, 142
Burke, Kenneth, 9, 10, 11, 12, 22, 46, 56-57, 95n, 104, 105, 111, 160
Butler, Samuel, 34

Cairns, William B., 35
Campbell, George, 35
Campbell, Karlyn Kohrs, 19, 52
Capella, Martianus, 28
Carlisle, O. A., 87
Carothers, J. C., 3n
Cassirer, Ernst, 61, 71
"Channeling" of discourse functions, 86–88, 108
Character types, and motivational axes, 78-79
Chase, J. Richard, 141n, 145
Chaucer, Geoffrey, 40
Cherwitz, Richard A., 77n

Motivational Axes, 10–12, 55–80,
107–8, 113–14, 115, 116,
121–22, 123, 133, 145–46,
152, 155, 160, 163–71

Narrative mode, 40–42
New journalism, 42, 134
New Yorker, 103
Niebuhr, Reinhold, 84
Nietzsche, Friederich, 43
Novak, Michael, 43

Oakshott, Michael, 9n
Occasion and context, as
distinctive feature of aims,
101–2
Ong, Walter J., 3n, 5, 6, 22n,
33n, 42n, 47, 51, 74, 89, 168
Openness and centrality, as
principle of rhetoric, 105–6,
113, 119, 163
Organicism, as world hypothesis, 71–73
Orwell, George, 153n, 155

Panter-Downes, Mollie, 138–41
Paradox, in reflective/exploratory
rhetoric, 154
Participation and non-participation, as axes of discourse,
62–63
Pascal, Blaise, 68
Peirce, C. S., 71
Pepper, Stephen, 67, 69–73,
76–78
Perelman, Chaim, 77, 101, 104,
111, 142, 146
Performative rhetoric, 110–11,
113–14, 122, 133, 141–52;
examples and analyses,
146–52; types of, 144–46
Personal contact, 47
Philology, as branch of criticism,
166

Piers Plowman, 40n
Pike, Kenneth, 22, 24–25, 44, 78,
85
Pitkin, Willis, 21n, 22n
Plato, 8, 18, 70, 75, 77, 79, 90,
160, 163; *Gorgias*, 79; *Phae-
drus*, 81; *Republic*, 79
Pluralism, 77–79, 106, 163
Poetic discourse, 94–104, 113
Policy deliberation, 121
Postman, Neil, 7
Practical criticism, 166–67
Pragmatic theory, 1–4, 171
Pragmatism, 71. *See also*
Contextualism
Predicables, 35n
Probability scale. *See* Scale of
probability
Prophet, character type, 78–79
Propositional status, as predictor
of subgenres, 116, 120
Proto-discourse, 82–83
Proto-genres, 82–83
Provenance, as determinant of
style, 52
Publicity, as feature of discourse
performance, 84
Purpose, as distinctive feature of
aims, 95–96

Quintilian, 4n, 81, 117

Realism: as "out there" orientation, 66–69; philosophical,
163
Referentiality and non-referentiality, as axes of discourse,
61–62
Reflective/exploratory rhetoric,
111–13, 115, 121, 133,
152–59; conceptual patterns
in, 154–55; example and
analysis, 156–59; types of,
155–56

Walter H. Beale received his Ph.D. in 1971 from the University of Michigan. He has taught since then at the University of North Carolina, Greensboro, where he currently holds the rank of Professor of English. His previous publications include "Rhetorical Performative Discourse: A New Theory of Epideictic" (*Philosophy and Rhetoric*, 1978), *Old and Middle English Poetry* (Gale Research, 1976), and *Real Writing: Argumentation, Reflection, Information* (Scott, Foresman; 2nd ed., 1985).

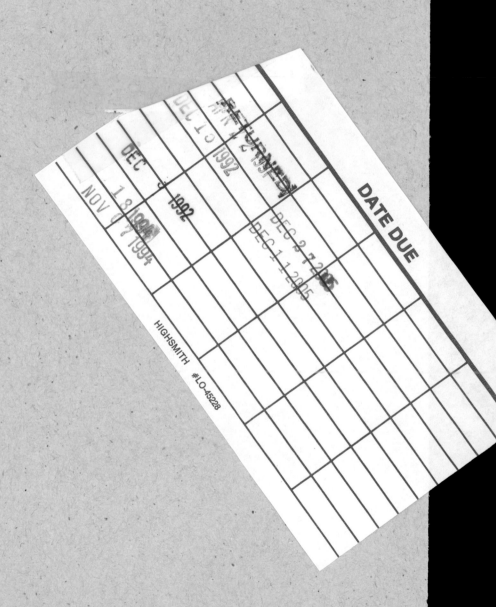

308035